MERCHANTS, MAMLUKS, AND MURDER

SUNY series in the Social and Economic History of the Middle East

Donald Quataert, editor

MERCHANTS, MAMLUKS, AND MURDER

The Political Economy of Trade in Eighteenth-Century Basra

THABIT A. J. ABDULLAH

State University
of New York
Press

Published by
State University of New York Press, Albany

Production by Susan Geraghty
Marketing by Patrick Durocher

Printed in the United States of America

For information, address State University of New York Press,
90 State Street, Suite 700, Albany, NY 12207

Library of Congress Cataloging-in-Publication Data

Abdullah, Thabit.
Merchants, Mamluks, and murder : the political economy of trade in eighteenth century Basra / Thabit A.J. Abdullah.
p. cm. — (SUNY series in the social and economic history of the Middle East)
Includes bibliographical references and index.
ISBN 0-7914-4807-X (alk. paper) — ISBN 0-7914-4808-8 (pbk. : alk. paper)
1. Basrah (Iraq)—Commerce—History—18th century. 2. Merchants—Iraq—Basrah—History—18th century. 3. Mamelukes. 4. Basrah (Iraq)—Ethnic relations—Economic aspects. 5. Basrah (Iraq)—History—18th century. I. Title. II. Series.

HF3770.Z9 B3715 2000
380.1′09567′5—dc21

00-026524

10 9 8 7 6 5 4 3 2 1

To My Beloved Samera

CONTENTS

MAPS, TABLES, AND FIGURES

MAPS

TABLES

FIGURES

ABBREVIATIONS

BA	Başbakanlık Arşivi, Istanbul
BSH	Basra Hazinesi
DBŞM	Bab-ı Defteri, Başmuhasebe Kalemi
IOR	India Office Records, London
MM	Maliyeden Müdevver
MSA	Maharashtra State Archives, Bombay
NAI	National Archives of India, New Delhi
OC	Occasional Correspondence

NOTE ON TRANSLITERATION

Attempting to achieve consistency in transliteration when dealing with Arabic, Persian, and Turkish words in the same study is not easy. Words that have a familiar English spelling, such as Oman, Kuwait, or Basra, are retained in that form. Aside from these, I have used the Arabic transliteration system of the *International Journal of Middle East Studies*. To maintain a sense of consistency, I have used the same system when transliterating Turkish or Persian words commonly used in Basra. The only modifications are the following: "ch" is used for the Turkish "ç," and "g" and "p" are retained in Turkish words. Thus, the Turkish words *saliyane*, *çelebi*, *akçe*, and *kürüş* are rendered *saliyanah*, *chalabi*, *aqchah*, and *ghurush*.

NOTE ON CURRENCTY

A large number of different currencies were used in eighteenth-century Basra, and their values constantly fluctuated. During the middle of the century, however, most currencies did achieve some degree of stability. Nevertheless, the figures given below are only meant to give the reader some rough sense of the equivalent values and should not be considered precise exchange ratios:

1 *rupee* = 0.11 sterling = 0.05 *tuman* = 5.5 *maḥmudi*

There were many types of *ghurush* (the most common being the ghurush asadi). Normally, 1 ghurush = 120 aqchah = 40 parah. The value of 1 ghurush = 1 rupee can be taken only as a very rough estimate.

ACKNOWLEDGMENTS

The research and writing of this work was assisted by a number of fine individuals and organizations, and I would like to take this opportunity to thank them all. The research in London was partially funded by a generous grant from the Department of History at Georgetown University. In India I was assisted by a grant from the Joint Committee on the Near and Middle East of the American Council of Learned Societies and the Social Science Research Council with funds provided by the William and Flora Hewlett Foundation. The work in Istanbul was assisted by grants from the American University in Cairo, the Oklahoma Foundation for the Humanities, the Department of History at Oklahoma State University, and the Dean's Incentive Grant at Oklahoma State University.

This work certainly owes a great deal to Professor Hanna Batatu. His kindness, advice, and unwavering commitment to excellence, so evident in his own work, were a continuous source of inspiration and help. I thank my brother Haitham for his beautiful cover illustration and extensive copyediting of the manuscript. The work was greatly improved by the suggestions and criticisms of Hala Fattah, Dina Khoury, Aziz Sbahi, Afaf Marsot, Halil Sahillioglu, Thomas Lier, Judith Tucker, Hisham Sharabi, the late Albert Hourani, and the readers of SUNY Press. Malcolm Yapp and K.N. Chaudhuri provided helpful comments on research in England and India. While in India I received much help from Professor Om Prakash of the Delhi School of Economics and Dr. Pradeep Mehendiratta of the American Institute of Indian Studies. Tony Green was kind enough to permit me to stay at the American Research Institute in Turkey and to use their fine library.

I was also greatly assisted by the many scholars and employees of the India Office Records, the British Museum, the library of the School of Oriental and African Studies, the National Archives of India, the National Museum of India, the Maharashtra State Archives, and the Başbakanlik Arşivi. I thank the Ministry of Human Resource Development of the Indian government for granting me a research permit and the Delhi School of Economics for acting as my sponsors. The History Department of Bombay University provided me with valuable assistance during my stay in Bombay. Lastly, I am grateful to Maria DenBoer for the fine work she put in copyediting the manuscript.

INTRODUCTION

On the evening of March 22, 1791, a body was found near the rubbish dump on the outskirts of the city of Basra.[1] A laborer at one of the brick kilns nearby made the discovery when returning home from work and immediately informed the authorities. The body, clearly that of a wealthy man, was soon brought before a stunned *mutasallim*[2] and his aides. After some probing, the victim, apparently strangled to death, was identified as a Jewish merchant by the name of Sallum. His wife had been asking concerning his whereabouts for several days and word would now confirm her worst fears. While crimes were not uncommon in late-eighteenth-century Basra, the mutasallim must have felt that the murder of a wealthy merchant was the last thing his beleaguered city needed. For the past two decades it seemed as if scarcely a year passed without the visitation of some terrible disaster, either natural or man-made. Plague, war with Persia, tribal raids, highway banditry, piracy, and constant political turmoil had all contributed to commercial decline and a good deal of frayed nerves. Now, with the monsoon winds just beginning to shift, news of this murder carried by the departing ships would certainly not reflect well on the port's reputation for security.

The very next day a prominent figure in the Jewish community of Basra, Khawjah ᶜAbdullah ibn Yusuf, publicly accused the Armenians of committing the crime. A charismatic and strong-willed man, Khawjah ᶜAbdullah had endeared himself to the Ottoman authorities and made a fortune through commerce. That evening, as the authorities scrambled to contain the growing crisis, about five hundred Jews, including women and children, marched up to the mutasallim's house and demanded the immediate punishment of the entire Armenian community. This was followed by another demonstration the next morning with Khawjah ᶜAbdullah and other Jewish notables leading the march. The mutasallim, much to the surprise of many merchants, finally gave in to the pressure and ordered the arrest of several Armenians. As they were being interrogated, Samuel Manesty, the English resident, suddenly entered the fray. Manesty, a man of extreme arrogance who styled himself in the manner of an oriental despot, vigorously protested government actions on the grounds that the Armenians enjoyed British protection and could not be detained by Ottoman officials. After several days of rising sectarian tensions and the danger of a developing conflict between the mutasallim and the English resident, it became clear that even the *wali* of distant Baghdad, Sulayman Pasha, had some hand in this increasingly complex case. Notwithstanding his province's growing dependency on English shipping for its lucrative trade with India, Sulayman Pasha stood firmly behind the Jewish leaders in their conflict with the powerful English resident.

Essentially, this book is an attempt to untangle the knot of political, social, and economic factors that lay at the heart of the curious murder case that opens this chapter. The extraordinary animosity between the Armenian and Jewish communities, both prominent in the trade of Basra, suggests tensions that go well beyond the death of one merchant. The readiness of the authorities in Basra and Baghdad to support the Jews and the determined English support of the Armenians points to other than mere altruistic interests. Lastly, the stubborn standoff between the pasha of Baghdad and the English resident at Basra is certainly an indication that not all was right with England's growing role in the commerce of the region. To deal effectively with these questions, this study shifts from the specific to the general by examining the overall economic and political conditions that affected the major merchant communities of Basra at the end of the eighteenth century. Three broad, interrelated issues, all of which have a direct bearing on the above case of the Jewish merchant, are explored.

The first is the overall nature of Basra's import-export trade during the eighteenth century, its rise and decline, the various regional networks with which it was tied, and the structural changes affecting its performance. The second looks at the role of the wholesale merchants in charge of the city's long-distance trade (the *tujjar*). This includes a discussion of the merchant communities, their regional connections, and their relationships with the Ottoman authorities and the growing European presence. The third issue, discussed throughout the work, deals with the gradual development in Basra of what M. N. Pearson has called the "soft areas" in Asian economies through which European articulation, followed by incorporation into the capitalist world economy, took place.[3] In other words, rather than examining the full process of Basra's incorporation, the main focus is on the indigenous and regional factors (especially those affecting long-distance trade) that provided the opportunity for later incorporation into the world economy.

Throughout its history Basra has belonged to two worlds: the Middle East and the Indian Ocean. It is, therefore, quite natural that this study should be affected by the historiographic contributions of both areas. The issue of long-distance trade in particular has recently received much attention in studies on the Indian Ocean. Historians such as M. N. Pearson, K. N. Chaudhuri, S. Arasaratnam, and, most recently, P. Risso have argued for the viability of the Indian Ocean as a single unit of historical study.[4] While some, like Andre Wink, have called into question the plausibility of including the Far East in such a unit,[5] few have questioned its applicability to the western half of the Indian Ocean. C. A. Bayly has even gone so far as to argue in favor of "viewing the colonial conquest of India in a west Asian context" due to the great historical interaction between the two societies.[6] The regularity of the monsoons and the relative ease of sailing from port to port created a certain economic, social, and cultural cohesion quite evident in the eighteenth century. It was not uncommon for an eighteenth-century traveler to note Arab sailors navigating ships from Surat and Surati shipbuilders working on Omani vessels owned by merchants from Basra. Muslim *ʿulama'* were found in all the major ports while Arabic and Persian were the recognized languages of commerce, politics, and religion from Bengal to the Swahili coast.

An issue unique to maritime history and important in the historiography of the Indian Ocean is "the problem of where the coast ends and the hinterland begins and how much of the hinterland is relevant to an understanding of the coast and ocean."[7] Historians of India's maritime trade have increasingly united their efforts with those dealing with such inland issues as agrarian structure, land revenue, administration, and political structures. The significance of the inland distribution of goods, the political and social impact of maritime merchants, and the effects of trade on the production of goods became more apparent when viewed through the broad, comparative space of the Indian Ocean. In this manner "the Indian Ocean links of . . . states became intrinsic to an understanding of what went on in them, to an analysis of their rise and decline."[8]

The role that Surat played, for example, in the economic life of the Mughal Empire was one of the questions raised by Ashin Das Gupta's study, *Indian Merchants and the Decline of Surat, 1700–1740*.[9] In this work, Das Gupta successfully argues that the rise and decline of Surat can only be understood when viewed through a broad regional perspective, taking into consideration both political and economic factors from local as well as distant locations such as Egypt, the Ottoman Empire, Persia, and Yemen. Niels Steensgaard, on the other hand, explores the relationship between coast and hinterland by discussing the so-called Asian trade revolution of the seventeenth century.[10] Steensgaard argues that the entrance of the Dutch and English trading companies in the Indian Ocean galvanized maritime trade at the expense of long-established caravan routes. Specifically, Steensgaard refers to the decline of the caravan silk trade between Persia and Syria and its shift to the maritime trade under European control. This, in turn, affected power relations in the hinterland and, more important, bolstered the power of the Europeans in the region.

The question of European penetration is one of numerous issues that have preoccupied historians of both the Indian Ocean and the Middle East. In both camps the question most frequently raised in this regard is how such sophisticated societies as those of the Mughals, Ottomans, and Safavids ultimately succumbed to European domination.[11] In recent times the most influential approach used to deal with this issue has been the world-systems perspective initially put forth by Immanuel Wallerstein.[12] Since this theory has been reviewed and debated in countless fine works, it would not serve much to do so here. Suffice it to say that historians of the Indian Ocean and the Middle East have found much utility in the theory's global perspective and its emphasis on the development and expansion of the European world-capitalist system (the prime mover in modern world history) after the sixteenth century. As societies came in contact with European expansion, their various economic, political, and social structures were transformed to accommodate their inclusion into the world-capitalist system. This transformation, termed "incorporation," has been a favorite focus of historians.

Despite its many strengths the world-systems perspective has recently come into some rough waters. In several works M. N. Pearson convincingly called into question the extent of European influence prior to the mid-eighteenth century, let alone the sixteenth as Wallerstein claims.[13] Here, Pearson builds on Eric Wolf's argument that European capitalism did not appear "as a qualitatively new phenomenon," capable of world domination, until the dawn of the industrial revolution at the end of the eighteenth century.[14] The sixteenth through the eighteenth centuries are described as an "age of partnership," during which Europeans were "simply living in Asia, and working, with varying degrees of success."[15] In other words, rather than firmly establishing their domination, European merchants at the time were simply part (and, up to the eighteenth century, a minute part) of the Asian world. From the perspective of the Middle East, Islamoglu-Inan criticized the world-systems approach for being "one-sided and 'economistic.'"[16] It "fails to explain the specific local (regional) histories and class relations in pre-capitalist societies, and therefore it cannot account for the diverse development patterns in the periphery."[17] In this manner, it portrays Asian or Middle Eastern societies as "passive recipients of the impulses from the [European] core."[18]

To correct this bias several works have appeared that seek to understand the dynamics of Asian economies during the "early modern" period, just prior to incorporation in the world economy. The argument is basically that only by doing so can we understand the process by which European capitalist expansion "fit" into the preexisting economic systems. In other words, the early modern period gives us the opportunity to view incorporation more dialectically as it gradually takes shape through the interaction and articulation of European and Asian commercial interests. The emphasis has largely been on the eighteenth century since this was the century that immediately predated European domination and during which many of the early, more subtle transformations took place. Much of the work here has been on commerce and the commercial classes through which European articulation initially took place. Andre Raymond's meticulous work on Cairo was among the earliest to highlight the importance of this issue.[19] More recently, works by Dina Khoury, Frangakis-Syrett on Smyrna (Izmir), and separate works on Aleppo by Bruce Masters and Abraham Marcus also emphasized, with varying degrees of success, the importance of understanding the economic and social developments of the eighteenth century as the prelude to European dominance.[20] The present work seeks to bring this interest in the early modern period to a region of the Ottoman Empire and the Indian Ocean that has received little attention despite its obvious importance.

The literature on the economic history of early modern Iraq is extremely limited. Aside from general remarks on the economic policies of individual rulers,[21] there are hardly any works that systematically deal with Iraq's economy during this period. To be sure, the turmoil surrounding the country's recent unhappy history with the resulting inaccessibility of Iraqi archives has figured prominently in this dearth of literature. Yet, there is also a methodological problem. In the past, studies of the Ottoman Empire have been tainted with the notion that, during their early period the Ottomans, imbued with the "Ghazi spirit," were primarily interested in westward expansion.[22] The empire's relations with the East were often reduced to a history of defensive wars against first, rival Turkic states, then the Safavids in Persia, aimed at freeing the Ottomans for their primary mission in Europe. Thus, the empire's provinces of Mosul, Baghdad, and Basra were often regarded as significant only in a military sense.

While this view has recently begun to change, the remaining lacunae, particularly with respect to Iraq, are still prominent. Two recent works illustrate this problem. In an edited volume by Halil Inalcik and Donald Quaeteart, pre-nineteenth-century Iraq is mentioned only briefly, particularly when compared with the work's treatment of Syria and Egypt.[23] Likewise, Daniel Panzac's article on Ottoman maritime trade mentions the empire's eastern trade only briefly, preferring to focus mainly on the Mediterranean trade with Europe.[24] Undoubtedly, the authors of these works were hampered by the overall dearth of published material on Iraq.

An exception to this neglect are recent works dealing with trade in early modern southern Iraq by Yılmaz, Khoury, and Fattah. The latter two authors have also taken the lead in attempting to establish links between Ottoman and Indian Ocean historiographies. Serap Yılmaz's article on Ottoman trade with India underlines the importance and complexity of this trade during the eighteenth century.[25] Using mainly French reports and some Ottoman sources, Yılmaz highlights Basra's central role as a transit port in the India trade link. Despite its brevity, Dina Khoury's article on the merchants of Mosul and Basra in the sixteenth and seventeenth centuries raises several issues.[26] Most important is her use of Fredric Lane's concept of "protection rent" and Niels Steensgaard's elaboration on this concept through his discussion of the "sellers of protection" in Asia.[27] By viewing both the Ottoman state and the tribes, which often collected safe passage fees from merchants, as sellers of protection, Khoury attempts to "move away from statements that see the economic life of the Ottoman Arab provinces as determined by a general polarization of interests between the political elite and the merchants."[28]

Lastly, Hala Fattah's study of the political economy of the Persian

Gulf, Arabia, and southern Iraq focuses on two primary issues.[29] The first, reiterated in this work, is her regional approach to the study of the area which breaks with "the assumption that the economic history of the Ottoman provinces necessitates the study of each province on its own, as distinct from the region of which it formed a part."[30] This practice of imposing "barriers on regions that had none,"[31] still apparent in most works on Middle Eastern history, has confused our understanding of the area. The second point that Fattah stresses during her discussion of the various regional networks of trade and the local market towns is their "resiliency and endurance" in the face of British economic penetration. The various tactics employed to resist British penetration eventually helped shape the manner and extent of the region's incorporation into the world economy.[32]

In this sense, Fattah's focus on the process of incorporation picks up where the present work leaves off. This study of Basra's trade in the eighteenth century focuses on a period in which structural changes affected the trade of the region as a whole and provided the opportunity for significant British penetration. Chapter 1 takes a broad survey of Basra's history, followed by a discussion of the paramount role of its geographic position. It also looks at the structure of the city, as well as the nature of its population and administration in the eighteenth century. The conclusion of this chapter is that Basra's fortunes were certainly on the wane by the end of the century. In Chapter 2 the focus is on the overall nature of Basra's import-export trade, with particular attention given to maritime shipping figures. Once again, notwithstanding an earlier boom, the evidence points to a decline in trade at the end of the century.

It is not until the third chapter that the causes for this decline are analyzed. This is done by looking at the different networks of trade to which Basra was tied. For each of these networks, information is given concerning the merchandise exchanged, patterns of trade, and the structural shifts that affected their health. Among the paramount causes of these structural shifts were the waves of tribal migrations from Arabia which affected the entire region, particularly in the second half of the century. The chapter concludes that the trade of Basra declined, among other reasons, primarily because of the long-term disruptions caused by these migrations as well as by the collapse of the central state in Persia. The increasing role of Britain in Basra's maritime trade is also analyzed. The role which Basra's big wholesale merchants played is treated in Chapters 4 and 5. The emphasis is on the contradictory interests of the main merchant communities which reflected the different trade networks in which they operated. These contradictions, which were particularly obvious on the political level, allowed the British to gain greater influence and paved the way for the eventual incorporation of southern Iraq.

Endeavoring to write about an area that has been largely ignored poses numerous risks. There are few works with which to compare findings. Also, the dearth of research on the economic history of the Persian Gulf region prior to the nineteenth century makes it difficult to place the present study within a broader time frame. It is possible, though, to draw comparisons with similar studies of other areas. In keeping with one of the goals of this study of placing Basra's economic history within both Middle Eastern and Indian Ocean historiography, comparisions are made, wherever possible, with studies in both areas. The result, while far from sufficient will, hopefully, add to the understanding and debates of both areas.

CHAPTER 1

Al-Baṣrah Al-Fayḥa'[1]

HISTORY UP TO 1700

Eighteenth-century Basra descended from a line of port cities going back to pre-Islamic times. Yaᶜqub Sarkis argues that the very name of the city is derived from the ancient Aramaic *Basriyatha* or *Basriyi*, meaning "the place of huts" or a "settlement."[2] Alexander the Great named it Teredon,[3] while the name of Charax Spasinou was in use prior to the Sassanian invasion of A.D. 225.[4] By the time the Arabs arrived, some four centuries later, the port of al-'Ubulla had supplanted Charax. In 638, the Arab army established a camp several miles to the southwest of the port near the small Persian settlement of Vaheshtabad Ardashir.[5] Historians usually refer to the decision of the Caliph ᶜUmar ibn al-Khaṭṭab in 638 to establish this military base as the date for the foundation of the Islamic city of Basra.[6]

The diverse cultural and ethnic mixture of its inhabitants, born of its nature as a port and caravan city, created a social dynamism that would bring Basra both greatness and ruin. Throughout the Islamic period the city was a constant source of instability for the central authorities. It was at Basra, in 656, that the first major inter-Muslim conflict took place in the famous Battle of the Camel. Revolutionary movements, such as that of Ibn al-Ashᶜath in 701, the Zott in 820–835, the Zanj in 869–883, and the Qaramiṭah in 923, repeatedly brought havoc to the city. It was also at this time, however, that the city achieved much of its greatness. During the eighth and ninth centuries Basra developed into one of the leading commercial cities of the Middle Ages and the chief port supplying Baghdad, the new Abbasid capital. Its commercial success was accompanied by a vibrant intellectual life. It was at Basra that Arabic grammar became standardized by Sibawayh and al-Khalil ibn Aḥmad. Philosophers and theologians such as the Muᶜtazilah and Ikhwan al-Ṣafa debated and discussed, while poets and belletrists like Abu Nuwas and al-Jaḥiẓ created some of the greatest works of Arabic literature.

Basra, along with the rest of Abbasid Iraq, was already in decline long before the Mongol invasion of 1258. During the following century the canals and dams that had provided the city's freshwater supply were neglected and gradually deteriorated. When Ibn Battuta visited the city in the mid-fourteenth century, he found it in ruins and its few inhabitants in the process of relocating closer to the river near its present site. Hamid al-Bazi argues that the foundations of modern Basra, located about seven miles to the northeast of the medieval city, were actually established in 885 by the Caliph al-Muwafaq. Al-Muwafaq's town was known as "al-Muwafaqiyyah" or "al-Baṣirah."[7] By the fifteenth century the city's canals had deteriorated to the extent that fresh water became exceedingly difficult to find. The status of the relocated city did not improve until its occupation by Safavid Persia in 1508, when a limited commercial regeneration took place. Ottoman conquests in 1534 and 1546 hastened the process of integrating Basra within the developing commercial networks of the empire. Politically, though, Ottoman rule remained nominal despite several unsuccessful attempts at creating a navy capable of driving the Portuguese out of the Gulf.[8] In the absence of a firm government, Basra was left to contend with periods of tribal domination and Persian threats without much assistance from the Porte.[9]

During the early seventeenth century, Basra gained a further degree of autonomy under the rule of one of its own natives.[10] In 1596, the Ottoman governor, plagued by an inability to control the city, simply sold his governorship to a local official by the name of Afrasiyab and left for Istanbul.[11] Unfortunately very little is known about this lively period, but under Afrasiyab's son ᶜAli, and grandson Husayn, Basra enjoyed a renaissance of sorts, with increased security, trade, construction, and literary output. This coincided with a general rise in the trade of the Indian Ocean brought about by the consolidation of the Mughal, Safavid, and Ottoman Empires, and the increasing participation of Europeans in inter-Asian trade.

Basra's independence was cut short when, in 1668, the wali of Baghdad led a force that overthrew the Afrasiyab dynasty and ushered in a new period of uncertainty punctuated by plague, Persian occupation, and tribal control. It was not until the signing of the Karlowitz peace treaty in 1699 that the Ottomans were able to deal more effectively with their unruly provinces in Iraq.[12] A fresh campaign was launched from Baghdad in 1701 that expelled the Muntafiq tribes of Shaykh Maniᶜ ibn Mughamis and installed ᶜAli Pasha as wali of an area stretching from Qurnah at the intersection of the Tigris and Euphrates to the Persian Gulf. Five years later Basra was officially incorporated into the province (*pashalik* or *wilayah*) of Baghdad.[13]

HASAN PASHA AND THE MAMLUKS

In 1704, the Ottoman Porte finally found, in Ḥasan Pasha, the individual with the skills required to govern the troublesome province of Baghdad. His appointment undoubtedly signaled the beginning of a new and significant era in the history of Basra and modern Iraq as a whole. For the next forty years he and his son and successor, Aḥmad Pasha, gradually built a powerful military-administrative apparatus based largely on imported Georgian slaves, or *mamluks*.[14] The use of slave soldiers (usually of Turkish origins) to serve as the elite corps of the army, or as a sort of praetorian guard, dates back to the late Abbasid period. The most famous chapter in this uniquely Islamic institution was the establishment of a mamluk-administered sultanate in Egypt between 1250 and 1516.[15]

Initially, Basra continued to vacillate between being a dependency of Baghdad and being a separate province in its own right. In 1733, however, it was placed firmly under the jurisdiction of the province of Baghdad and remained so for the next ninety-eight years.[16] Ḥasan Pasha and his mamluk army proved quite successful in "raising the standard of obedience" throughout the province despite the steadily growing strength of the tribes and the increasingly chaotic situation in neighboring Persia.[17] Under him and his son Aḥmad the territory of the province was extended to include roughly the area of modern Iraq, with the notable exception of the province of Mosul in the north (Map 1.1). The new mamluk army also showed its worth in defending the borders against invasions from Persia. During the course of the century, the Ottoman Empire repeatedly went to war against the successors of the Safavids in Persia. The most serious threat came from Nadir Shah, who invaded Iraq twice in 1733 and once in 1743. While most of the great battles took place around Baghdad and Mosul, Basra also saw its share of bloodshed during these years. It was not until the rise of Karim Khan Zand in the 1760s, however, that Basra became the central focus of renewed war. Notwithstanding the many conflicts and wars of the eighteenth century, Basra seemed to enjoy a period of relative pros-

MAP 1.1
Approximate Boundaries of the Province of Baghdad and Basra, c.1780

perity up to the early 1770s. By that time several factors, which will be discussed later, led to the decline of the city's trade until well into the next century, when the Ottomans embarked on the wide-scale *tanzimat* reforms.

As with Egypt in 1250, the increasing reliance on mamluk forces led, ultimately, to their direct rule of the province. In 1750, soon after the death of Aḥmad Pasha, Sulayman Abu Layla became the first mamluk wali of Baghdad and Basra. For the next eighty years, the province passed from one mamluk officer to the other, often contrary to the Porte's wishes. Their end came in 1831, when nature and excessive insubordination conspired to ensure their downfall. In that year, a terrible plague ravaged Baghdad just as Ḍawud Pasha, the last mamluk wali, moved Iraq closer toward outright secession. The approaching Ottoman army found little difficulty in dispersing the mamluks and reestablishing the Porte's direct control of the province of Baghdad and Basra.

LOCATION AND CLIMATE

Throughout its history, Basra's strategic location played a paramount role in the port's commercial viability (Maps 1.2, 1.3). While the eighteenth-century city was but a shadow of its more celebrated medieval ancestor, the importance of this location continued to act as a guarantor of its survival in the face of recurring disasters. Basra's location near the northernmost point of the Persian Gulf was ideal as a transit area in East-West trade. The elongated shape of the Persian Gulf, with Masqat at its entrance and Basra at its terminus, linked the Middle East to the Indian Ocean. This, however, only justified the general location of the city. More important, Basra, like many other Indian Ocean ports, stood some sixty miles up the mouth of a navigable river. Shaṭṭ al-ᶜArab, formed from the union of the Tigris and Euphrates fifty or sixty miles north of Basra, could easily accommodate the five hundred-ton ships of the eighteenth century.[18] Through this river the city had easy access to its hinterland to the north. Baghdad, some three hundred miles to the northwest of Basra, was reached by either the Tigris or the Euphrates. Shaṭṭ al-ᶜArab is also joined by the Karun (or Ḥaffar) River just below Basra. This river, which originates from the mountains of western Persia, provided easy communication with Shuster and other areas of southwestern Persia. Beyond Baghdad and Shuster there were routes to the northern parts of Persia, Kurdistan, Armenia, Georgia, and Anatolia.[19]

Despite its many benefits, Shaṭṭ al-ᶜArab also presented some significant difficulties. During the rainy season, in the winter, the river would usually overflow, causing the people to cut trenches that let the water flow into the desert. The stagnant pools that were formed around the city acted as breeding grounds for several deadly diseases, including malaria.[20] The head of the Carmelite order at Basra described one such flooding which occurred in June 1727 as "making the desert look more like a sea."[21] By September a terrible fever had taken hold of the city, causing the Carmelite priest to nearly lose his life.[22] The Persian traveler, Mirza Abu Ṭalib Khan, commented that the diseases caused by these pools were nearly as bad as the plague.[23] The tribes around

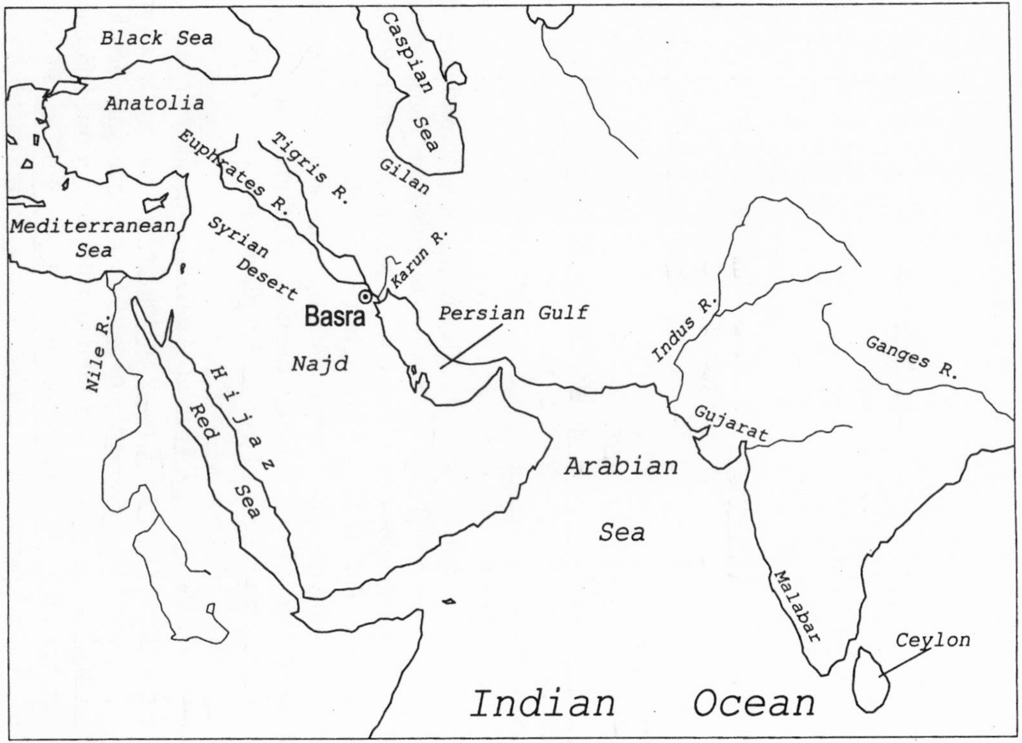

MAP 1.2
Geographic Location of Basra

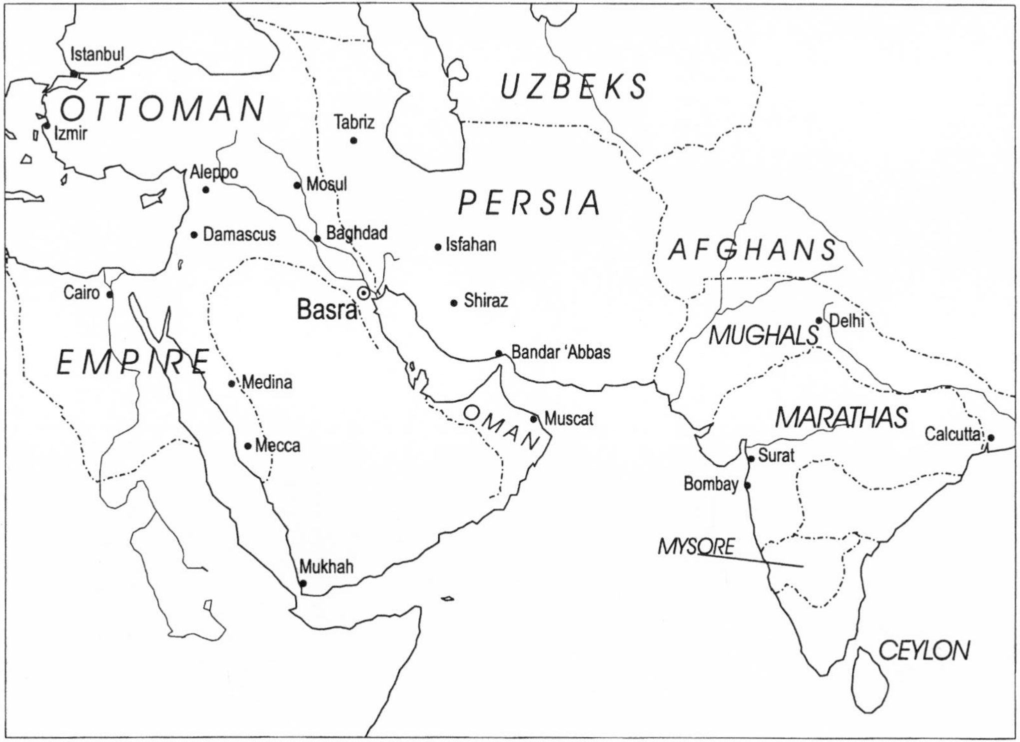

MAP 1.3
Political Location of Basra

Basra often used the threat of flooding the desert as an additional weapon in their frequent conflicts with the government.[24]

While the river itself was quite navigable, its mouth at Khawr al-Baṣrah was obstructed by a number of reefs and shoals formed by the silt deposits. The problem of maneuvering a large sailing vessel into the mouth of the river represented a great challenge even to the most experienced sailor, particularly during periods of high winds. Reports of ships running aground or breaking up were not uncommon. On April 28, 1757, a "large" ship belonging to Ṣalah Chalabi, one of the greatest shipowners of Surat, struck one of these reefs and sank, losing most of its cargo.[25] Likewise, on August 17, 1786, a ship from Mysore in southern India reported running aground twice in the Khawr al-Baṣrah on its way up the river.[26]

The location of Basra on the west bank of the Shaṭṭ al-ᶜArab had much to do with the security of the city. K. N. Chaudhuri mentions that "inland ports" could be defended more easily from pirates and warships by using chains stretched across the river and by mounting guns on shore-batteries.[27] At times, though, this strategy backfired. In October and November 1768, for example, the Kaᶜb tribe placed a chain across the Karun River and built several batteries below Basra. These actions succeeded in severely disrupting trade and the city had to give in to the shaykh's demands.[28] Likewise, a strong naval presence at the mouth of the river could put a total stop to all traffic to and from the Gulf. The Portuguese, the Dutch, and the English availed themselves of this opportunity several times during the century. In 1754, for example, the Dutch succeeded in blocking Khawr al-Baṣrah for six months, during which time they seized around eight vessels and two large ships.[29]

The proximity of Basra to the Persian border was regarded as both a blessing and a curse. Despite the generally lucrative nature of the Persian market, the frequent hostilities between the Persian and Ottoman Empires cast a constant shadow over the security of the frontier areas. These conflicts were particularly frequent and devastating in the eighteenth century, during which Basra alone suffered from three major Persian campaigns. In this respect, the river also acted as a natural barrier to possible invasions from the east. The armies of Nadir Shah in 1743 and Karim Khan Zand in 1775 encountered difficulties crossing the river in their attempts to take the city.[30] Not surprisingly, these wars left a deep impression on Iraqis as noted by the popular Iraqi, saying, "بين العجم و الروم بلوه إبتلينا" (Between the Persians and the Turks, what a calamity!).[31]

In addition to being a sea port, Basra was unique in that it was also a "desert port" or a caravan city. Located at the intersection of the Syrian and Arabian deserts, Basra enjoyed easy caravan communication with both Aleppo and the Arabian peninsula. Beyond Aleppo lay Alexandretta, western Anatolia, Istanbul, and Europe. Once again, though, this represented a mixed blessing. While it was generally easy for caravans to cross the desert, it was nearly impossible for the Ottomans to bring it under firm control. Tribal raids originating from the depths of Najd constantly harassed the city, particularly at the end of the century with the rise of the Wahhabis.[32]

The climate of the region also had a mixed effect on the fortunes of the city. Summer lasts from May until October, during which time the shores of the Persian Gulf become one of the hottest places in the world.[33] Temperatures around Basra have been known to go above 125°F, and it is not uncommon to have readings above 100°F in every month but December, January, and February.[34] Autumn and spring are pleasant, but barely last a month each, and winter arrives suddenly around November, bringing rain and temperatures that, at times, go below freezing. The rain, when heavy, turns the surrounding country into a morass of mud, causing trouble for all forms of land transport. Likewise, the desert near Basra is prone to the occurrence of sandstorms year-round.[35] The aridity and intense heat from the sun easily break the alluvium into fine dust. In the summer, when the winds are stronger, these storms can reduce visibility to twenty yards.[36] None of these storms were considered very dangerous, but in the eighteenth century they, at times, caused travelers great discomfort and often delayed caravans bound for Baghdad, Aleppo, or Persia.

The entire Indian Ocean region, including the Persian Gulf, is affected by the annual monsoons (Maps 1.4, 1.5).[37] The southwest monsoon, known to the Arabs in the Middle Ages as *mawsim al-kaws*, prevails from April to September. This was generally the season for eastward sailing. Yet, in June, July, and August the winds become too strong for safe sailing and most of the ports in western India were closed during these months. The winds shift around October, when a high pressure system develops in central Asia. The resulting mild northeast winds (*riḥ al-saba*) ending in March, inaugurate the season for traveling from east to west. These general wind patterns had important local variations.[38] A northwest wind prevails year-round over most of the Persian Gulf. In winter, these winds are regularly interrupted by southeasterly winds drawn by depressions in the Mediterranean. The

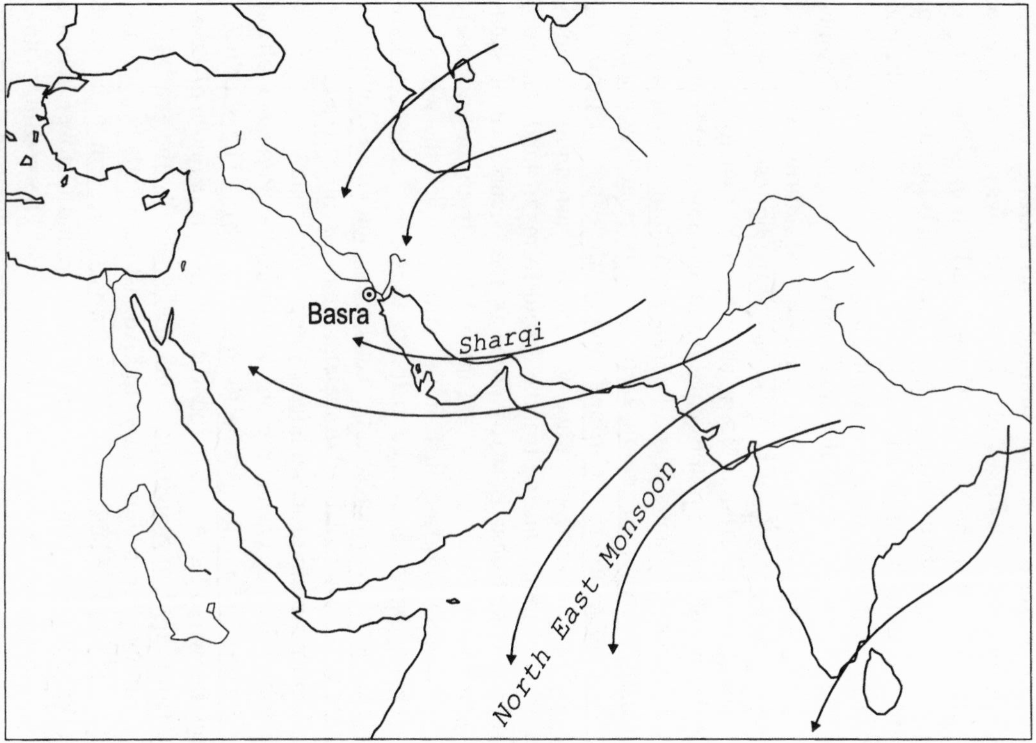

MAP 1.4
Wind Patterns in January

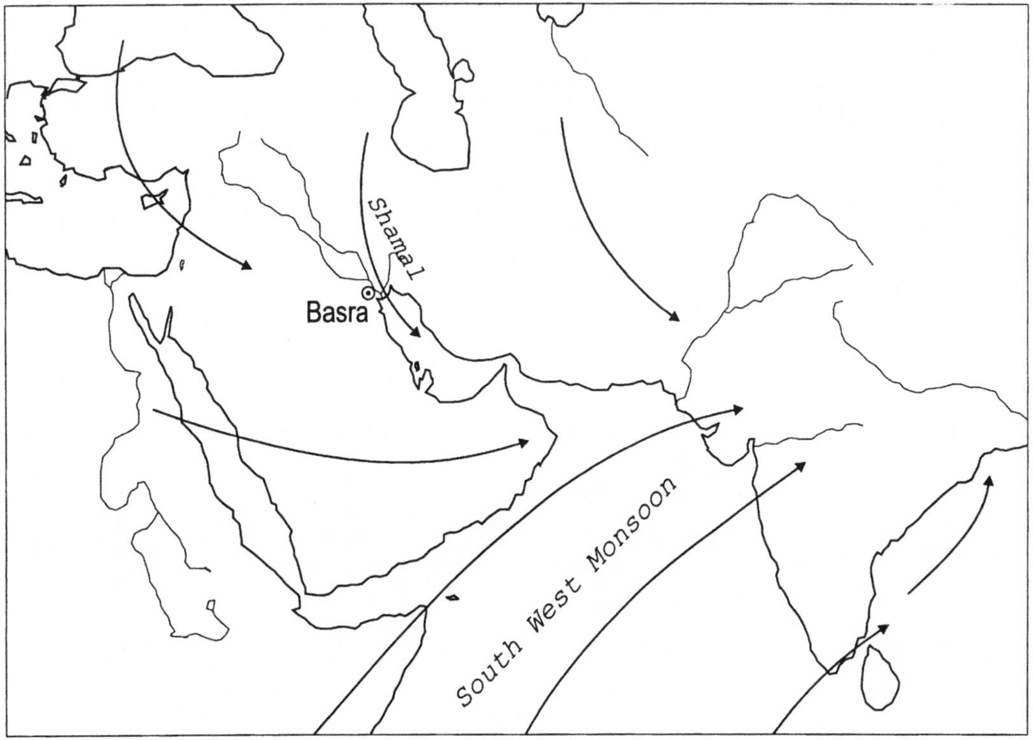

MAP 1.5
Wind Patterns in July

sharqi, as these southeasterly winds are called, are sometimes followed by a strong southwesterly gale known as the *suwayḥili*. The suwayḥili was, and remains, quite dangerous to sailing vessels. Sailors depended on the sharqi for their voyages up the Gulf despite its irregularity and the dangers of the suwayḥili.

During the summer months a low pressure system over the Indian subcontinent brings northwesterly winds down the southern part of today's Iraq and the Gulf. These winds are quite strong and have been called the *shamal* (or *dabur*)[39] to distinguish them from the weaker and less regular winter winds. The shamal normally arrives in June and is greeted by the people of Basra for the relative relief it brings from the oppressive heat. In the eighteenth century it was also greeted because it signaled the start of the sailing season to India.

A good understanding of these wind patterns was absolutely essential for a safe and prosperous voyage. A ship bound for Bengal on the eastern side of India, for example, had to leave Basra as soon as the shamal arrived and no later than mid-July so that it might round Ceylon prior to the onset of the northeast monsoon in October. If the intention was to make a stop at Surat or Bombay on the way to Bengal, the ship had to leave no later than February, make it to the Arabian sea as the northeast monsoon began to die out in March, and reach the coast before the end of April, when the southwest winds became too dangerous.[40] The great "Muscat fleet," which nearly monopolized the coffee trade from Mukha, usually left Yemen at the end of the southwest monsoon in September, arriving at the entrance of the Gulf just as the winds shifted in October and reached Basra by the middle of October.[41]

THE CITY

Notwithstanding these difficulties, eighteenth-century Basra was considered by its contemporaries as one of the important ports of the Indian Ocean. Various travelers from different backgrounds have left vivid accounts of this mercantile city, its administration, and its multiple communities. Those who visited the city during the first half of the century had, on the whole, a favorable impression of its overall conditions. This impression, however, would change by the end of the century.

The center of Basra was located two miles from Shatt al-ᶜArab and some eight miles northeast of the ruins of the medieval city (Map 1.6).[42] Its walls, built during the rule of Ḥusayn Pasha Afrisayab

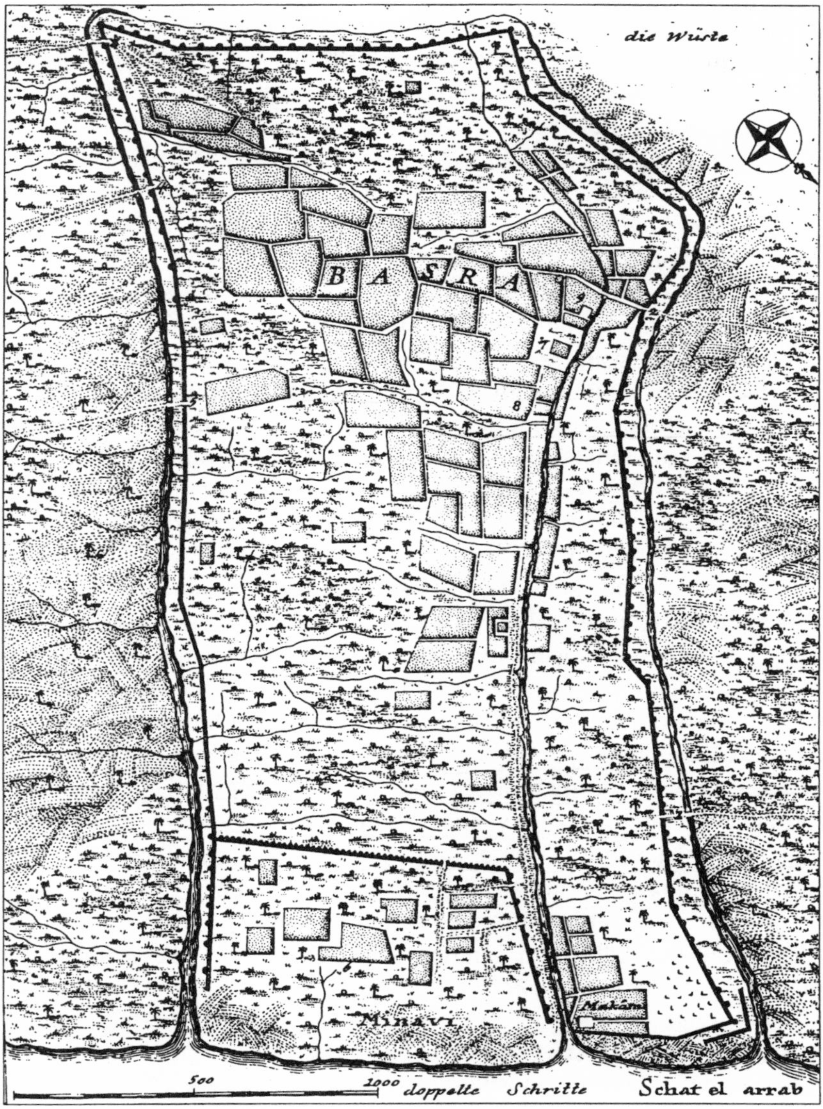

MAP 1.6
The City of Basra as Drawn by Carsten Niebuhr, c.1768
(*Source:* Carsten Niebuhr, *Voyage en Arabie*, p. 170)

(1650–68), were made from mud and sun-dried bricks.[43] They had five gates and 131 armed towers and surrounded the city from three sides, extending east all the way to Shatt al-ᶜArab.[44] William Heude in 1817 and George Kepple in 1824 both estimated the walls' circumference at eight miles.[45] This agrees with the measurement of the ditch that surrounded the city outside the walls and is still observable today.[46] The only source which contradicted this estimate was al-Bazi. He stated that Basra's walls measured four-by-three miles. Unfortunately, he did not mention how he reached this figure.[47] Maintaining the walls was a duty incumbent upon all the male inhabitants of the city. Even the wali would occasionally appear, working to repair some gap or remove accumulated sand from the foot of the walls.[48] Despite their mean appearance, the walls withstood the three-month siege of Nadir Shah in 1743 and held off Karim Khan's forces for thirteen months before the starving city surrendered in 1776. By the end of the century, though, its maintenance appears to have been neglected.

In 1786–1787, a traveler from India noted that many of the guns were unserviceable and that the walls and the towers were in a dilapidated condition.[49] The Ottoman Porte also registered its concern regarding the condition of the walls through several letters urging the wali to remedy the situation.[50] Still, in 1817, Heude estimated that only one-half of the walls were in proper condition.[51] The situation seemed to have gotten even worse by 1860, when the *qaḍi* of Basra, Aḥmad Nur al-Anṣari, complained about their state to the Ottoman governor.[52] There is little doubt that the state of the walls at the end of the century is indicative of the overall decline in the health of the city. While Ottoman security generally made many city walls unnecessary, this was not the case with frontier cities like Basra, particularly when the threat from Persia remained real throughout the century.[53]

Unfortunately, the Ottomans did not conduct a census for Basra throughout the eighteenth century. The nearest, taken in 1689, listed eighty-eight quarters (*maḥallat*).[54] By the time Niebuhr visited the city in 1764, there were seventy-two quarters.[55] Some, like Maḥallat Maydan al-ᶜAbid (Slave Market) or Maḥallat Sabbaghan ᶜAtiq (Old Dyers), refer to sites which at some time were known for a peculiar economic activity. Others, like Maḥallat Jamiᶜ al-Shaykh Aḥmad or Maḥallat Maqam ᶜAli, refer to important religious sites. Interestingly, in both the Ottoman census of 1689 and Niebuhr's list, there are hardly any quarters named after a religious, ethnic, or tribal community. Niebuhr's list contains one reference to a Maḥallat al-Yahud (Jewish quarter)and the

Ottoman census of 1689 refers to a quarter possibly belonging to the Sabeans, although the script is not legible. Nevertheless, these are the only two.[56] The great majority bore the name of a neighborhood notable, usually a religious figure. Commenting on this fact (although in reference to the previous century), Dina Khoury mentions that this could be an indication of "the openness of the city and the fluidity in the social relations of its residents."[57]

The size of these quarters varied greatly, from as few as ten to as much as four hundred houses. Each quarter had one large street from which numerous narrow winding alleys (*ʿuqud*) branched out. This, coupled with the absence of proper methods for the disposal of filth, caused most travelers to complain of the terrible stench in the center of the city. Ives mentioned that the streets "stink abominably," while Keppel thought it was "the dirtiest town even in the Turkish dominions."[58] The situation would become particularly oppressive when the winds died down. The medieval city apparently suffered similar problems, leading the Basrawi poet ibn Lanak to write the following verses:[59]

يخنُ في البصرةِ لونٌ   من العيشِ ظريفِ
نحنُ ما هبّتْ شمالٌ   بينَ جناتٍ و ريفِ
فإذا هبّتْ جنوبٌ   فكأنّا في كنيفِ

It seems that life in Basra can be very funny
If the north wind blows it feels like paradise or the countryside
But if the south wind blows it feels as though we were in a toilet

These unsanitary conditions certainly contributed to the recurring visitations of various diseases that would carry off great numbers of people. As late as 1850, an Ottoman report considered the possibility of relocating the city to escape the unhealthy climate.[60]

Most houses were very mean, constructed simply with mud and a few sun-dried bricks. It is not known exactly when the peculiar enclosed wooden balconies, typical of Basra's old upper-class houses, were first introduced. Al-Bazi believes that they were first introduced during the late Il-Khanid period. Their local name, *shanashil*, which is derived from two Turco-Mongol words (*shah*, or king, and *nashan*, or sitting area), seems to suggest an Il-Khanid origin.[61] In 1751, John Carmichael commented on the scarcity of wood and stones for construction.[62] A year prior to this, Bartholomew Plaisted had similar perceptions: "Though the city is large it has the meanest aspect. . . . The houses are generally two stories high [but built] in such a clumsy manner that the Governor's own house was no better than a dog-hole."[63]

This view was by no means held only by Europeans. Mirza Khan wrote that he "never saw a house [in Basra] that a person of moderate fortune in Lucknow would have considered respectable."[64] Nevertheless, we have no reports of dilapidated conditions until the end of the century. By 1860, al-Anṣari wrote that "nine-tenths" of the houses were totally ruined.[65]

In central Basra there were eighteen large bazaars, each specializing in one or two items. At Suq al-Qazzazah, for example, one could find silk and materials for embroidery, while Suq al-Ṣafafir specialized in copperware. There were also markets for cloth, knives, pens, camels, sheep, horses, fish, vegetables, incense, and many other articles. The bazaars opened early in the morning and closed at midday. A watchman guarded each from evening until the next morning.[66] At times when robberies increased, Basra's governors were known to have ordered the execution of anyone found in the bazaar after dark.[67] Other public buildings included about ten large mosques and over forty smaller ones, eighty-nine coffeehouses, thirty-five barber shops, several brothels, and nine bathhouses.[68] The baths opened morning to noon for women and noon to evening for men.[69]

The city was noted for the great number of religious shrines (*mazars*). The tombs of al-Zubayr ibn al-ᶜAwam and Talḥa ibn ᶜUbaydullah, two of the Prophet's companions, lie some six miles southwest of Basra. In that same location lies the tomb of Ḥasan al-Basri, whom many believe to be the founder of sufism. Within the walls the most famous mazar was that of Maqam ᶜAli, situated near Shaṭṭ al-ᶜArab. This mazar, built in honor of the Prophet's cousin and the first imam of the Shiᶜah, was said to contain ᶜAli's footprint.[70] Other mazars include the tomb of Yaḥya ibn Musa al-Kazim, the son of the seventh imam of the Shiᶜah,[71] and the circular tomb of Shaykh Muḥammad Amin al-Kawaz, head of the Shadhili sufi order of Basra, who died in 1547. The latter is located in the al-Kawaz mosque, whose fifteen-meter-high minaret was probably the tallest building in eighteenth-century Basra.[72]

Basra was famous for its many canals and creeks, leading some to have called it "the Venice of the East."[73] The most important of these was the al-ᶜAshar canal, which ran from Shaṭṭ al-ᶜArab through the length of the city. Numerous smaller canals branched out from al-ᶜAshar and Shaṭṭ al-ᶜArab to irrigate the many groves, gardens, and fields inside the city walls. In 1758 Edward Ives was moved to write that the "large vineyards, interspersed with rose-trees, fields of corn scattered up and down, and the view of the river at the same time form a picturesque and delightful landscape."[74] The gardens also produced pomegranates, figs, vegetables, and, most important, dates. Outside the walls there were large groves of date trees as well as fields of wheat, corn, and rice.[75] By the end of the century and well into the next, these canals seemed to have suffered from the same neglect that afflicted the city in general. In 1863 Pelly mentioned that the city was in ruins, with its canals "half-discarded."[76]

THE PEOPLE

Like most Ottoman cities of its time, Basra saw its population constantly fluctuate over the course of the century. Wars and the usual ups and downs of trade must have had a great impact on the number of people residing in the city at any given time. But plague, in particular, was the most ominous cause for a sudden drop in the population. In this sense, Basra was no different from the larger Ottoman cities like Istanbul, Cairo, and Izmir (Smyrna).[77] Between 1690 and 1800 there were at least six major outbreaks of plague, with numerous minor ones occurring in between.[78] During the plague of 1773, for example, nearly one-third of the inhabitants perished.[79] Most of the rest fled the city and did not return until several months after the plague had died out.

The Ottoman census of 1689 lists 5,557 households (*ḥanah*) plus 1,757 individuals (*mujarrad*).[80] Assuming that each household consisted of an average of 6 individuals, the total population would be 35,099. Ives, in 1758, mentioned that it was a "large, populous" city, and gives a rather inflated estimate of 60 or 70,000 inhabitants.[81] Niebuhr, a more careful observer, put the figure at 40,000 to 50,000 some 7 years later. His estimate, which tends to agree more with the Ottoman census (taking into consideration the time difference), assumed that the average number of houses were about 100 in each quarter, with each house containing 7 individuals.[82] The Iraqi historian ᶜAbdul-Qadir Bash-Aᶜyan al-ᶜAbbasi states that the population in 1765 was 60,000, but does not say how he arrived at such a figure,[83] while Yılmaz, quoting a 1768 French report, puts the figure at 70,000.[84]

Although Niebuhr's estimate seems the most reasonable, all these figures represent a significant increase in the population over the previous two centuries.

In the middle of the sixteenth century, it was estimated at only 16,000 residents living in 28 quarters.[85] By the end of the sixteenth century, Ottoman sources show that the population had climbed to nearly 20,000 before reaching the figures quoted above in the following two centuries.[86] In comparison, Baghdad in the late sixteenth century had a population of around 68,600,[87] climbing to 80,000 two centuries later.[88] This pattern is also visible in other Arab cities of the Ottoman Empire. Aleppo's population climbed from 80,000 in 1537 to 120,000 at the end of the eighteenth century, Damascus witnessed a rise from 52,000 in the early sixteenth century to 90,000 by 1800, and Cairo's population grew from 150,000 in 1517 to 263,000 in 1798.[89]

Also typical of other Ottoman cities (but perhaps more so), Basra's population represented a mosaic of religions, cultures and races.[90] Most travelers found Basrawis to have been quite friendly and hospitable to strangers.[91] Others, like Mirza Khan, would only say that the "majority . . . are low minded and of avaricious dispositions."[92] Most of the residents were Arabs, Turks, Persians, Jews, and Armenians, although "on close inquiry . . . [one could find] natives of every country in Asia."[93] Unfortunately, there are no consistent numerical estimations of each group. The great majority of the population were Arabs. Al-Ḥaydari mentions that the original inhabitants of the city were Sunni Shafiᶜis, whereas the people in the surrounding country were mainly "*rafaḍah*."[94] Many of Basra's Shiᶜis were of Persian origin.[95] There were also a number of Turks and Georgians, who were mainly government officials and soldiers.

The original Arab Sunni inhabitants of Basra trace their ancestry back to the tribes that came out of Arabia during the Islamic conquest of Iraq in A.D. 636. The majority believe that they descended from either Kalb or Tamim.[96] Sunni Arab families were the most powerful in the city and they dominated the *aᶜyan*, or urban men of influence. Among the best known were al-Kawazi, al-Rudayni, al-Kanᶜani, al-Naqib, and Rizq.[97] During the eighteenth century, however, there was growing reference to the Najadah, or people from Najd in Arabia. By the early nineteenth century their number and prestige had reached the point where they were able to directly challenge the governor's troops in a blood feud.[98] Among their leading families were al-Faddagh, Waṭban, al-Samiṭ, Mubarak, and ᶜAbdul-Razaq.[99]

The Arab Shiᶜis usually belonged to the surrounding tribes, the largest of which were the Muntafiq and Kaᶜb. Most tribesmen were in the city as temporary laborers. They maintained strong contacts with their kinsmen outside the city walls, and often called upon their tribe's aid when threatened. Hamilton, referring to the Kaᶜb people in Basra, mentioned that they "are not to be rigorously dealt with, for they are a people very bold, revengeful and cunning."[100] In April 1774, the city paid dearly for executing a member of the Kaᶜb tribe, suffering from various acts of retaliation, including the burning and plundering of several bazaars.[101] In addition to their tribal loyalties, there was considerable tension between Sunni and Shiᶜi Arabs. The Armenian traveler Joseph Emin recalled how during his trip down the Euphrates the Sunni merchants that accompanied him had to pretend to be Shiᶜi for fear of being killed by the surrounding tribes.[102]

Travelers also noted the large numbers of resident Armenians and Jews, both of whom could claim a number of Basra's wealthiest merchants. Most Armenians came from the quarter of New Julfa in Isfahan.[103] In addition to being merchants, many were shopowners, jewelers, brokers, and translators. Other Christians included several Syrians and a community of about sixty to seventy Catholics.[104] The Jews had a longer history in Basra. They practiced brokerage, money-lending, and exchange (*ṣarrafs*), and had a strong influence on the government, particularly at the end of the century.[105] Other communities included about one hundred *banyans*[106] and several hundred Sabeans.

Otter mentioned that "all" the ṣarrafs of Basra were Indians. While this is a bit of an exaggeration, it does highlight the importance of money transfers to India.[107] In the early seventeenth century the prestige of the Indian community reached a point where they were allowed, notwithstanding traditional Islamic sensitivities, to import a representation of the deity Govindaraj from India.[108] The Carmelite Fathers wrote much about the religion of the Sabeans (or Mandaeans) of Basra, but very little about their social conditions. Niebuhr mentioned that most of them were poor and generally held in low esteem by the inhabitants.[109] In general, the Sabeans of Iraq at this time were usually artisans, carpenters, boat-builders, and, later on, silversmiths.[110] Dina Khoury, citing the Carmelite Fathers, mentions that some were engaged in long-distance trade,[111] yet a consultation of the same source did not substantiate this claim.[112]

Like most other port cities, Basra had a large number of foreigners who came as traders, travelers, and sailors. Throughout the eighteenth century the records refer to the presence of merchants from Greece, Italy (especially Venice), Portugal, Holland, France, and England. In the eighteenth century, the most active European power in the Gulf was England. By the middle of the century, it had clearly become the most important European nation in Basra.[113] English commercial relations with Basra went back to 1635, yet it was not until 1723, one year after the fall of the Safavids, that the English East India Company established its first permanent factory there.[114] Beginning in 1744, the English and French repeatedly fought over the control of southern India. After defeating France in 1761, the Company began to rapidly increase its commercial interests in Basra.[115] In 1763, Basra replaced Bandar ᶜAbbas as the Company's agency in the Persian Gulf, and a year later the Porte recognized the English agent as consul. At the end of the century Basra's declining trade resulted in the agency's reduction to the level of a residency, and there was even some discussion of closing it down altogether. Nevertheless, the outbreak of war with France, Napoleon's invasion of Egypt, and the strategic importance of the port, especially for forwarding mail between England and India, kept the residency open.

The Dutch had also established commercial links with Basra as early as the middle of the seventeenth century. Their position, however, always seemed tentative. It was not until 1724 that the Dutch East India Company (VOC) began to show some "reasonable profits" from its Basra factory.[116] By 1752, however, a quarrel with the local authorities caused them to withdraw again. By the late 1750s it became clear that the VOC was no longer capable of competing with the English, and Dutch ships were rarely seen in the Gulf. The last time they were heard from was in 1793, when they decided to reject an offer by the wali of Baghdad to return to Basra due to the poor commercial outlook in that city.[117] The only other European power that attempted to establish a firm commercial relationship with Basra at this time was France. The earliest French contacts date back to 1638, when the Vatican appointed the first Latin bishop of Babylon to Basra.[118] Several years later, the French assigned the head of the Carmelite order in Basra as consul.[119] Despite their early presence and numerous attempts, the French never established a consistent trade with Basra, and by the middle of the eighteenth century even the occasional visit by a merchant ship had become a rarity.

ADMINISTRATION AND POWER

After the Ottoman conquest of Iraq in the sixteenth century, Basra was designated a *saliyanah* province (or a province with a salary).[120] This meant that the governor of Basra, after paying his administrative expenses, was required to remit to Istanbul a pre-set sum known as the *irsaliyah.* This pre-set sum was collected through a system of tax-farms known as the *iltizam* system.[121] According to this system the state would lease some revenue-making object (land or customs), known as a *muqaṭaʿah*, to a tax-farmer. In return, the tax-farmer agreed to pay the state some agreed-upon sum, keeping for himself anything in excess of that sum. Administratively, Basra had three pillars of political power. At the top stood the governor (whether wali or mutasallim) and his military-administrative establishment, manned primarily by mamluks and local militia of various forms. The judicial establishment occupied the next level, with the qadi, appointed directly by the Porte, at its helm. Lastly, representatives of the aʿyan acted as an advisory group to the governor. Inevitably, though, the system functioned in a much more complex manner, where contacts, relations, tribal origin, and family background mattered more than membership in any of the above bodies.

For most of the eighteenth century, Basra was governed by a mutasallim appointed by the wali of Baghdad. Initially, the mutasallim's primary function was to take over the rule of the province in the event of the wali's removal. He would remain in this "caretaker" role until the appointment of a new wali by the Porte.[122] By the eighteenth century the post had become permanent and its functions had likewise changed. In the province of Baghdad and Basra the mutasallim soon became the third most powerful official after the wali and the *kahyah.*[123] In addition to its high rank, this post also provided aspiring officials the opportunity to develop, independently of Baghdad, the networks and contacts necessary for advancement to the post of wali. Both Sulayman Abu Laylah and Sulayman the Great, two of the greatest mamluk walis, were mutasallims of Basra prior to their accession to the post of wali of Baghdad. The same was true of Aḥmad Pasha, the last nonmamluk Ottoman wali of Baghdad in the eighteenth century. Aḥmad Pasha became the wali of Basra in 1716 and of Baghdad in 1724.[124]

The relative importance of government posts at the beginning of the century can be gathered by observing a list of the presents which the English East India Company representative gave the leading officials of Basra in 1702 (Table 1.1). At the time, Basra was still a separate province.

What is interesting about this list is the importance awarded to the qubṭan pasha, who had his own kahyah. In a separate letter the English representative mentions that the qubṭan pasha was a person of great power and influence in the city.[125] This post refers to the commander of the fleet stationed at Shaṭṭ al-ᶜArab. The Carmelite Fathers recorded that in 1702 the fleet consisted of "forty warships with the same number of smaller vessels."[126] During the early part of the century the qubṭan pasha was considered second only to the mutasallim in the hierarchy of Basra's government, with a generous share of the city's tax-farms held in his name.[127] In addition, the qubṭan pasha also received a handsome salary, which for 1741 totaled 15,000 ghurush.[128] Initially the order for his appointment or removal came directly from Istanbul. In 1741, for example, when the wali needed a more reliable qubṭan pasha to face a tribal threat, he was forced to petition the Porte in Istanbul rather than take any action directly.[129] By the second half of the century, however, Baghdad's influence over Basra increased and with it the power to appoint the qubṭan pasha.[130] Baghdad's control seemed to have reduced his power, as subsequent sources do not portray him in the same light. The decline in his power is evident from the reduction in the size of Basra's fleet. Early in the century, the qubṭan pasha commanded fifty to sixty ships; by the 1780s the fleet was reduced to twelve ships.[131]

TABLE 1.1
Gifts (in rupees) Given by the
English East India Company to Basra Officials, 1702

Pasha	350
Qubṭan pasha	150
Kahyah and *shahbandar*	70 each
Khaznadar, *diwan effendi*, two officials of the custom house, and the kahyah of the qubṭan pasha	30 each

Source: IOR, Occasional Correspondence, E/3/65, Letter from Bussora dated December 22, 1702, no. 8094.

The mutasallim's post was always tenuous. Baghdad, fearing the development of an independent power base, seldom allowed a mutasallim to remain at his post for long. This naturally caused much anxiety and instability, particularly because the first demand of a new mutasallim was usually in the form of financial gifts. The wali also sought to gain financially by constantly replacing officials since most of the important posts were farmed out to the highest bidder. By the end of the century, this practice seemed to have become more common. Once appointed, a new mutasallim soon found out that he was not able to command much power on his own. In 1786, ᶜAbdul-Qadir observed that the mutasallim was "the ruler of Basra only in name."[132] The people, in general, had a much greater sense of loyalty toward their local neighborhood leaders, tribal shaykhs and landowners, or the heads of their religious communities, rather than to a governor who was usually a total stranger. Still, a successful mutasallim was able to increase his powers by exploiting the differences among these local leaders.

The mutasallim's right-hand man in Basra was the shahbandar. Like the qubṭan pasha, he had a seat on the city's *diwan*, or assembly of leading notables including some of the leading aᶜyan, the qaḍi, the *muftis*, and the top government officers. The main role of the shahbandar was to ensure the orderly functioning of the custom house, represent the government to the merchants, and help mediate their conflicts. The Carmelite Fathers referred to him as the "judge of the merchants."[133] When Ḥajji Ismaᶜil, a merchant of some note, petitioned the government on a contractual dispute with a number of English merchants in 1726, the shahbandar was appointed to look into the matter.[134]

The janissaries represented the main military force of the government. In 1721, Hamilton estimated their numbers at three thousand, with one thousand more at Qurnah.[135] It is doubtful, however, that such a large force was maintained near Basra during peacetime. Neither the Ottoman, European, or local sources clarify whether these janissaries were the local descendants of Ottoman soldiers (known as the *yerli kullari*), or whether they might have been sent directly from Istanbul (*kapi kullari*).[136] None of the officers, with the exception of the *agha* of the janissaries, who had a seat on the diwan, were permitted to enter Basra without special authorization.[137] Basrawis generally regarded them with some apprehension since they were often prone to mischief and plunder, particularly if their pay was delayed. The mutasallim usually had a difficult time controlling their *'urṭas*,[138] which tended to act like gangs, constantly harassing the merchants and shopkeepers for protection money. After the death of Sulayman Abu Laylah in 1762, the mutasallim was powerless to prevent them from plundering a great number of homes and shops. At times, the 'urṭas even fought each other for control of certain quarters.[139] By the end of the century, though, Sulayman the Great successfully disbanded most of the janissary 'urṭas.[140] The city also had an irregular militia called, most likely, the *lawand*.[141] Niebuhr mentions that within this militia one could find a number of merchants as well as simple seamen, porters, and others of the lower classes.[142] Membership was voluntary and none of the men received pay for their services.

Travelers have always said much about the unstable nature of Ottoman provincial governments and the frequency with which they changed. Few, however, have commented on the stability and continuity that the aᶜyan presented.[143] The aᶜyan are a difficult group to define precisely because the meaning of the term tended to change over time and place. In general they were (for various reasons) prestigious members of the community, or men of great influence. Their influence meant that they formed an intermediary group between the government and the people and were regularly consulted on matters affecting the general population. In Basra, they tended to be, with few exceptions, a mostly urban phenomenon. The eighteenth century, in particular, witnessed a significant rise in the power of the aᶜyan throughout the Ottoman Empire. Historians have argued that there were two major causes for this. The first relates to the empire's gradual shift to the system of tax-farming during the seventeenth century. This, in turn, tended to open up "opportunities for the local population to obtain access to resources previously monopolized by the state and its agents."[144] The Porte also encouraged the growth of the political power of the aᶜyan as a counterforce to that of the increasingly independent-minded walis.[145] The title was, for example, recognized by the Porte, but it did not carry with it any official post.

The aᶜyan of Basra, in this respect, were not unlike their counterparts in other Ottoman cities. Niebuhr mentions that the real power in Basra was divided between the aᶜyan[146] and the janissary troops. The wali (or later, the mutasallim) usually called on the aᶜyan (most of whom were merchants) whenever he was faced with a tough decision requiring the active support of the inhabitants.[147] At other times, the aᶜyan had the power to elect a temporary wali after the death of the one sent by the Porte.[148] The number of those considered members of the aᶜyan varied from year to year, but in 1775 twenty-nine people sat on the Basra diwan.[149] Of these, eleven were representatives of Basra's aᶜyan while the rest were government officials, some of whom might also have been local aᶜyan. By the middle of the century, the aᶜyan's already considerable influence and power appeared to be increasing. They even managed, at times, to openly challenge the will of the wali of Baghdad who now controlled Basra. In 1773, for example, the aᶜyan succeeded in demanding that the wali reinstate the popular mutasallim Sulayman Agha (later the wali Sulayman the Great) who had been recalled earlier in the year.[150]

Throughout the eighteenth century the head of the aᶜyan always came from the al-Kawazi family. In recognition of his family's influence, the Porte, in 1706, granted Shaykh ᶜAbdul-Laṭif al-Kawazi (a prominent sayyid)[151] the hereditary title of "Bash Aᶜyan al-Baṣrah."[152] For much of the century this post was occupied by his son, Shaykh Darwish al-Kawazi, who constantly mediated conflicts with the tribes, argued on behalf of the merchants, and generally played a prominent political role. The extent of his influence can be gathered from an event in 1769 when the leading aᶜyan and the mutasallim conspired with Shaykh ᶜAbdullah of the Muntafiq tribe against the wali of Baghdad. In the aftermath of their failed conspiracy, the wali executed most of the government officials, including the mutasallim, yet he merely chastised Shaykh Darwish al-Kawazi and then set him free.[153]

Another important member of the aᶜyan was the *naqib al-ashraf*, who presided over the community of sayyids. In the eighteenth century, this post was always occupied by a member of the al-Rifaᶜi family.[154] In addition to the prestige gained by handling the affairs of the sayyids and checking their lineages, the Rifaᶜi family also brought the post increased influence due to their position as shaykhs of the Rifaᶜiyyah sufi order. This order, established in the twelfth century by Shaykh Aḥmad al-Rifaᶜi, was the most important sufi order in Basra.[155] Although the information here is limited, it is known that the Rifaᶜiyyah order included members from various social classes, such as artisans, peddlers, lower ᶜulama', dervishes, and others from the lower classes.[156] Many of the guilds, or *aṣnaf*, of Basra also acknowledged the leadership of the Rifaᶜiyyah shaykhs.[157] The shaykhs of the Rifaᶜiyyah order also gained power through the enormous wealth that they commanded. Much of this wealth came from their role as caretakers of the many endowments that were presented to the order, all of which were exempt from taxation. Among the most noted naqib al-ashraf of Basra in the eighteenth century was Shaykh Mahdi al-Rifaᶜi who, at the end of the century, succeeded in establishing a *zawiyah* for his order in Baghdad.[158]

The diwan also included the so-called caravan *bashi* and, in rare instances, leaders of *dhimmi* communities. The caravan bashi, usually a shaykh of one of the important tribes inhabiting the Syrian desert, was responsible for organizing the biannual caravans to Aleppo.[159] The leaders of the Jewish and Armenian communities were, at times, invited to attend a meeting of the diwan when issues concerning their communities were discussed. At the end of the century, though, when the influence of the Jewish merchants increased, the head of the Jewish community became a regular member of the diwan.[160]

At the head of the religious and judiciary establishments were the qaḍi and mufti. Unlike the qaḍi of Baghdad, who was from the elite of Ottoman qaḍis, Basra's qaḍi usually came from the lower ranks. He was rarely Arab (although later in the century many were) and gained his income from fees, charity, fines, and, sometimes, bribes.[161] Since he usually did not speak the local Arabic dialect, his *na'ib* (assistant), a native of Basra, attended to most of the cases himself.[162] Although the qaḍi was supposed to receive his appointment from the Porte, Baghdad always had an important say in the matter, especially during the mamluk period. In 1773, for example, the qaḍi ᶜAbdul-Raḥman al-Suwaydi received his appointment directly from Baghdad's wali, ᶜUmar Pasha, without the Porte's prior knowledge.[163] Basra also had two muftis, a Ḥanafi, representing the official Ottoman *madhhab*, and a Shafiᶜi, representing the madhhab of the majority of Basrawis. Both sat on the diwan, although the Ḥanafi mufti enjoyed a higher status. The office of the Hanafi mufti became hereditary sometime in the mid-sixteenth century after the Ottoman conquest of Iraq, while that of the Shafiᶜi mufti became hereditary during the first decade of Sulayman Abu-Laylah's rule in the 1750s.[164] Each had a na'ib which assisted him in all his duties.[163] The Shiᶜis had no representative in the diwan, nor were they recognized as a legitimate Islamic madhhab.

The surrounding tribal confederacies represented another important political force. Large migrations from Arabia along with continued low urbanization allowed the tribes to constitute the great majority of the people in the province of Baghdad and Basra. ᶜAli al-Wardi estimates that in the nineteenth century up to three-fourths of the people in Iraq had rural tribal affiliation.[166] This great demographic upheaval began, most likely, early in the seventeenth century as a result of a prolonged drought affecting Najd in central Arabia. Entire tribes were forced to move out of Najd in search of water and forage driving, in their turn, other tribes from their lands. In the process the tribal population of Iraq and Syria rapidly multiplied.[167] Najdi tribes, however, were unable to outrightly occupy southern Iraq due to the existence of the great Muntafiq tribes. This confederacy, the largest of the southern tribal confederacies, occupied areas between Qurnah and present-day Nasiriyyah and Kut. The origin of the Banu al-Muntafiq goes back to pre-Islamic times, when they inhabited areas of central Arabia. The tribe participated in the Islamic conquest of Iraq and as a result, settled into the marshy area north of Basra.[168] By the sixteenth century, the Muntafiq had grown into a large confederation of over twenty tribes under the paramount shaykhs of Al Saᶜdun.[169] The most important of these tribes were Banu Malik, Banu Saᶜid, and al-Ajwad.[170] During the sixteenth and seventeenth centuries, Basra repeatedly fell under the direct rule of the Muntafiq shaykhs, the last of which was Shaykh Maniᶜ ibn Mughamis, who captured the city in 1690.[171]

Despite Ottoman control of the region during most of the eighteenth century, the Muntafiq rarely lost their independence, as can be seen in the numerous letters exchanged between Basra and Istanbul complaining of their insubordination.[172] Even then the Muntafiq shaykhs continued to enjoy a powerful influence over the government of Basra. In 1729, the English agent convinced the mutasallim of the necessity of having the ships of Basra take English passes for protection. He soon found out, however, that the mutasallim's decision was worthless without the approval of Shaykh Muḥammad ibn Maniᶜ.[173] Their word also carried much weight with the wali of Baghdad. Soon after the above-mentioned incident, the aᶜyan complained to Shaykh Muḥammad ibn Maniᶜ about the "evil administration" of the mutasallim. After receiving Shaykh Muḥammad's complaints, the wali had the mutasallim strangled.[174] Five decades later ᶜAbdul-Qadir would still note that Shaykh Thuwayni of the Muntafiq "virtually rules the vilayet."[175] By the end of the century the Muntafiq's growing strength led Shaykh Thuwayni to actually seize power in Basra and apply to the Porte for recognition as a wali independent of Baghdad. Even after Baghdad's wali, Sulayman the Great, defeated him, he still could not afford to alienate the tribe and agreed to reinstate Thuwayni to the shaykhdom of the Muntafiq.[176]

A final word should be mentioned concerning the political and social weight of the English agent. Notwithstanding the natural tendency of English sources to exaggerate their influence, there is little doubt that by the second half of the century the agent was recognized as one of the most influential figures in Basra. Mirza Khan remarked that Samuel Manesty, perhaps the most influential English agent at this time, was "considered by the inhabitants . . . as a person of great consequence," and "always addressed him in an adulatory and flattering manner."[177]

His influence was derived from several sources. Possibly the most important was England's growing control of the freight trade with India. By the second half of the century the agent could put the city in a panic by threatening to move his operations to Kuwait.[178] The English also made use of their overwhelming naval strength several times by coming to the assistance of Basra in conflicts with the Kaᶜb.[179] This, naturally, won them many favors. English influence over the Porte was generally growing during this period, and this was reflected, although in a limited way, in their dealings with the Basra government. The personal power of the agent, or resident as he came to be known by the end of the century, grew particularly after 1764. In that year, the resident of Basra was recognized as a British consul, making him eligible for several immunities with respect to trade duties. Being a consul also meant that all merchants trading under English protection were required to pay a "consulage" duty to the Company's resident.[180] Residents, such as Samuel Manesty, took full advantage of these rights to accumulate a huge fortune, which they used to buy influence and power.

Of all the local inhabitants the Armenians seemed to have established the closest relationship with the English resident. By 1790, the agent was being invited to the diwan as a "representative of the Christians" whenever a problem developed that involved the Armenian community.[181] It also became difficult for a mutasallim to retain his post unless he was on good terms with the resident. In one incident related by Mirza Khan in 1803, the resident had the qaḍi turned out of office as a result of a dispute between the two. This led Mirza Khan to comment that "this circumstance shows that the English possess nearly as much power in Bussora as they have in India."[182]

Basra, in the eighteenth century, was apparently defined by a myriad of contradictions. Its ideal location invited both merchant and marauder; its generally predictable wind patterns were, at times, suddenly interrupted by a destructive suwayḥili gale; and the numerous competing powers within and without the city kept alive an atmosphere of both vigilance and apprehension. Its distance from the Ottoman capital made it more susceptible to competing local interests. Nevertheless, its inhabitants rarely turned against each other in a violent manner despite their broad social diversity and the tensions in their region brought about by the fall of the Safavid Empire and the great tribal migrations from Arabia. Many of Basra's merchants successfully amassed great wealth during this century despite their unpredictable surroundings. The most successful merchant had to tread cautiously among the different powers and establish the widest possible contacts. These contacts usually involved distant and widely dispersed regions and countries tied together by trade.

CHAPTER 2

The Shifting Fortunes of Trade

For most of its history southern Iraq sat at the center of a large region tied together by trade. Many of these commercial links were as old as the earliest Mesopotamian civilizations. Evidence of caravans crossing the Syrian desert and shipping contacts with the Indus Valley abounds in ancient Sumer and Babylon.[1] During that period, raw materials, like bitumen, seem to have been the primary exports, while imports included hard rock from Iran, copper from Oman, and timber from Lebanon and the Indus Valley. Soon after its foundation in the seventh century, Basra's fame for its excellent dates reached as far as China, and its imports included numerous items destined for the great markets of Abbasid Baghdad.[2] Reflecting its extensive commercial activity during this period, the great Arab belletrist al-Jaḥiẓ referred to Basra as the "city of commerce."[3] Under Ottoman rule Basra never regained its past role as one of the paramount ports in the Middle East. Nevertheless, it continued to be an important gateway for the empire's trade with India.

Numerous travelers have reported that Basra's trade with places like India, Aleppo, and Baghdad operated on a strict timetable determined by the annual monsoon winds. The large Aleppo caravans and the "Baghdad boats" would ideally reach the city just as the India ships arrived around June or July. In reality, though, delays were common on any of these routes, causing the entire schedule to be delayed or rearranged. In addition to this, a significant amount of merchandise was distributed throughout the region in a totally unplanned and unpredictable manner through piracy, banditry, and wars. The fate of the *Islamabad* clearly illustrates how this happened. In February 1765, the ship suffered a mutiny while anchored off the southern Persian coast. After killing the captain and seizing its precious cargo of pearls, the mutinous crew sailed to the island of "Khist" (Qeshm?), near the entrance of the Gulf, where they, in turn, were seized and stripped of their treasure by the shaykh of that island. Not long after, the island was invaded by the combined forces of Nasir Khan, the ruler of a southern Persian province, and Shaykh ʿAbdullah of Hurmuz, and the treasure was divided between the two. In early autumn, Karim Khan Zand succeeded in subduing Nasir Khan and promptly took his share of the treasure to Shiraz.[4]

EXPORTS

As in the past, eighteenth-century Basra functioned primarily as a transit port between India, Yemen, and Masqat, on the one hand, and Persia, Syria, Iraq, and Anatolia on the other.[5] According to contemporary French estimates only one-sixteenth of imported goods were actually consumed in Basra; the remainder was shipped elsewhere.[6] Those articles that were produced locally for export included gall nuts (used for making ink) and rose water. There are also sundry references to maritime shipments of Arabian horses to India despite the Porte's prohibition on their export. This trade appeared to be of greater importance in the sixteenth century and it was not until the nineteenth century, fueled by British military demands in India, that the horse trade would actually take off.[7] Some of the city's surrounding fields also produced a number of crops, some of which were exported, particularly rice and barley.

The overall importance of these local exports, however, paled in comparison with the city's chief crop: dates. While the value of this commodity certainly cannot be compared to the pepper of Malabar or the textiles of Izmir or Surat, dates still played a central role in the economic, social, and even literary life of southern Iraq.[8] Travelers who visited Basra could not help but comment extensively on the beauty of the date groves that covered both banks of the Shaṭṭ al-ᶜArab. Even in the eighteenth century the region was known to produce more dates than any other area in the world.[9] There are over one hundred different varieties of dates known in Iraq today, eighty-six of which come from the Shaṭṭ al-ᶜArab region.[10] Niebuhr listed nineteen of the most popular types, including the Khaḍrawi, Ḥillawi, and Zahdi.[11] The Ḥillawi and the Jibjab were the most common date types in Basra and its immediate surroundings.[12] In 1721, Alexander Hamilton estimated that Basra exported ten thousand tons of dates annually.[13] Toward the middle of the century date exports earned an estimated 100,000 pounds sterling.[14] The state also benefited by directly taxing the producers. In 1669 owners were paying a total of 22 aqchahs (Turkish *akçe*) a year per date tree.[15] Otter observed in 1734 that there were many buildings in the city where dates were stored for later export to Baghdad, the Gulf, and India.[16] A constant worry for merchants was whether they would be able to ship the dates before they start going bad. In an interesting letter written by a number of Basrawi merchants to the Porte, this was listed as one of their main concerns.[17]

In addition to their good taste and high nutritional value,[18] dates were highly valued by shipowners for use as ballast to stabilize their ships. Rather than stones, heavy metals, or even jars of water, dates were preferred because they could be sold at a handsome profit while also serving an indispensable purpose. It was not unusual, therefore, for ships bound for India to delay their departures as long as possible until the date baskets arrived from the surrounding countryside. One indication of how important dates were as a ballast was that "baskets of dates provided the standard measurement of shipping space and of the size of the vessel" throughout the Persian Gulf.[19] This type of demand had the effect of employing a large number of the population in the various stages associated with fertilization, care, harvest, packing, and shipping.[20] Cultivators had to artificially fertilize the female inflorescence with pollen.[21] This usually took place in April, and in August or September a large number of seasonal laborers from the surrounding tribes arrived to take part in the harvesting and packing. By late autumn or early winter ships bound for India were invariably loaded with dates.[22]

Some of the harvest was preserved through drying (*khalal maṭbukh*), or by extracting a syrup from the dates (*dibs*). In addition, dates were used in making vinegar, oil, and alcoholic drinks such as wine and *ʿaraq*.[23] The employment that the date tree provided was not limited to the fruit. Nearly every part of the tree was used in some fashion. The trunk provided wood for building houses, furniture, and small boats. Date stones were pounded and turned into cattle fodder. The large leaves made baskets, mats, and roofing material, while the outer fibers provided the raw material for rope-making.[24]

Basra had no port for large ships to dock at directly. Instead, ships would anchor in the middle of the river and unload their cargo onto a fleet of small boats for transport to the city. Some of this unloading would take place two miles below Basra at the village of Saraji. The village of Mannawi also played this role, and in the 1650s Basra's wall was extended to include it within the city.[25] The ʿAshar canal was used for transporting goods to the center of the city. Keeping this canal open was obviously a top priority requiring massive expenditure. In 1724, for example, the wali, ᶜAbdul-Raḥman Pasha, collected 12,000 ghurush from the inhabitants of the city (primarily the merchants) to cover the expenses of cleaning the canal.[26] A custom house, protected by three guns, was located at the entrance of this canal.[27] The main custom house (*gumruk*), however, was located in the center of the town.[28]

CUSTOMS DUTIES

Import and export duties at Basra changed constantly, but were considered fairly high for the time.[29] Before unloading, ships had to first pay an entry toll of unknown amount.[30] Most merchandise examined by the customs official was then divided into two classes: "fine" goods, such as most kinds of cloth, and "gruff" goods, which included such "heavy" items as metals, coffee, and spices. For most of the century, Europeans, enjoying special commercial rights granted by the Capitulations agreements,[31] paid only 3 percent duty on all goods imported or exported. The import duty was figured from the actual selling price of the items. Non-Europeans paid as high as 7.5 percent import duty on "fine" goods and 8.5 percent on "gruff" goods. This, however, was figured through an old scale of values that usually listed the value of an item below its actual worth.[32] They also paid 5.5 percent for all items exported by sea.[33]

These duties became even heavier when considering that merchants also paid various amounts at Baghdad, Aleppo, Isfahan, and Surat, allowing the aggregate duty on transported goods to reach as high as 17 percent of their original value.[34] In addition to (or often in lieu of) these official duties, merchants normally paid various unofficial fees in the form of presents and bribes. In 1756, the agent reported that merchants were obliged to give the mutasallim a "present" of 744 rupees for each "small" ship and 1,240 rupees for each "large" ship.[35] Needless to say, many merchants preferred to take their chances on smuggling, often with the connivance of the authorities. While figures on smuggling are obviously unavailable, it is likely that smugglers usually unloaded Indian goods at night at some point along the Shaṭṭ al-ᶜArab and carried them by camel into the city or to the village of Zubayr for later transport to Aleppo or Baghdad. During the second half of the century, Kuwait also served as a port for smugglers.[36]

The commercial customs duties that Basra collected were the city's most important source of revenue. In 1707 almost half of the city's 215,335 ghurush in revenues came from the customs duties.[37] Although the total amounts collected were much higher in 1707, this percentage was about the same in 1551 when Basra's revenues were 2,935,551 aqchah.[38] Even in 1704, when Basra's trade declined sharply due to conflicts with the Muntafiq tribe, Basra's customs revenue recorded 153,351.5 ghurush.[39] Unfortunately, the available Ottoman documents do not show whether this percentage or actual amount changed over the course of the eighteenth century. As Mehmet Genc points out, the tax-farming system tended to freeze the recorded revenues and the amount sent to the Porte so that "no matter how much the actual tax revenues collected from any economic activity may have increased in time, the amount of revenues handed over to the [central] Treasury did not change."[40] Most of the customs revenues came from ships arriving from India. In 1707, for example, the Basra authorities collected the handsome total of 7,807.5 ghurush from only one ship loaded mainly with lead, tin, sugar, and other goods.[41] Of this, 1,102.5 ghurush was categorized as iltizam (tax-farm), 284 ghurush went to the *miri* (collected directly by the Porte), and 394.5 ghurush taken as court expenses, with the remainder going to the city's treasury.

THE SHIPS AND THEIR SAILORS

Maritime trade, clearly the most important part of Basra's commercial activities, was carried out by numerous types of vessels. Information on the types of ships that sailed the Persian Gulf in the eighteenth century is extremely rare. Most of the local vessels used in the eighteenth century disappeared or changed radically by the nineteenth century.[42] References to the names of the vessels by contemporary travelers must be viewed cautiously since these names changed greatly over the years so that one used in the eighteenth century might mean something totally different in the twentieth. Also, the names of vessels differed from port to port so that a description of a *dhow* off the African coast might not necessarily be applicable to the Gulf.[43] The available information suggests that during the medieval period the hulls of Indo-Arab ships were double-ended, and planks and other parts were stitched or sewn together with "cairo" or twine made of the fiber of the coconut tree.[44]

Portuguese influence in the sixteenth century led to several important changes, such as the use of nails and the appearance of the square stern (*al-kashtil*). Between the sixteenth and eighteenth centuries, most

Indo-Arab trading vessels were between one hundred tons and two hundred tons in size and had a single mast with one large lateen sail. To increase their carrying capacity, most ships were not decked.[45] The vessels were likely built at Surat, along the Indus River, or at ports along the Malabar coast, using teak or coconut wood.[46] Among the most common types that operated in the Persian Gulf were the *tranki*, *ghrab*, *ghalafah*, and the smaller *dinghy*.[47] Larger vessels included the *baghalah*, *ganja*, *sanbuq*, dhow, and *jihazi*. Unfortunately, most of these names "remain as terms without much indication of what they actually were."[48] The available information suggests that the tranki, ghrab, and ghalafah all used both a sail and oars.[49] According to one contemporary source, the dinghy had

> no deck except just abaft, which covers the man at the helm below which there is a place to put goods that might suffer materially by the rain; the stern is much higher than any other part, and are altogether, most clumsy, inconvenient, unmanageable things.[50]

J. A. Stocqueler, an English traveler, left the following description of the baghalah in 1831:

> Buggales are large boats averaging from one to two hundred tons burthen; they have high sterns and pointed prows, one large cabin on a somewhat inclined plane, galleries and stern windows; they usually carry two large latteen sails, and occasionally a jib; are generally built at Cochin and other places on the Malabar coast. . . . The Nasserie, on which I engaged a passage, . . . was manned by about forty or fifty natives of Grane, or Koete [Kuwait].[51]

The other large native vessel that was common in the eighteenth century, the *dhow*, was "about 150 to 250 tons burthen."[52] They were "distinguished from baghalahs by a long gallery projecting from the stern, which is their peculiar characteristic."[53]

The captain of the ship was known as the *nakhudhah*, a title common in the Indian Ocean. The most important factor that separated the nakhudhah from his European counterpart was the nature of his relationship with the sailors. As Stocqueler relates, the lack of a system of strict hierarchy on board Arab ships seemed quite similar to those within the tribal societies of the Gulf and Arabia:

> The sailors acknowledged a kind of paternal authority on the part of the commander, and mixed with their ready obedience to his mandates a familiarity quite foreign to English notions of respect, and the due maintenance of subordination.[54]

In most cases the nakhudhah owned his own ship and was hired by a merchant or governor. This was usually the case with the Masqat fleet of the eighteenth century. In 1796, for example, the Omani nakhudhahs Ibrahim, Maḥmud Bashir, and Abdul-Laṭif, owned the *Raḥmani*, *Idrisi*, and *ᶜUthmani*, respectively.[55] The exception was represented by such great Indian shipowning families as the ᶜAbdul-Ghafurs and Chalabis of Surat. Here, the nakhudhahs did not own the vessels but were simply employees of the owners. The nakhudhahs and the sailors were, however, allowed to bring a limited cargo, free of charge, which they sold or traded during their voyage.[56]

If the information on the ships is meager, then the knowledge of the sailors of Basra or the Persian Gulf in the eighteenth century is practically nonexistent. An average large ship trading with India had a crew of fifty to eighty men in addition to the nakhudhah and two mates.[57] K. N. Chaudhuri argued that the danger and unpredictable nature of the sea generally led sailors in the Indian Ocean to resort to "semi-magic rituals and ceremonies."[58] In addition to local vessels, many of Basra's sailors were widely employed on European ships and, at times, played a role in influencing policy. In 1743, for example, the English agent at Basra, sensing the approach of Nadir Shah's army and wishing to uphold a policy of neutrality, ordered the EEIC ship *Francis & Mary* out to sea. He was surprised that five days later the ship reappeared in the river. The captain explained that "his Lascars,[59] who were all Bussorah people, had obliged him to return here again," so that the ship may join in the defense of their city.[60]

BASRA'S OVERALL TRADE PATTERNS

The task of presenting an accurate view of the nature of eighteenth-century trade is severely handicapped by the dearth of dependable data over a reasonable period of time. Ottoman financial documents on Basra do not help much since the tax-farms rarely changed throughout the century. Thus, from 1701 to 1754 the total recorded revenues of the Basra treasury did not change from 75,000 ghurush per year, which is certainly too low a sum anyway. In 1755 it went up to 97,252 ghurush and remained that way throughout the century.[61] To make matters worse, Basra's incorporation within the province of Baghdad, and Baghdad's growing autonomy during this period, meant that there were very few detailed reports from Basra that were reaching Istanbul.

Locally the merchants rarely relied upon written agreements or documents. Likewise, Basra's custom house (or gumruk) records did not survive long beyond their date of entry. Usually, most of the gumruk muqaṭaᶜah was held by the wali or the mutasallim, which he then farmed out to various individuals. Records of these agreements have not survived.

The sources suggest that Basra's commercial health during the first decade of the eighteenth century was not good. At the turn of the century Basra was under Persian rule. While the early years of this rule appear to have brought some prosperity to the city, it later grew sour due to poor relations with the surrounding tribes and the appointment of a more heavy-handed governor. Throughout 1700, the Muntafiq tribes led by Shaykh Mahanna harassed the city, practically cutting off all trade routes.[62] The Ottoman reconquest of Basra in 1701 did not lead to an immediate commercial revival. In 1707 an interesting meeting took place between the Ottoman wali, Khalil Pasha, and the city's leading merchants to discuss the causes behind the depressed state of Basra's trade.[63] During the meeting the merchants complained that only four ships had arrived from India in the past two years and these were loaded to only one-third capacity. They also mentioned that they had written to their partners in Baghdad, Mosul, Diyarbakr, and Aleppo, telling them not to come because there was nothing for them to buy at Basra. In listing the causes for this situation, the merchants mentioned, above all, the lack of security in the countryside and the Persian Gulf due to the hostility of the Muntafiq tribes and the imam of Masqat. While Basra's trade began to pick up in the years following this meeting, Ottoman sources still complained of insubordinate tribes interfering with trade during the second decade of the century.[64]

It was not until the early part of the second decade that trade began to significantly pick up. The collapse of the Safavid Empire was accompanied by the decline of the empire's primary port of Bandar ᶜAbbas, allowing Basra to become the leading commercial port in the Persian Gulf.[65] In addition the Ottomans had, by now, successfully established a fair amount of security in the hinterland, allowing for a relatively free flow of trade. There is, for the remainder of the century, an almost unbroken record of Basra's trade. Representatives of the English East India Company (EEIC), who remained in Basra for most of the eighteenth century, recorded the arrival and departure of most ships above one hundred tons in size. By comparing the diaries of the English agent at Basra with those at Bandar ᶜAbbas[66] (which also reported on Basra's shipping) and the monthly reports sent to London, a rough picture of the volume of shipping from 1724 to 1793 can be established. These dates represent a period where the records appear mostly in order, albeit with some breaks.

The volume of shipping fails to take into account the riverine and caravan trade, although, by all accounts, these depended directly on the India trade. The amounts of imports and exports involved are also not mentioned, yet it is unlikely that ships, over a seventy-year period, would continue to arrive if they were not selling and buying profitably. Also, by not taking into consideration the number of small vessels that traded at Basra, an important element of the port's maritime trade, particularly within the Persian Gulf, will be missing. This is a problem commonly encountered by Indian Ocean historians where there are no reliable estimates of the numbers of small vessels. A similar problem exists with respect to smuggling, which was also widespread. Since the goal here, however, is to establish only a sense of the general patterns of trade over the century, these deficiencies can be partially offset by accompanying the discussion of the data with eyewitness accounts and contemporary reports.

Perhaps the first recognizable feature in Figure 2.1 is the overall instability of eighteenth-century trade. Rarely were there two or three years of sustained growth or stability. Rather, the number of vessels trading at Basra rose and fell sharply from year to year, usually as a result of the frequent swings in the security of the trading routes. Such fluctuations were typical of trade in the Indian Ocean region, where the lack of accurate estimates concerning levels of demand led, time and again, to a glut in the market followed by a drastic reduction in commercial activity. In 1729, for example, the number of ships calling at Basra was relatively high. During that same year the English agent reported that the "vast quantity of [imported] goods [were] sinking" the market.[67] The following year the number of ships declined sharply, with several arriving and departing without unloading their merchandise. Figure 2.1 also illustrates the detrimental consequences of recurring disease (especially plague), tribal revolts, and war with Persia. The war with the Kaʿb in 1765 led the agent to report that, "during these commotions little or no business can be transacted in town, no money to be had and those that have any are afraid to show it, the Government's demands being very great."[68] Likewise, each war with Persia was preceded by rising tensions followed by continuing fears, both of which contributed to the depression of trade beyond the immediate

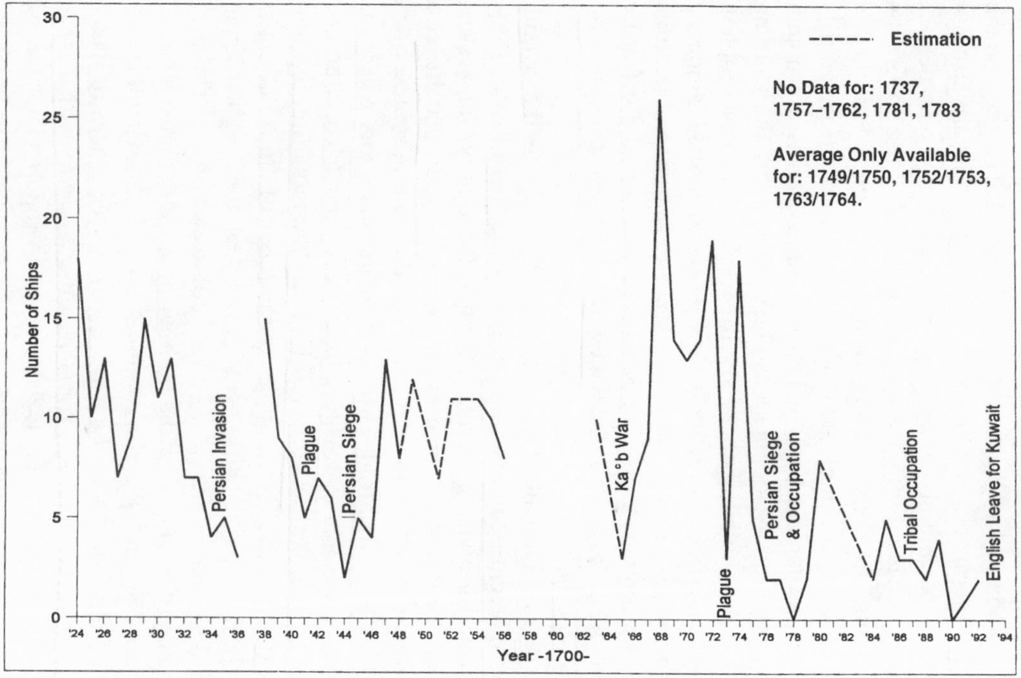

FIGURE 2.1
Total Volume of Basra Shipping, 1724–1792
(*Sources: MSA*, Bussora Factory Diaries, nos. 193–202; *MSA*, Gombroon Factory Diaries, nos. 112–118; *IOR*, Letters from Basra, nos. G/29/18–22)

period of hostilities. While a small minority of merchants benefited from these wars by winning the contracts to supply the pasha's army with provisions, the vast majority considered war one of the worse scourges of the time.

Based on the available shipping figures, presented in Figure 2.1, Basra's trade for the remainder of the century can be divided into three distinct intervals: 1724–56, 1766–74, and 1775–93.

RISE: 1724–1756

The available figures begin two years after the Afghan conquest of Iran and the subsequent civil war between the various successors of the Safavid Empire. During this period trade appears to have progressed in a relatively consistent manner, with the notable exception of the years in which Iraq became the field for the Ottoman Empire's battles with Nadir Shah's Persia.[69] In 1733, after years of foreign invasions and civil war, a resurgent Persia under Nadir Shah took the offensive against the Ottoman Empire. For the next three years several great battles were fought, Baghdad suffered a painful siege, and several attempts were made to capture Basra. As peace appeared near in 1736, the English agent wrote that the past years saw "very little trade" in Basra.[70] The figures for 1738 show that trade recovered nicely after the cessation of hostilities. The peace treaty of 1736, however, collapsed in 1743 when Nadir Shah's armies crossed the border once again. While this time the main campaigns took place in the north around Mosul, Basra also suffered from a harsh three-month siege. Once again, the letters of the English agent speak of a stagnation of trade: "There is such a scarcity of money in the place that there is hardly enough to bear the dayly expenses of the inhabitants . . . [the ships] have not carryed back any return for their cargos."[71]

The impact that these campaigns had on trade continued far beyond the immediate period of hostilities. Nearly a year after Nadir Shah's forces quit Basra, the English agent continued to complain that "the frequent alarms that we have at this place of the Persians coming tho' with ever so little foundation occasions an entire stagnation of trade and most of the principal inhabitants merchants and others have quitted the port."[72] Nevertheless, such drops in commercial activity do not appear to have been anything more than temporary disruptions. By 1746, the figures suggest that the merchants did return and trade picked up once again. Likewise, it does not appear that the various visitations of the plague had any lasting impact on trade. During the first half of the century Basra suffered from at least three major plague epidemics, each lasting two or three months. According to the head of the Carmelite church, the plague of 1727 brought trade to a virtual stop between September and November and carried off around eight thousand people.[73] Still, the figures show that once the disease had died out, trade resumed as before. If the tumultuous years of Nadir Shah's invasions were ignored, the number of large ships arriving at Basra would average around eleven per year. This figure agrees with that mentioned by Manesty and Jones in their report of 1791, in which they state that the number of large ships calling annually at Basra during the first half of the century numbered between ten and twelve.[74] According to an Ottoman source, however, Basra normally received sixteen to seventeen ships each year prior to the Persian occupation of 1697.[75]

BOOM: 1766–1774

This period begins as the wali's war with the Kaᶜb tribes begins to level off and ends with the Persian occupation of the city. During most of this period the port enjoyed a spectacular boom in trade occasioned by increased English shipping and the rise of the Masqat fleet, which monopolized the Mukha coffee trade. Such a boom is not surprising given that the mid-eighteenth century witnessed a general rise in commercial activity all over the Indian Ocean due partially to increased European, especially English, involvement. Other causes for this boom in Basra were increased security after the end of the major campaigns against the Kaᶜb, the withdrawal of Persia into a state of internal fragmentation, and the increasing involvement of the English East India Company's navy in ensuring the safety of the sea lanes.

This period of relative security was preceded by the rise of two indigenous maritime powers that temporarily threatened the shipping lanes around Basra. Between 1754 and 1766, Mir Mahanna, the shaykh of Bandar Riq, developed a strong navy that did not hesitate to challenge European ships.[76] He successfully expelled the English from Bandar Riq and seized the nearby Dutch island of Kharg. From his new well-fortified base at Kharg, Mir Mahanna attempted to attract Gulf trade and repeatedly harassed Basra's shipping until he was overthrown by his own commanders. In 1769, he was captured and executed by the mutasallim's forces while seeking asylum among the Muntafiq tribes.[77] The second power developed under the leadership of Shaykh Sulayman of the Kaᶜb. Making use of the inaccessibility of their territory deep in the marshes of present-day Khuzistan, and by playing Ottoman against Persian, the Kaᶜb were able to establish a semi-independent principality. Their navy soon began to prey on Basra's thriving maritime trade, prompting the mutasallim to launch several campaigns against their strongholds. While no decisive victory was achieved, the mutasallim, with English help, was able to limit their threat, particularly after the death of Shaykh Sulayman in 1767.[78]

The rise of these local maritime powers gradually drew the English into a more active military role. Up to the early 1760s, the EEIC presidency in Bombay had repeatedly reminded the agent at Basra to avoid all activities save those directly associated with the company's trade. In 1765, after the Kaᶜb seized two EEIC ships near Basra, this policy was abandoned in favor of providing direct support for the mutasallim's war against the Kaᶜb and protecting Basra's ships from Mir Mahanna's navy.[79] Two years later, the two sides formalized this cooperation in the form of a treaty whereby the English agreed to provide a small fleet for the protection of the port and in return the government would cover the fleet's expenses.[80] These measures apparently paid off, with trade reaching new heights in the following years.

The English navy was not the sole factor in bringing about favorable trade conditions. In 1765, the city had the fortune of having one of the best governors in its history. Sulayman Agha, who would later become Sulayman Pasha the Great, wali of Baghdad, was appointed mutasallim just as the conflict with the Kaᶜb was reaching a critical point. Originally one of Ḥasan Pasha's Georgian mamluks, the young Sulayman gradually moved up the ranks during the time of Sulayman Abu Laylah.[81] Sir H. J. Brydges, who knew him for many years, left a vivid description of one of the giants of early modern Iraq shortly after his death in 1802:

> Suleiman was, perhaps, as fine a specimen of a Turkish Pasha as ever existed. Born a Georgian, he was possessed of great manly beauty—his stature and form were such as to give the greatest effect to the magnificence of the Turkish dress—he was as expert in all military and field exercises and sports as those who made them their employment and profession—sincere and warm in the exercise and belief of his own religion, he was as tolerant as a Turk could be towards those whom an article of his own faith bound him to consider as infidels—

> exact and economical in his expenses, he was accused of avarice, but when he considered his country to be in danger, he freely and readily parted with that which he had amassed slowly and by degrees.[82]

At Basra Sulayman proved to be an excellent administrator with a special talent for mediating conflicts and gaining support for his policies through argument rather than coercion. The English agent recorded an example of his method in 1767:

> We cannot avoid observing Bussora has never known a Mussaleem more truly attachment [sic] to its interest than [Sulayman Agha] is. A few days past he assembled the several merchants of the place, set forth to them the troubles of the country and the loss in revenue that the ravages of the Chaub [Kaᶜb] had occassioned [sic] he observed to them the necessity he was under of satisfying the English their demands the impossibility of doing it and at the same time supporting his government with credit unless they contributed thereto—Mahomet Kia the late Mussaleem would the reason of force, Soliman Aga, the milder methods of persuasion.[83]

As a result the merchants agreed to pay a "free gift" to the mutasallim on each imported bale until the situation improved.[84] Such methods increased his popularity among the population in general and the merchants in particular, who normally favored a steady, cautious ruler. ᶜAbdul-Raḥman al-Suwaydi (Basra's qaḍi during part of Sulayman's governorship), who was rarely kind to his contemporary rulers, repeatedly praised Sulayman's character and leadership abilities.[85]

This fortune was suddenly interrupted by the terrible plague of 1773. The disease (probably smallpox or bubonic plague) arrived in northern Iraq from Istanbul in 1772. It rapidly spread, decimating the population of major cities and wiping out entire villages.[86] By early 1773, it reached Baghdad, where it raged for over two months. Abu Chafchir,[87] as this plague was called, arrived at Basra in early April and did not die out until the end of May.[88] There are no reliable figures on the casualties, but contemporary accounts do give a sense of the scope of the devastation. Al-Suwaydi mentioned that the plague carried away the "majority" of the residents of al-Qiblah, the quarter in which he resided during his stay in Basra.[89] After his departure to Bushire, the English agent wrote several moving letters describing the scene he had left behind:

> Neither it is in our power sufficiently to describe to you the horrid scene that we had hourly before our eyes and the dreadful accounts

> which we dayly received from Bussora . . . the inhabitants were carried off in such numbers that for several days very few could be found who were daring enough to pay the last duties to their departed friends and relations . . . the creek which runs through the town . . . was covered with clothes and beds of deceased persons, and numbers of baskets with dead bodies were seen floating up and down in it undirected but by the wind and tide—the dead were probably the owners, and had been suddenly struck whilst they were earning their daily substance.[90]

Basra's ordeal did not end with the plague's departure. The mutasallim, now with a much depleted guard, requested the aid of the Muntafiq to police the city. Instead, the tribesmen under Shaykh ᶜAbdullah committed several robberies and extortions.[91] Not to be outdone, the Kaᶜb also seized the opportunity by destroying the qubṭan pasha's fleet and house, and pillaged some of the city's suburbs. The government had to finally purchase peace with them at a very high price.[92] Describing the situation after his return to Basra, the English agent wrote:

> On our arrival here the 5th instant [January 1774] we found a great alteration indeed in the town; it appeared the picture of desolation and ruin—scarce a family but what had suffered most considerably, and amongst the rest most of our servants and dependents, the greatest part of the town uninhabited, and the few inhabitants in the other for the most part the poor remains of the villages around Bussora, whom fear had drove into the town for protection.[93]

Several years later, Manesty and Jones estimated that one-third of the population had perished as a result of the plague of Abu Chafchir.[94] The merchants bore the financial burden of the loss. Short of cash due to the closure of the custom house, the government repeatedly pressed the merchants for money. Those that fled did not fare much better since most returned to find little left in their homes. "In short," wrote the English agent, "the town [is] in so wretched a condition that it will take many years to put it into as flourishing a state as it was even some months ago."[95] The sources (Figure 2.1) show, however, that as news of the end of the plague reached India, the ships returned to Basra in numbers nearly matching those of 1772. These figures are backed by several reports of the merchants returning and trade picking up again.[96] At the end of 1774, Parsons, the English traveler, was so impressed by the revived trade of the city that he wrote: "This is the grand mart for the produce of India and Persia, Constantinople, Aleppo and Damascus; in short it is the grand oriental depository."[97]

DECLINE: 1775–1793

While the city had little problems rebounding from the effects of the plague, other, more ominous events were about to seriously damage the port's commercial livelihood. The Ottoman Empire's wars with Russia, which ended in the humiliating treaty of Kuchuk-Kainarji in 1774, certainly had a negative impact on the economy of the central provinces due to overtaxation and the devaluation of the currency.[48] These economic changes were hardly felt in distant Basra, but the war encouraged other enemies of the empire to act. Basra's rich trade revenues did not go unnoticed by a resurgent Persia under Karim Khan Zand, whose own port of Bushire was not doing nearly as well. Taking advantage of Ottoman preoccupation in Europe, Karim Khan mobilized his troops for the conquest of Basra. The cause behind Karim Khan's attack on Basra involved several issues, such as old border disputes, the rights of Iranian pilgrims in Najaf and Karbala', and the continuing power struggle in Persia.[99] The most important consideration, though, was Karim Khan's desires to revive Persia's trade. During the civil war that followed Nadir Shah's death in 1747, "trade had crept steadily away from marauding brigands and extortionate warlords to the security of Basra."[100] By 1770, the English no longer saw a profit in trading at Bushire and closed down their factory. This move, in particular, infuriated Karim Khan and he vowed to destroy Basra, which he referred to as "a great eyesore."[101]

As the Persians were beating the drums of war, Basra's charismatic mutasallim, Sulayman Agha, was busy preparing the city for a long siege, and by early 1775, the entire city had been mobilized for war. The following month, a thirty thousand strong Persian army crossed the Shaṭṭ al-ᶜArab.[102] During the siege that followed, Sulayman Agha proved to be as great a military leader as he was an administrator, holding the invaders at bay for thirteen grueling months. His hopes were kept alive by repeated promises from Baghdad that an army would soon be sent to relieve the increasingly desperate city. The army never arrived, and on April 20, 1776, the starving city surrendered.[103] During the ensuing Persian occupation, trade declined to a trickle despite attempts by Karim Khan to promote Basra as Persia's new emporium. The initial rule of Sadiq Khan, Karim Khan's brother, was generally tolerable. Matters changed, however, under the governorship of ʿAli Muḥammad Khan, who is universally described as a brutal tyrant.[104] Under his rule, taxes were raised, properties confiscated, and families scandalized.

Within three years the people of Basra had suffered from the ravages of plague, tribal attacks, siege, starvation, and a harsh occupation. Just when their fate seemed hopelessly sealed, help arrived from the Muntafiq under Shaykh Thamir. In September 1778, the Persians were totally routed by the tribal army in the marshes north of Basra.[105] After hearing of the death of Karim Khan, in March of the following year, the remnants of the Persian occupation force withdrew, leaving Basra "a depopulated and ruinous city."[106]

As brutal as these events were, previous experiences with plagues and wars suggest that the city would have been poised for commercial growth once the danger had passed. This time, however, the commercial decline persisted, with a limited recovery in 1780 proving to be short-lived. Prior to the Persian occupation Basra's custom house collected a healthy three thousand to four thousand tumans annually from European ships alone. In 1785, this amount had dwindled to only five hundred tumans or less.[107] After 1780 profits for English merchants fell sharply and the French (who were planing to reestablish trade links with the region) now considered sending their ships up the Red Sea instead of the Gulf due to the decline of Basra's trade.[108] The weakness that these conditions caused allowed the Muntafiq to capture Basra in 1787, dealing yet another blow to any recovery for some time. By 1789, Basra's pre-1773 annual importation of three thousand bales of Indian piece goods was reduced to less than eight hundred bales.[109] This decline, unlike others that had occurred throughout the century, continued well into the nineteenth century. As late as 1840, a French consular agent reported that Basra's population had fallen to only five thousand inhabitants.[110] According to Muḥammad Salman Ḥasan, Iraq's trade with India did not begin to rise again until the 1860s.[111] By that time, however, English economic penetration and the Ottoman Tanzimat had fundamentally altered the nature of Basra's trade.

While this decline seemed quite severe, it clearly was not due to some general crisis affecting the Ottoman Empire as a whole.[112] For Manesty and Jones, who wrote a report on the trade of the region, there was little doubt that the plague and the Persian occupation represented two of the chief causes of the decline of Basra's trade.[113] Given the above accounts of these events, it is not surprising that many historians have accepted this assessment.[114] Iraqi historians have tended to emphasize the devastating role of the Persian occupation of 1776–79. Others, like Daniel Panzac, tend to focus on the role that natural disasters play in disrupting trade. In this respect he argues that the plague of Abu Chafchir was the chief cause of the decline of Basra's fortunes.[115] The preceding outline of Basra's trade in the eighteenth century, however, speaks against the idea that epidemics and wars, no matter how severe, can cause more than a temporary interruption of commerce in this strategic area of the Persian Gulf.

It appears that the major obstacle to unraveling the cause for the decline of Basra's trade in the late eighteenth century has more to do with methodology than with limited data. When dealing with the Middle East, most historians have tended to situate the subject of their study within an administrative rather than an economic perspective. In two of the most influential works on the economic history of the early modern Middle East, the authors deal with Basra within the framework of "Iraq," or "The Iraqi Provinces."[116] Such an approach assumes that it would be more fruitful to study Basra's economy along with that of Mosul, rather than, say, Oman, when the opposite is in fact true. Thus, to understand the causes of the decline of Basra's trade there is a need to look at the wider region to which the city's economy belonged and the different trade networks with which it was tied.

CHAPTER 3

Networks of Trade

In the eighteenth century, Basra was linked to six major trading areas. India was certainly the most famous, with its much-coveted merchandise of spices and fabrics. Of almost equal fame was the city's biannual caravan trade with Aleppo. The coffee of Mukha created the demand for trade with Yemen, usually via Masqat. The Tigris and Euphrates provided the highways for Basra's trade with Baghdad and points north, while southern Persia was reached through either caravans or the Karun River. And lastly, Basra traded extensively with other ports on the Persian Gulf. Of less importance were the trade routes to Arabia and Damascus, both of which were linked to the Aleppo trade. For Basra's merchants this was usually an open region with hardly any notion of national or ethnic boundaries.[1]

In the early part of the eighteenth century this trading region could be viewed as a subset within an emerging self-contained Indian Ocean "world system" with its center at Surat.[2] It is now well known that by the end of the century this emerging world system was gradually incorporated within a European-dominated world economy. According to Niels Steensgaard, the eighteenth century witnessed a "number of apparently unconnected phenomena" that ultimately led to a structurally more vulnerable multipolar world system in the Indian Ocean.[3] These "unconnected phenomena" include a major increase in European demand for Asian products, the indigenous development of a number of competing naval powers, and the weakening or collapse of the Muslim empires.[4] Variations on all of these factors, plus some local ones, played a role in the structural transformation of Basra's trade networks. To understand how this transformation came about, each one of the six networks will be examined separately.

THE MARITIME TRADE WITH INDIA

There is little doubt that Basra's maritime trade with India constituted the most important part of the city's commerce. There were three main terminal points for Indian goods imported into the Ottoman Empire: Istanbul, Aleppo, and Cairo. The first two received most of their goods via Basra, particularly during the eighteenth century, when the Red Sea route appeared to have stagnated.[5] Indian textiles were usually in high demand, competing quite successfully with local products.[6] In 1785 it was estimated that the total annual imports of Indian goods into Istanbul alone equaled some 5 million ghurush. This was slightly under the amount of total imports from Europe during the same period.[7] The traveler Mehmet Emin effendi, who visited Surat in 1749, saw a number of merchants from Baghdad and Basra purchasing goods and preparing to ship them to the Middle East.[8]

The India ships brought large quantities of merchandise of various types. On average, the large ships brought more than one thousand bales[9] of goods each.[10] From Bengal, Basra imported rice, sugar, sugar candy, iron, tin, lead, lumber, chinaware, and piece goods of "near fifty different kinds."[11] The Coromandel coast provided chintz of different kinds, cotton, and cotton yarn. Musk, henna, lump lac, Kashmir shawls, Gujarat piece goods, and various cotton fabrics came from Surat and the Malabar coast. Indian spices, including pepper, cassia, turmeric, indigo, cardamum, cloves, nutmeg, cinnamon, and ginger, came from various parts of the subcontinent. Some shipments of cloves and nutmeg also originated from places as far away as Indonesia. The only important European commodities shipped from India and sold at Basra were English woolens and firearms. In 1707, a ship owned by the well-known Surati merchant Ahmad Chalabi unloaded Indian merchandise which brought in 15,494.25 ghurush in customs duties.[12] Assuming that this merchandise was taxed at the normal 8 percent of its value, the estimated value of the goods must have been around 193,678 ghurush. Now considering that this ship was loaded with only one-third its normal capacity, the figure for the value of Indian goods brought on a ship loaded up to half or three-fourths capacity (which was the normal amount) would have been in the range of 290,517 ghurush to 435,775.5 ghurush. Most of this merchandise was transported to Aleppo, Baghdad, and Persia.[13] After unloading, many ships left a *wakil* (agent or broker) behind to dispose of the cargo in the most profitable manner. This trade with India resulted in a chronic deficit for the Ottomans.[14] While the Ottomans were eagerly paying for Indian goods there was hardly any product that was exported in return. The result was a regular cash flow from the Middle East to India. This was also the case at Basra notwithstanding Basra's export of dates and some Arabian stallions.

India, for most of its history, had two distinct trading areas. Gujarat, Malabar, West India, and the Persian Gulf represented one region, while Bengal, Coromandel, and eastern India constituted a second, separate area.[15] By taking the aggregate number of ships and their dates of departure and arrival, a sense of the annual shipping schedules between Basra and India can be established. As is evident in Figure 3.1, the ships from Bengal and East India rode the northeast monsoon and arrived at Basra between April and July, peaking in June, just as the winds began to shift.[16] This guaranteed that they did not have to waste too much time at Basra. In fact, those returning directly to Bengal usually departed within a couple of weeks of their arrival since the voyage took nearly four months and passing Ceylon was quite difficult after October. Rarely did a small vessel attempt this voyage. Communication with western India was much easier and more frequent.

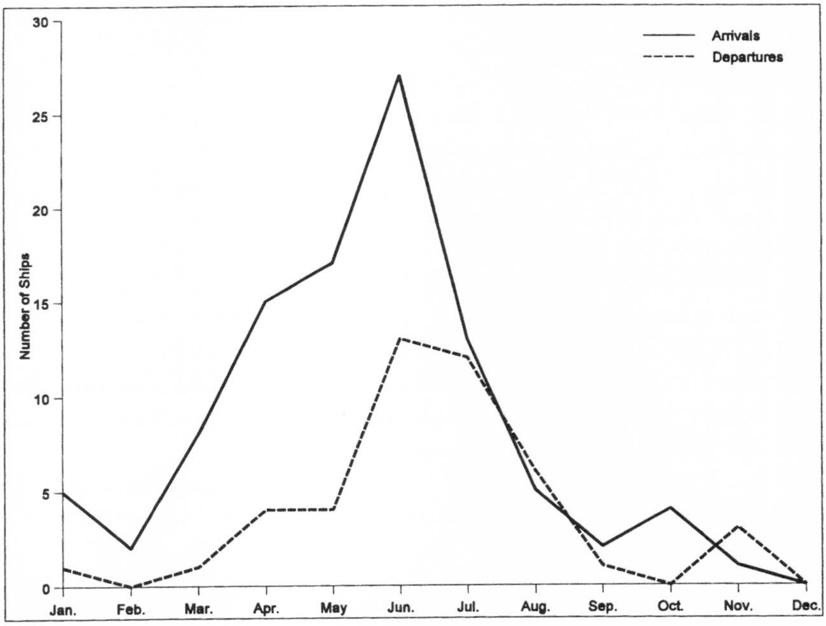

FIGURE 3.1
Basra's Shipping Patterns with East India, 1724–1792
(*Sources: MSA*, Bussora Factory Diaries, nos. 193–202; *MSA*, Gombroon Factory Diaries, nos. 112–118; *IOR*, Letters from Basra, nos. G/29/18–22)

Although the majority of ships arrived in July and August, a fair number also appeared between December and April (Figure 3.2). Departures peaked twice, around August and November. The latter probably included ships ultimately heading for Bengal with long stops at India's western ports. There were no noticeable differences in the schedules of European and Indo-Arab shipping to India.

While a great deal of the merchandise from East India was transported in stages by native Indo-Arab ships, Europeans dominated the direct shipping routes throughout the century. This, however, was not true of the trade with West India. Although the earliest dependable figures available are for 1724, the sources still suggest that Indo-Arab shipping dominated this route throughout the first third of the century (Figure 3.3). In 1690, despite a harsh bout with the plague, as many as sixteen or seventeen ships arrived at Basra from the various parts of India.[17] By 1707, due to the conflicts with Persia and the Muntafiq

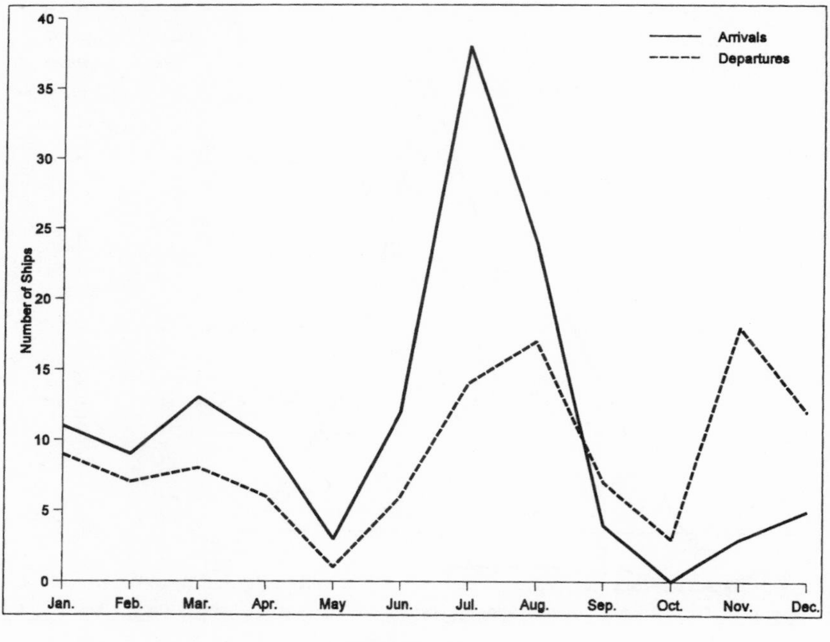

FIGURE 3.2
Basra's Shipping Patterns with East India, 1724–1792
(*Sources: MSA*, Bussora Factory Diaries, nos. 193–202; *MSA*, Gombroon Factory Diaries, nos. 112–118; *IOR*, Letters from Basra, nos. G/29/18–22)

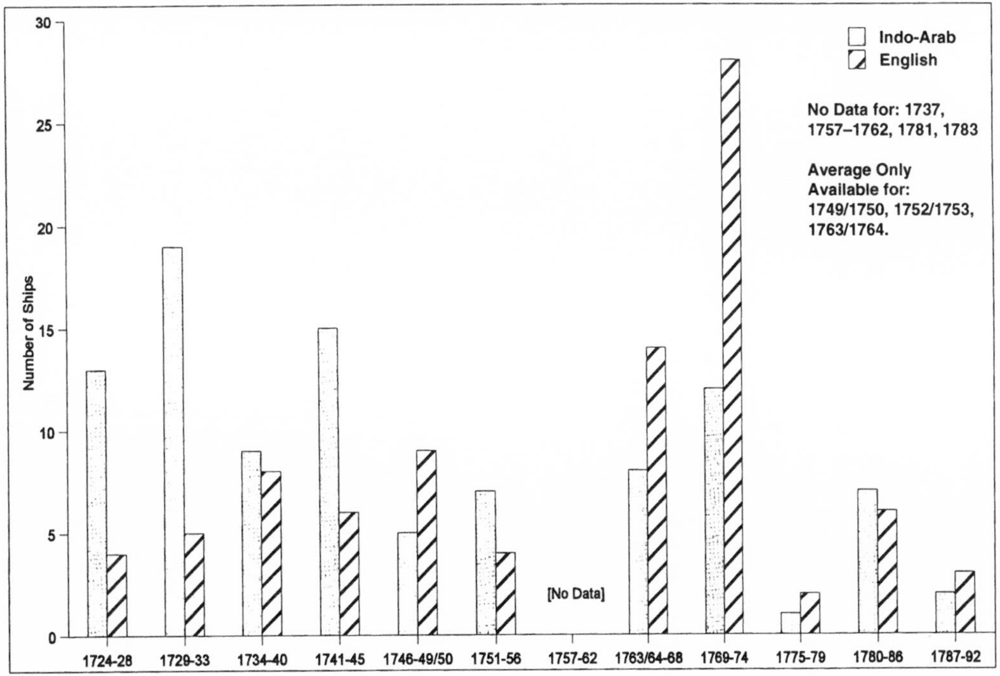

FIGURE 3.3

Comparative Volume of Basra Shipping with West India, 1724–1790

(*Sources: MSA*, Bussora Factory Diaries, nos. 193–202; *MSA*, Gombroon Factory Diaries, nos. 112–118; *IOR*, Letters from Basra, nos. G/29/18–22)

tribes, this number had dropped to six.[18] Several years later trade began to pick up, thanks to the establishment of security, so that a total of eleven ships were reported to have arrived in 1720.[19] Favorable trade during this period also corresponded to its general rise in West India, particularly in Malabar, which enjoyed a boom in commercial activities around 1730.[20]

The most important of the Indo-Arab ships that traded between Basra and West India were those owned by the Chalabi family of Surat.[21] Each year Basra waited anxiously for the arrival of Chalabi's two ships that regularly made the voyage from Surat. During the first decade of the eighteenth century, when the Ottomans were still busy trying to establish control over southern Iraq, Chalabi's two ships were the only ones from India still calling regularly at Basra.[22] The size of these ships was considered larger than most European vessels trading in this area. The *Fath al-Raḥman*, which ran this route throughout the first half of the century, had a carrying capacity of five hundred tons. The same was true of the *Islambuli* and the *Salamani*, which operated in the second half of the century.[23] The importance of these ships to the merchants of Basra was clearly demonstrated in 1754, when the Dutch seized them as the result of a previous dispute with the mutasallim. The panic that this action created was enough to force the mutasallim to give in to Dutch demands.[24] Basra's commercial performance for the rest of the century again showed its great sensitivity to developments in India. After the boom of the 1730s, Malabar's trade began to stagnate as a result of the instability and increasing regulations brought about by the rising state of Travancore. It revived again around 1773/1774 before declining sharply for the rest of the century and beyond.[25] In both, its rise in the early 1770s and its subsequent decline, Malabar's trade practically mirrored that of Basra.

Figure 3.3 also shows that while Indo-Arab shipping with West India exceeded that of the Europeans up to the mid-1740s, it was generally declining throughout most of the first half of the century. The ratio of European (especially English) to native shipping continued to shift in favor of the former until the Persian occupation of 1776 and the subsequent overall decline in trade. The English had achieved this domination of the European trade with Basra as a result of their defeat of France in the long struggle for mastery over India. During the first Anglo-French war in India in 1744, the English navy succeeded in establishing its control of the seas.[26] By the end of the Seven Years War (1756–63), England emerged as the paramount European power in

India. This "greater power for the English at Surat and Bombay naturally carried with it greater power in the Red Sea and Persian Gulf."[27] Thus, while France's trade with the Ottoman Empire accounted for nearly 50 percent to 60 percent of the empire's trade with western Europe, it was practically nonexistent at Basra.[28] Several years before the Seven Years War, the Dutch were expelled from Malabar after losing the war with the kingdom of Travancore, allowing the English to become the unrivaled European commercial power in the Gulf.[29]

There is much evidence that points to a growing European control of the Indian Ocean freight trade, becoming quite evident by the second half of the eighteenth century.[30] Lakshmi Subramanian argues that English control of Surat's shipping and freight trade became particularly pronounced after 1759.[31] Not surprisingly, the sources confirm that this was also the case with respect to the Persian Gulf and Basra at the same time.[32] In a number of letters from both Surati merchants who traded at Basra and Basrawi merchants specializing in the Indian trade, these merchants mentioned their intention to freight exclusively on English ships.[33] The number of English and Indo-Arab ships arriving in Basra from India (evident in Figure 3.3) lends further credence to this claim. Lastly, the French, who in a 1768 report were considering reestablishing their trade with the Gulf, repeatedly complained of English domination of the freight trade between Basra and India.[34] While this European (English) domination never reached the same level as it did in the Mediterranean, there is little doubt that increased English shipping played a decisive role in Basra's trade boom of 1768–74.[35]

THE COFFEE TRADE AND THE ROLE OF THE OMANIS

The other important source for this boom was the rise of the Masqat fleet in the second half of the century. Despite the numerous works that make passing reference to the great fleet of Oman and its successful expeditions against the Portuguese in the seventeenth century, not much is known about its role in the trade of the region.[36] Clearly, the Yaᶜrubi sultans, who came to prominence in the mid-seventeenth century under the leadership of Imam Sultan ibn Sayf I, succeeded in developing a strong fleet built largely at the port of Surat.[37] In 1650, they took Masqat from the Portuguese and began a series of naval expeditions that soon drove the Portuguese from the Gulf and most of

East Africa. El-Ashban believes that by the turn of the century Omani naval power had become "stronger than any of the native rulers along the entire shores of the Indian Ocean."[38] The rise of Masqat soon attracted a large trade with India, Yemen, Africa, and the Gulf. In the attempt to establish their claim over part of this trade, the Omanis also challenged the two great Islamic empires in the area. In 1707, the merchants of Basra complained that hostilities with the imam of Masqat was one of the primary causes behind the stagnation of Basra's trade after the Ottoman reconquest.[39] While a lucrative, peaceful relationship was eventually established with Ottoman Basra, Masqat's intense conflict with Safavid Persia lasted much longer. During the first two decades of the century, the Omanis sacked several Persian ports, culminating in their occupation of the island of Bahrayn in 1717.

The power of the Ya^{c}rubis declined during the 1720s as rival claimants to the throne plunged the country into a prolonged civil war which was only temporarily interrupted by Nadir Shah's invasion in 1738. The throne finally fell to the Al Bu Sa^{c}id clan in 1749, marking the start of a new period of relative stability in Masqat. Under the wise leadership of the Sa^{c}id imams, Masqat reclaimed its position as one of the paramount ports of the Indian Ocean. Their trading empire soon spread from South Arabia to East Africa, with the imam's representatives present in all the main ports of West India and the Persian Gulf, including Basra. The enterprising skills which the merchants of Masqat exhibited allowed their trade to continue to flourish even after its decline in the Persian Gulf at the end of the century. In 1791, the EEIC agents at Basra wrote that "whilst trade languishes and an increasing scarcity of specie prevails in the Turkish and Persian dominions, the merchants of Muscat are engaged in capital commercial enterprizes."[40]

Masqat's primary export to the Persian Gulf during this period included slaves, ivory, some Batavian sugar, and, most important, coffee. After successfully driving out the Portuguese from East Africa in the seventeenth century, the Omanis established several trading colonies, including those at Zanzibar, Kilwa, Pate, and Mombasa, from which slaves and ivory were exported to the Persian Gulf, Arabia, and India.[41] Among the vessels used to transport East African slaves were the dhow, baghalah, and *sunbuk*. The slave dhows ranged in size from "mere boats" to 350 tons and were noted for being "enormously swift."[42] Information on the size and nature of this trade to Basra remains scanty. Otter, in 1734, mentioned that the Masqat fleet had brought in a shipment of slaves while he was there, yet he failed to mention anything else on the subject.[43] There were numerous Ottoman regulations for the sale of slaves in Basra in the sixteenth century, but they give little indication of the scale of the slave trade in the eighteenth century.[44]

The available information indicates that Omani vessels sailed for East Africa, with the northeast monsoon, in early November and returned during the summer months with the southwest monsoon. Many slaves were usually held in Masqat for some time before being sold in the various ports of the Persian Gulf.[45] In Basra, most of the slave ships returned loaded with dates. While estimates have varied greatly, the most convincing ones suggest that this trade was not very large in the eighteenth century. It was not until the following century, particularly between 1840 and the late 1880s, that the slave trade picked up considerably. Even here, however, historians have differed over the numbers involved.

According to Austen, a total of about two thousand slaves were sold in the "Upper Persian Gulf" (mainly Basra, Kuwait, Bushire, and Bahrayn) between 1830 and 1866.[46] Toledano, on the other hand, writes that four thousand to five thousand slaves were sold in 1840 alone, "most of them in Basra, Kuwait, Bahrayn and Bushire."[47] In one of the few estimates available for the eighteenth century, Ricks states that between 1722 and 1822 the number of slaves exported to the entire Persian Gulf did not exceed five hundred to six hundred each year, with most years registering figures far below this.[48] Jwaideh and Cox have argued convincingly that demand for slaves in southern Iraq was never high due to tribal customs that objected to concubinage and slave labor in agriculture.[49] This argument is supported by the lack of eighteenth-century Ottoman or EEIC documents referring to the slave trade at Basra. The few slaves that were sold in Basra were mostly employed as domestic servants.[50]

The primary trading commodity of the Omanis, however, was the coffee of Mukha, over which they developed a virtual monopoly in the second half of the century.[51] It was estimated that the Masqat fleet carried "near one half of the quantity [of coffee] annually produced in Yemeen."[52] This, in turn, was "sufficient for the full consumption thereof in the countries of Persia, Arabia Deserta, Mesopotamia, Courdistan, Armenia, Georgia and Natelia."[53] Some of this "article of luxury" reached as far as Germany, Poland, and Russia.[54] Prior to the rise of the Masqat fleet, Mukha coffee reached Basra mainly through Indian ships belonging to Surat. According to one English report written in

1721, ten thousand bales of coffee were exported annually from Yemen to Basra.[55] The authorities at Basra estimated that the customs revenues from coffee imports at the end of the seventeenth century equaled 50,000 ghurush to 60,000 ghurush per year.[56] Not surprisingly, Yemen's commercial ties with Basra were strong enough for news from one to affect the market of the other. In 1701, for example, the merchants of Mukha rejoiced at news of Ottoman reoccupation of Basra, which they felt would surely boost their coffee exports.[57] This trade apparently suffered a decline in the middle of the century partially due to the civil war that erupted in Yemen and culminated in 1759 with the millenarian movement of Abu ᶜAlamah.[58] By the 1760s, however, the impact of the new Masqat coffee fleet became apparent. In normal years, it numbered some fifty trankis,[59] most of which were quite small.[60] On their return they carried off the bulk of Basra's date exports, which they sold in various parts of Arabia, East Africa, and India.

Thanks to the continuing vibrancy of Masqat's economy, the coffee trade did not suffer a sharp decline similar to that of the India trade toward the close of the century. Nevertheless, there is evidence that there was a reduction in the amounts imported by Basra. Other than a decline in demand due to the overall difficult conditions at Basra, there might have also been a problem in the supply. Between 1785 and 1820 the Al Bu Saᶜids took a series of aggressive steps (including military confrontation) designed to ensure their control of the carrying trade to the Persian Gulf.[61] The chief enemies of the Omanis at this time were the ᶜUtub of Bahrayn, the Qawasim of Ra's al-Khaymah, and their powerful Wahhabi allies from Najd.

The Wahhabis appeared in the middle of the century as an Islamic reform movement with a message emphasizing puritanicalism. Shortly after its establishment, most of the tribal factions and city-states of Najd, through conviction or intimidation, swore allegiance to its doctrines. Under the leadership of the Al Saᶜud family, they were organized into a powerful confederation primed for expansion. By the turn of the century, they had established their overlordship over central and eastern Arabia and threatened Oman, Syria, Kuwait, Basra, and all of southern Iraq. The apogee of Wahhabi power came in 1802, when they sacked the Shiᶜi city of Karbala', causing much distress all over southern Iraq.[62] In the Gulf, their influence was felt through an "ironclad association" with most of the coastal tribes.[63] The Wahhabi tide was not halted until 1818, when their imam surrendered to the forces of Muhammad ᶜAli of Egypt.

Arguably, their strongest allies in the Gulf were the Qawasim (singular Qasimi), a section of the Hawalah tribes originally inhabiting the Persian side of the Gulf. The power of the Qawasim became apparent in the Gulf with the decline of effective Persian control, especially after the death of Karim Khan Zand in 1779.[64] Masqat's conflict with the Qawasim and the Wahhabis was most intense between 1800 and 1820.[65] The ebb and flow of this war did not end until the Wahhabi defeat at the hands of the Egyptians in 1818. Only then did the English and Omani navies succeed in destroying the Qasimi fleet and fortifying their main ports.[66] In 1819, the Qawasim were forced to sign a General Treaty of Peace which effectively neutralized their challenge. During this long conflict the Omani fleet was unable to reach Basra with the same regularity and ease, causing an overall decline in Basra's coffee imports. In addition to this, Yemen's coffee exports suffered a major blow at precisely the same time as Masqat's war with the Qawasim. Paul Dresch mentions that increased competition from Java and Caribbean coffee (which were not imported at Basra) led to a worldwide drop in coffee prices. In the early nineteenth century they suffered a serious crash, leading to a drop in exports.[67]

The close commercial ties between Masqat and Basra were also evident in their political relations. Under the Al Bu Saʿids the friendship between the two ports grew into an active military alliance against Persia. During Karim Khan's siege of Basra, the imam of Oman sent a large fleet composed of two "large ships" and numerous "small craft" under the command of his son to help repel the invaders.[68] The participation of the Omani fleet temporarily turned the tide, lifting the spirits of the besieged Basawis and allowing them to hold on for several months longer. The Ottoman sultan was reportedly so delighted with this gesture that he ordered Baghdad's wali to send the *kharaj* tax of Basra to the imam and to grant Masqat's merchants favorable terms of trade.[69] In reply the imam described the two ports as "a single body sharing both good and bad."[70] This friendship was again tested in 1809 when the Wahhabis requested Masqat's assistance in attacking Basra. The imam's refusal infuriated the Wahhabis and led to their invasion of Oman the following year.[71]

THE REGIONAL TRADE WITH THE GULF

Lack of information on the number of small vessels trading at Basra becomes critical when considering the nature of maritime trade within the Persian Gulf. There is little doubt that the merchandise transported by these vessels within the Gulf exceeded that of the larger ships recorded by the English agents. According to one estimate, the Arabs had over four hundred small vessels operating in the Gulf, West India, and East Africa in the eighteenth century.[72] Contemporary Dutch sources indicate that several hundred more ships (mainly small trankis) operated in the Gulf.[73] The majority of the Arab inhabitants of the coast who owned these boats lived in extreme poverty. Their main sources of livelihood were fishing, pearling, all sorts of petty trade, and piracy. Fiercely independent, they often sailed with their entire families and meager belongings from shore to shore to avoid state control or to seek new fortunes.[74]

Throughout most of the century, Basra acted as the major "international port" for the Persian Gulf (Map 3.1). Countless fleets of small

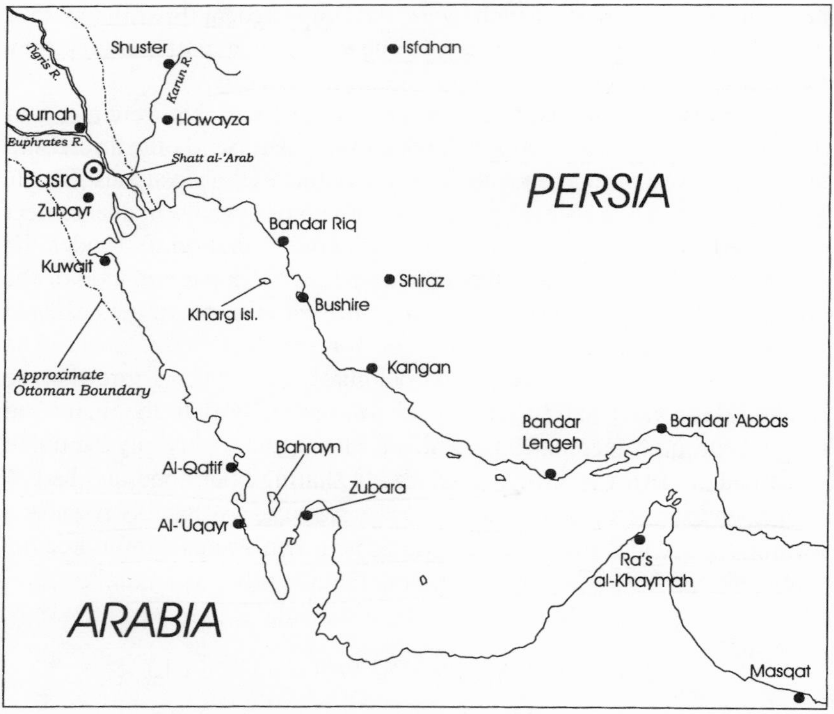

MAP 3.1
Ports of the Persian Gulf, c.1780

boats from all over the Gulf brought the products of the Gulf to Basra for export to India or the hinterland. Bandar ᶜAbbas remained active, especially during the first half of the century, but the heights which it had enjoyed under the Safavids had long since passed. In its stead, Nadir Shah encouraged the development of Bushire in the northern part of the Gulf. Under the Matarish Arabs and their shaykh, Nasir al-Madhkur, it soon became Persia's paramount port and a competitor of Basra for the India trade.[75] Bushire also had a limited local trade with Basra and was often used by merchants interested in smuggling their goods into southern Iraq through Persia.[76] Near Bushire, the island of Kharg briefly rose to prominence in the middle of the century, first under the Dutch and then under the ruthlessly ambitious Mir Muhanna. Other ports on the Persian side that were active during this period were Bandar Riq under the Banu Saᶜb Arabs, Lengeh, and Kangan.

On the Arab side of the Gulf, the island of Bahrayn, with its rich pearl fisheries,[77] and al-Qaṭif in the area of al-Ḥasa between Kuwait and Qatar, were the oldest established ports. During the first two decades of the eighteenth century, control over Bahrayn changed hands several times between Persia and Oman. In 1753, as part of his aggressive policy in the Gulf, Nadir Shah seized the island after several decades of Arab rule. Bahrayn would not revert back to Arab rule until 1783, when the Khalifah section of the ᶜUtub Arabs occupied it.[78] The port of Qatif, on the other hand, remained under the control of Banu Khalid up to the closing years of the century, when it fell to the Wahhabis from Najd. By the turn of the century, the port of al-ᶜUqayr was superseding al-Qaṭif as the paramount port in eastern Arabia. Its main exports were dates plus various types of gums and incense.[79]

The Najdi tribal migrations of the seventeenth and eighteenth centuries had a profound impact on the rise of new ports in the Gulf. During the century, the above-mentioned ᶜUtub, who originated in Najd, settled into Kuwait (al-Qurayn) and Qatar (Zubara) before seizing Bahrayn. By the middle of the century, Kuwait, with an excellent natural harbor and strong leadership under the Al Ṣabaḥ shaykhs, became home to one of the finest fleets in the Gulf.[80] Around 1760, the Khalifah section of the ᶜUtub, followed by the Jalahimah, left Kuwait for Qatar. Together they transformed the small town of Zubara into an important center for the export of pearls.[81] Throughout the second half of the century, the Gulf became a stage for the ᶜUtub's prolonged struggle against the Hawalah Arabs, especially the Qawasim section around the Trucial and southern Persian coasts. Little is known of the history of the Hawalah other than that they were the long-established inhabitants of the southern Persian coast, some of whom returned to the Arab coast around the seventeenth and eighteenth centuries.[82] By the end of the century, the Qawasim, with their base at Ra's al-Khaymah, had become active in the pearl trade and, more important for Basra's trade, piracy.

Each of these, and numerous other smaller settlements, had a fleet of small vessels active in the carrying trade of the Gulf. As the larger ships unloaded their goods from India at Masqat, Bushire, or Basra, these fleets would then disperse the merchandise throughout the region. Their most profitable export, pearls, was often the cause of many of the conflicts. In 1767, for example, the ᶜUtbi fleet was sent to bring a large freight of pearls from Qatar to Basra. Upon their arrival, they discovered that the Qawasim had attacked the place and made off with an enormous amount of pearls and money estimated at 30,000 tumans.[83] These pearls were most probably later smuggled into Masqat and secretly sold or taken directly to India.

The season for pearl fishing began around the middle of May and ended in late September.[84] At the end of the season the pearls were sold to the merchants in the various Gulf ports, who then shipped them to Basra, Bushire, or Masqat for export. The pearl trade was undoubtedly one of Basra's most important assets. Even when this trade suffered a decline at the end of the century, some pearl merchants like ᶜAbdul-Jalil al-Ṭabaṭaba'i still continued to make handsome profits.[85] Over the course of the century, larger native vessels, of over one hundred tons, were increasingly used in the carrying trade of the Gulf. The main cause for this increase was the rise of the ᶜUtbi and Masqat fleets in the second half of the century. The ᶜUtub, in particular, dominated the pearl trade to Basra in the second half of the century.[86] Another reason for the frequent appearance of large native ships in the carrying trade of the Gulf could have been the transfer of the bulk of native shipping from the increasingly competitive India trade to that of the Gulf. The second half of the century also witnessed an increase in the number of English ships patrolling the Gulf, some of which inevitably (although in a limited fashion) became involved in the carrying trade. Their presence became particularly evident after 1765, as a result of British involvement in the protection of the trade of Basra.

The last decades of the century witnessed a sharp rise in the number of piratical attacks on Basra's shipping. While *piracy* is a word that conjures up various images, it should be noted that those who carried out these operations in the Gulf were quite different from the renegade and run-away sailors that made up European piracy at that time. Most of the raids were carried out in the course of intertribal conflicts or by shaykhdoms attempting to control parts of the Gulf trade. In this sense, their practices differed little from those of the leading European powers of the time except that, at times, they degenerated into indiscriminate attacks on all vessels. Certainly the tribes themselves considered such attacks a "legitimate form of warfare and source of income."[87]

While piracy was nothing new to the Gulf, numerous factors contributed to its intensification toward the end of the century. One of the most important was the demographic upheaval of the preceding century and its culmination in the establishment of new shaykhdoms along the Gulf. Soon after its establishment, the ᶜUtbi shaykhdom in Bahrayn witnessed a protracted power struggle between the Khalifah and Jalahimah sections. After their eviction from the island, the Jalahimah, under their fiery leader Shaykh Raḥmah ibn Jabir, launched a relentless war against the maritime trade of Bahrayn and its allies (notably Kuwait), which inevitably affected Basra's trade.[88] In this campaign Shaykh Raḥmah often found support from the Qawasim. Unlike the Jalahimah, the Qawasim, under Shaykh Saqr ibn Rashid, rarely discriminated in their choice of victims, targeting ᶜUtbi, Omani, and European ships with equal zeal.[89] In 1808, for example, Qasimi attacks included an estimated twenty ships from India, with four belonging to the English.[90] As with the Qawasim, the Jalahimah benefited greatly from their alliance with the Wahhabis of Najd. But also like the Qawasim, the Jalahimah became increasingly isolated after the defeat of the Wahhabis in 1818. Nevertheless, Shaykh Raḥmah of the Jalahimah refused to give up. He continued his relentless war against the Al Khalifah, a willing ally of any of their enemies, until 1826 when, surrounded by ᶜUtbi ships, the now old and blind shaykh preferred to blow himself up rather than surrender to his bitter foes.[91] In the meantime, though, the trade of Basra and the Gulf in general "had dwindled to a trickle."[92]

Newly established shaykhdoms that maintained amiable relations with Basra nevertheless helped direct trade away from it. "Altho'," observed Manesty and Jones, "a favorable change has lately taken place in the commercial interests of Muscat, Bahreen, Zebarra [Qatar] and Grain [Kuwait], the commercial importance of Bussora has since the year 1773 most materially decreased."[93] Kuwait, in particular, seemed to benefit from Basra's decline by attracting a number of

Basra's principal merchants.[94] Resuming their comments on its growing importance, Manesty and Jones wrote in 1792: "Grain [Kuwait] has always had a free communication by the desart [sic], with Bagdad and Aleppo and very large and rich caravans . . . frequently passed to and from those cities."[95]

It would not be a great exaggeration to say that the development of Kuwait received a major boost directly as a result of the Persian occupation of Basra in 1776.[96] "The degree of [Kuwait's] importance," Manesty and Jones continued,

> must ever depend on the prosperity or distress of Bussora, during the time, in which the Persians were in possession of that city, Grain [Kuwait] was the port through which that part of the produce of India proper for the Bagdad, Damascus, Alepo [sic], Smyrna and Constantinople markets which is annually brought to Bussora, found its way to these places.[97]

After the Persians withdrew, Kuwait continued to attract trade away from Basra, thanks to its relative security, autonomy, and low customs duties. The flight of many of Basra's leading merchants to Kuwait continued to play a major role in the commercial stagnation of the city's trade well into the 1850s.[98] Bahrayn and Qatar benefited in a similar manner, accentuating Basra's decline.[99]

THE TRADE WITH SOUTHERN PERSIA

Basra's trade with southern Persia is testimony to the great commercial freedom enjoyed by the merchants of the area and the general lack of state intervention. Relations between the Ottomans and Persians were often extremely hostile, particularly around the vicinity of Basra. Nevertheless, the lively trade across the border appeared largely unaffected by the political hostilities, and travelers, like Mir ᶜAbdul-Laṭif al-Shustari who visited Basra in 1787, came and went with hardly any difficulties save those offered by bandits.[100] The existence of a wealthy Persian community in Basra, referred to earlier, certainly had commercial dealings with their kin across the border. In August 1729, the English agent reported that the route between Basra and Isfahan was now secure and that "many" merchants were going and coming "once again."[101] Khawjah Yaᶜqub, probably the most important Jewish merchant prior to the Persian occupation, and his partner, Khawjah Shahadah, regularly took Indian spices and cloth to Shuster and brought Gilan raw silk to

Basra.[102] The same was true of Basra's Armenian merchants, who kept up regular correspondence with their partners in Isfahan.

Merchandise from Basra was sent to either Shiraz or Isfahan via Shuster and Dizful.[103] The former, to the southeast, was reached directly by caravan, or by ship to Bushire then by caravan, while the latter, to the northeast, was reached by the Karun River and caravan. Closer to Basra was the city of Huwayza, just across the Shaṭṭ al-ᶜArab. Trade between Huwayza and Basra remained active despite several Ottoman attempts to take the city after the fall of the Safavids.[104] Unlike the mainly camel caravans of the Syrian desert, the mule was the most common means of transportation in Persia, with the usual size of a caravan not exceeding thirty or forty animals. Merchants operating along this route rarely owned their own animals, preferring to hire mules and muleteers for the trip. The mules of the village of Zarqan, north of Shiraz, were considered the most dependable and usually preferred by the merchants.[105] Basra's imports from Persia included dried fruits, pistachios, saffron, rhubarb, tobacco, drugs, sword blades, spear heads, gun barrels, caps, Kashmir shawls, lambskins, Kirman wool, carpets, and Gilan raw silk. Most of this material was reexported to the Gulf, Baghdad, and Aleppo, and from there to various other points. Basra's exports to Persia included Indian spices and piece goods, Mukha coffee, some English woolens, various piece goods from Aleppo and Baghdad, specie, and its own dates.[106]

In the seventeenth century, under the Safavids, the southern part of Persia flourished, with merchants from all over Asia and Europe flocking to Isfahan.[107] During this time, Basra benefited from the strong state of the Persian economy. The fall of the Safavids in 1722, and the ensuing civil strife culminating with the wars of Nadir Shah, obviously had a negative impact on this trade. The decline in Persia's economy, however, (especially in the south) was successfully checked under the rule of Karim Khan Zand (1750–79).[108] In addition to improving security, he moved the capital farther south to Shiraz, reduced the rate of taxation, encouraged handicrafts, repaired the irrigation networks, and granted merchants, particularly the Armenians, new privileges. These reforms soon had a favorable impact on trade, leading the EEIC's "Select Committee Appointed by the Court of Directors" to report: "under the last-mentioned prince [Karim Khan Zand], commerce had begun to revive, and very considerable progress had been made at his death."[109] It is no accident that this period, despite continuing border tensions and recurrent hostilities with the Kaᶜb tribes, coincided with Basra's trade boom prior to the Persian invasion of 1775. Between

December 1768 and March 1777, over 27 percent of the merchants that had dealings at the English factory in Basra were from Persia.[110]

After the death of Karim Khan Zand in 1779, Persia entered a new period of savage civil war. Government reports sent from Basra at this time are full of anxiety over the unstable conditions in Persia and the need for reinforcements.[111] Trade routes became increasingly insecure because of the Kaᶜb and Banu Lam tribes who, like the Qawasim in the Gulf, grew in strength and ambition after the collapse of central authority in Persia. The Kaᶜb's efforts at establishing an independent shaykhdom had a particularly negative impact on Basra's trade. Having emigrated from central and eastern Arabia to Persian Khuzistan sometime in the seventeenth century, the Banu Kaᶜb jealously guarded their independence by inhabiting the inaccessible marshlands along the Karun River all the way up to Ḥuwayza.[112] After the collapse of Nadir Shah's effort to reunify Persia, they gradually emerged, under Shaykh Salman, to become an important local naval power.[113] Karim Khan's attempts to bring them to heel were cut short by his death and the end of Persia's central authority. By 1780, Basra's administrators were again warning of the need for naval protection against the raids of the Banu Kaᶜb fleet.[114]

Persia's chaotic state did not end until 1794 and the establishment of the new Qajar dynasty. The story of the rise of the Qajars and the excessive cruelties of their leader, Agha Muhammad Khan, is well known. Agha Muhammad's fury, fueled by an unrelenting hatred for the Zands, fell heavily on the cities of southern Persia, particularly Shiraz and Kirman. Normally, Basra's trade with Persia would rapidly recover following such periods of instability, yet the rise of the Qajars fundamentally altered this relationship. Even prior to their ascendancy, the economic and demographic growth of the north at the expense of the south gradually increased after the fall of the Safavids. Under Qajari rule, the focus of Persia's political power and economy moved decisively from Isfahan, Kirman, and Shiraz, to Tabriz and, later, to the new capital of Tehran.[115] As the north benefited from the rapid growth of its trade with Russia, the south, upon which much of Basra's trade had traditionally depended, fell into "decay and depopulation."[116]

THE RIVERINE TRADE WITH BAGHDAD

In most of its essentials, the nature of the riverine trade between southern and northern Iraq remained unchanged until the introduction of steamship navigation in the nineteenth century. During the eighteenth century, Basra's riverine trade with Baghdad was carried by several fleets of mostly small boats called *takanahs* with a few larger ones called *shaykhas*.[117] Less common ships included the *daniq*, *barakshin*, baghalah, *sinik*, *ghalyawz*, and the *sa*ᶜ*d* on the Tigris, and the ghrab on the Euphrates.[118] In the 1760s there were about forty ships operating along the Tigris route, each capable of carrying three hundred to four hundred bales.[119] Under normal conditions, the "Baghdad Boats," as these ships were called, made the trip once a year down either the Tigris or the Euphrates depending on their respective security situation. The Euphrates route normally enjoyed better security due to the protection provided by the Muntafiq in return for a fee paid by the merchants. The Euphrates was also preferred for the return trip because its current was not as strong as that of the Tigris. If all went well, which was quite rare, the boats would leave Baghdad in June and arrive at Basra in July as the India ships were unloading and prices were generally at their lowest. As often happens, however, the Muntafiq shaykh would close the route at the last hour in the hopes of receiving additional payments. This is what happened in 1725, when Shaykh Muḥammad al-Maniᶜ forced the Baghdad boats to lay in the river "for months" until the merchants agreed to pay him "considerable sums" for their passage.[120]

Joseph Amin, who in 1768 came down to Basra on one of these boats, related that he first traveled by caravan for four days from Baghdad to Ḥilla, stopping each night at a caravansary. After paying the customs at Ḥilla, the boats took seventeen days to reach Samawa, where they again paid customs. Three days later they paid additional customs at Qurnah, before reaching Basra. The entire trip south took some twenty-five days, while going north could take up to twice that long.[121] The most important cargo that these boats brought from Baghdad included copper, specie, and various goods originating from Anatolia, Aleppo, and Persia. Ships waiting to return to India were particularly eager to get a good freight of specie. In March 1774, for example, seven large boats arrived from Baghdad with about 800,000 rupees in gold and silver specie.[122] They returned loaded with India goods, Mukha coffee, and pearls.

Copper, valued in the foundries of India, remained a strong export item throughout the century, even after the decline of maritime trade. The copper originated in mines around Diyarbakr in southern Anatolia.[123] They were all considered the property of the Porte and under the command of a "Pasha of the Mines." The mined copper was transferred by river or caravan to Mosul, where it was smelted and cast into cakes. From there it was transported by boat to Baghdad and then to Basra. The copper was subject to customs in each of the three cities. At Diyarbakr it paid an export duty of 2 percent, followed by an import duty of 2.25 percent at Mosul and 2 percent at Baghdad. At Basra it paid an import duty of 8.33 percent and an export duty of 5.5 percent. The estimated cost of transporting it from Diyarbakr to Basra (inclusive of duties and protection payments) amounted to some 50 percent of its original value. Nevertheless, the merchants at Baghdad who purchased the copper found it profitable enough to increase exports from 16,000 *attaree maunds*[124] in 1791 to 70,000 in 1796.[125]

The increased export of this item represented the exception rather than the rule. Beginning in the 1770s, the preferred Euphrates route began to lose its security due to the increasing rebelliousness of the various tribes that inhabited the region. The decline of state authority as a result of the Persian invasion goes only so far in explaining this tendency. Of greater significance were the tribal migrations of the past century and a half and their culmination, during the last third of the century, with the increasing boldness of tribes like the Khazaᶜil just above Qurnah. This tribe, located along the Euphrates from Diwaniyyah to Basra, constantly threatened the city's riverine communication with Baghdad. During the second half of the century, the Khazaᶜil built several fortresses along the Euphrates, forcing ships to pay for their protection.[126] By 1787 they had obstructed the trade along the Euphrates to the extent that merchants were forced to use the slower and more expensive Tigris River route.[127] As a result, provisions at Basra became critically low and prices increased dramatically. Sulayman Pasha, the wali of Baghdad, responded by personally commanding a large army to punish the rebellious tribes. The Khazaᶜil, however, led by their cunning shaykh, Hamad al-Humud, successfully evaded the wali's army.[128] For the remainder of the century and well into the next, campaigns were sent against them almost annually, but this only increased the violence of their raids.[129]

While the insubordination of the Khazaᶜil had the most direct effect on the riverine trade, other tribes also contributed to the disruption of communications. In 1786, the powerful ᶜUbayd tribe around Baghdad launched an ambitious movement to install their shaykh, Sulayman al-Shawi, as wali of Baghdad.[130] This rebellion continued for two years before it was finally subdued. In 1787, al-Shawi joined forces with Shaykh Thuwayni of the Muntafiq and seized Basra, prompting the wali to organize a large campaign to reoccupy the port.[131] This was also the period when Wahhabi raiding reached as far as the banks of the Euphrates. By the end of the century these rebellions and raids practically shut down the Euphrates route, contributing to the overall decline of Basra's trade.

THE CARAVAN TRADE WITH ALEPPO

Rivaling Baghdad as Basra's most important inland trading partner was the city of Aleppo in northern Syria. With a population of over one hundred thousand, Aleppo was easily the largest city in the Fertile Crescent. It was also the third largest city in the Ottoman Empire after Istanbul and Cairo.[132] Although the trade among India, the Ottoman provinces, and Europe went through several routes, the desert route between Basra and Aleppo was considered to be the safest, cheapest, and most direct in the eighteenth century. The commercial links between the two cities were underscored in 1781 when the government of Aleppo agreed to pay half the construction cost of a new fleet to protect Basra's shipping.[133]

The caravans that crossed the Syrian desert were among the largest and best organized in Asia. Camels took the merchandise of Basra, India, southern Persia, Yemen, Masqat, and the Gulf, and brought back goods from Syria, Anatolia, and Europe. The imports included gold and silver coins, French broadcloth, Venice ware, beads, looking glasses, stained glass, silks, satins, brass wire, cochineal, tobacco, and Aleppo flowered piece goods.[134] Another item brought by these caravans from Istanbul was the so-called gold thread that was used for decorative stitching and was always in high demand in India.[135] Three types of caravans traveled between Aleppo and Basra.[136] The large, so-called merchant caravan, which transported goods and specie, was the most important in terms of the amount and variety of the merchandise traded. This caravan took several months to prepare and, under normal conditions, made the trip twice a year. The second type was simply a smaller version of the merchant caravan; it usually left Aleppo to travel to Basra and returned with the merchant caravan. Lastly, the so-called light caravan contained unladen desert-bred camels for sale in Aleppo. This was the largest of the three and made the trip once a year.[137]

In the preliminary preparation for a merchant caravan the merchants and camel-owners would first choose a caravan leader, called a shaykh or bashi, who was then sanctioned by the wali. The choice of the bashi was a very delicate matter since one who did not command respect among the desert tribes might not prove effective in securing a safe journey. In addition to his tribal credentials, most merchants preferred that he also be a sharif with a reputation for honesty since it was not uncommon that caravans were pillaged through an agreement between the bashi and the tribes. In the eighteenth century, this position was usually held by a member of the ᶜUqayl tribe, who inhabited most of the towns along the route, including areas around Aleppo. In the middle of the century, most merchants preferred the services of a certain bashi named Sayyid Talib, whose reputation guaranteed him a substantial income.[138] The bashi would fix the schedule, pick the route, collect the necessary provisions, and "standardize the quality and size of each individual camel-load of goods."[139] The average camel-load measured some five hundred pounds although some camels were known to carry up to seven hundred pounds.[140] At the end of the century, merchants paid between 90 and 130 rupees for each camel-load, depending on the nature of the merchandise. This price is likely to have been lower in the 1760s and could be indicative of the higher protection costs required by the desert tribes.[141] The bashi also organized the caravan's protection by hiring squads of armed cameleers, each under the direct command of his own shaykh. Along the route the bashi's authority was absolute despite the presence of other officials such as the *mu'adhin*.[142]

The size of these merchant caravans varied greatly, depending on the state of trade and security. A "normal" size was around fifteen hundred camels, although some reached as many as four thousand. It was the "light caravans," however, that usually included the largest number of camels. In the seventeenth and eighteenth centuries, growing demand for camels throughout the Ottoman Empire brought annual caravans of three thousand to five thousand unladen camels from Basra to Aleppo. In 1745, William Beawes estimated that around eleven thousand camels were sold in Aleppo, while Plaisted estimated the figure at three thousand to four thousand annually.[143] The caravans originated from ᶜUqayr and other parts of southern Arabia, and moved north, picking up more camels around Zubara, Qaṭif, and Kuwait. The various caravans assembled at the town of Zubayr, to the southwest of Basra, prior to departing for Aleppo (Map 3.2). Ideally, the merchant caravans departed after the arrival of the Bengal ships, usually in July,

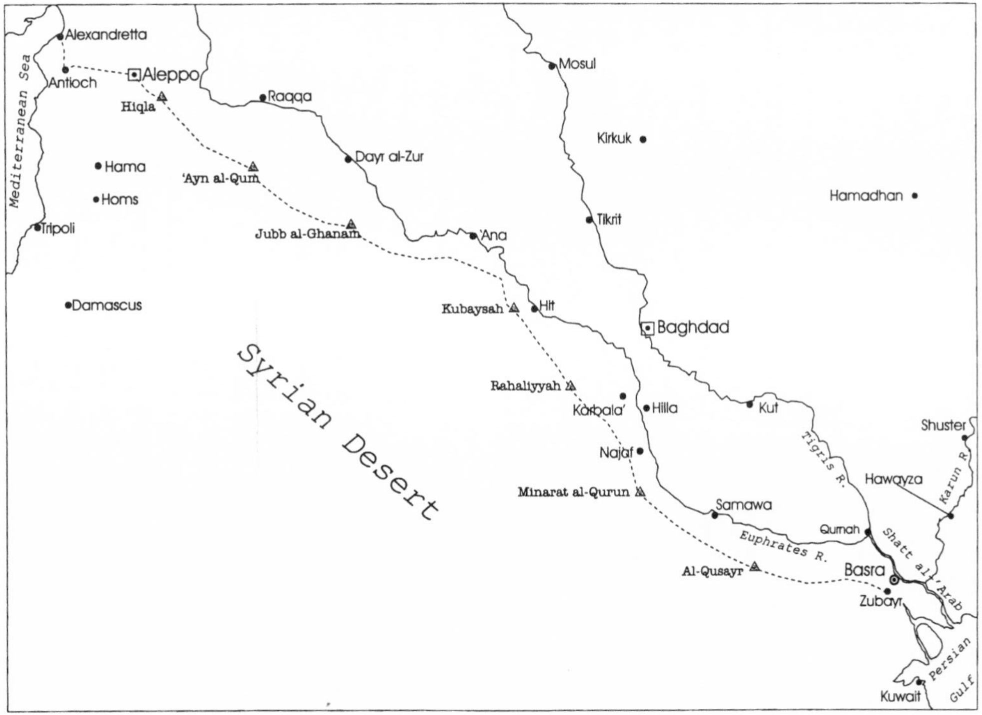

MAP 3.2

The Aleppo–Basra Caravan Route with Major Rest Areas

(*Source:* Based on the map in Douglas Carruthers, ed. *The Desert Route to India*)

while the light caravans normally left in April. This schedule, however, varied quite often due to the ever-changing political, economic, and security situation in Iraq, leading William Beawes, who traveled with a merchant caravan in 1745, to remark:

> nor have the caravans such regard to the seasons of shipping as I imagined, being here informed their setting out is far from depending upon the will of the merchants but entirely upon the will of the Bashaw of Bagdat and the agreement of the principal tribes of Arabs.[144]

The normal route, some 780 miles, ran parallel to the Euphrates. The caravans rarely approached the river because the muddy surface slowed the camels down and the desert provided a haven from the numerous customs points. The caravan continued to grow as it approached Najaf and Karbala', and at Kubaysah it was usually joined by the Baghdad caravan. The entire trip took between forty-five and seventy days for the large caravans, and some twenty-five days for the small ones.

Many merchants believed that Baghdad's control of Basra had a disruptive impact on the Aleppo caravan trade. As early as 1739, Baghdad's wali, Aḥmad Pasha, refused to allow caravans to go directly from Basra to Aleppo without first stopping at Baghdad to pay additional tolls.[145] During the century the Basra–Aleppo route functioned best when Baghdad's control of Basra was weak. By the middle of the century, Basra's merchants seem to have reached an agreement with the wali to pay the additional Baghdad customs up front at Basra, thus being spared the costly and time-consuming trip to Baghdad. Several caravans were allowed to proceed in this manner until the agreement was nullified due to problems in collection from Basra.[146] Prior to Persian occupation, the struggle between Basra's merchants and the central government in Baghdad over the Aleppo trade intensified greatly. In 1774, the wali refused a request from a number of merchants to organize a caravan to Aleppo, thereby increasing secessionist tendencies in Basra.[147] This conflict of interests had profound political implications, which will be discussed later.

Toward the end of the century Aleppo faced a growing economic crisis.[148] Among the numerous causes for this crisis were the civil war in Persia, which affected Aleppo's silk trade, the increasing power of the Najdi tribes in the countryside, and the rise of Izmir and Damascus as Aleppo's primary rivals for the European and Middle Eastern trades, respectively. Volney, who visited Aleppo at the end of the century, speaks of the utter devastation of the economy and the desolation of the city and its hinterland.[149] This alone would have guaranteed a reduction in Basra's caravan trade, yet the situation became quite critical when the rising power of the Najdi tribes affected the security of the caravan route. The greatest damage was certainly done by the Wahhabis and their allies, who succeeded, as noted earlier, in sacking Karbala' in 1802. Two years later they raided the southern suburbs of Basra, causing much damage and loss of life.[150]

In addition to this, the Persian occupation of 1776–79 had two immediate impacts on the Basra–Aleppo trade.[151] First, it encouraged the development of a Kuwait–Aleppo route, where Kuwait's relative isolation afforded it greater security and freedom of commerce. Second, the decline of the Basra–Aleppo trade gave a boost to the hitherto secondary Baghdad–Damascus trade. During the second half of the century Aleppo's trading position gradually gave way to the rise of Damascus as the primary commercial city of Syria.[152] This combination of increasing controls from Baghdad, a decline in the security of the caravan route, the development of an alternative route from Kuwait, the waning of Aleppo's commercial prominence, and the rise of Damascus, all contributed to the decline of Basra's caravan trade at the end of the century.

Three primary conclusions emerge from the discussion of Basra's trade networks. First, it is clear that Basra acted as the link between the two regions of the Persian Gulf and western India on the one hand, and Iraq, Persia, and Syria on the other. It is, therefore, quite natural that Basra's economy would react to any developments that might occur in any of these regions. Second, Basra's primary role in this trade was as a port-of-transit. Although Basra's dates were in demand, especially in India and the Persian Gulf, this alone did not justify the importance of the city in the trade networks of the region. The primary cause for the city's commercial prominence was its strategic location, which linked the various routes among Europe, the Ottoman Empire, Persia, and India. Lastly, while all indications point to the decline of Basra's trade after the plague of 1773 and the Persian occupation of 1776–79, these events represented only the short-term causes of this decline. More important were the significant structural transformations that affected the region after the rise of the Qajars in Persia, the decline of Aleppo, and the rising competitiveness of other ports in the Gulf. Likewise, the late eighteenth century witnessed the height of tribal power in southern Iraq, enabling tribes such as the Khazaᶜil, ᶜUbayd, and Muntafiq to flout central authority and disrupt the trade routes with Baghdad and Aleppo. As late as 1850 Basra's mutasallim, Maᶜshuq Pasha, was still complaining of the government's inability to control the tribes and secure the chief inland trade routes.[153]

Trade, however, did not take place simply by virtue of good location or the demand for certain products. In the final analysis the engine for trade was the individual merchant. Throughout the century, Basrawi merchants proved quite resilient in trying to make the best of a bad and rapidly worsening situation. How this class organized its activities and how it responded to the challenges facing its world at the end of the eighteenth century is the subject of the next two chapters.

CHAPTER 4

The Merchants (Tujjar) and Trade

Prior to the twentieth century, the merchants of Basra formed a highly amorphous group, which in many ways reflected the nature of their livelihood. According to Hanna Batatu, the "characteristic of the transit trade determined the nature of the merchants connected with it: they were basically a migratory class" and tended to shift "with the shift of the trade channels."[1] ᶜUthman ibn Sanad tells us of a merchant named ᶜAbdul-ᶜAziz ibn Musa al-Hujari who originally came to Basra from Najd. After spending several years there, he left for Baghdad, and by the end of the century was reported to be living in Qatar.[2] Such examples represented the norm rather than the exception. Strictly speaking, it can be said that Basrawi merchants actually belonged to a region rather than a city. For this reason their presence in Basra appeared extremely fluid, with new individuals suddenly taking center stage while other, well-known ones vanished from the scene. Their mobility over the region from West India to Istanbul and Yemen, described in the previous chapter, underlined their constant struggle for economic survival. As Hala Fattah so succinctly put it:

> Because of the vicissitudes of general supply (which was often tied to the chronic instability of the market, caused by plagues, droughts, and the military adventures of tribal chieftains), economic survival depended on open and easy access to a wide region in which secondary markets made up for traditional trade centers which became inoperative over time.[3]

It is also not always clear who, in the eighteenth century, was or was not a merchant. Trade in Basra played such an important role in the economy that nearly everyone with excess wealth invested in it. The distinction, therefore, between those whose livelihood depended primarily on trade and those to whom trade was a secondary source of income often appears blurred.[4] The sources do, however, reveal that Basra's wholesale merchants, their disparate loyalties notwithstanding, had a clear sense of their distinct mercantile identity. The tujjar, as these wholesale merchants were called, distinguished themselves through their command of large amounts of wealth and by having commercial interests far beyond the confines of the city. Unlike the grocers (*baqqalun*), butchers (*qaṣṣabun*), or various other small retail traders, the tujjar did not engage in manual work nor were they formally organized into guilds. They were usually well educated and quite religious.[5] Some, like the Naqib family, were distinguished as both successful merchants and respected ᶜulama'.[6] Out of the sixty-two tujjar mentioned by the English agent between 1768 and 1776, thirty-three carried the title of ḥajji, indicating that they had made the pilgrimage to Mecca. Another four had other religious titles such as sayyid, shaykh, and mullah.[7]

THE RISKS OF TRADE

Aspiring merchants chose from a variety of options when beginning their careers. The likely route was to start as an apprentice taking charge of a specific shipment. This was particularly common with the younger members of an established merchant family. In the 1760s, Yaᶜqub ben Aaron Gabbai, one of the foremost Jewish merchants of Basra, gave his nephew the responsibility of receiving and selling his merchandise in Istanbul. Later, the nephew became an established merchant in his own right.[8] Information on the Armenian merchants of New Julfa (many of whom were present in Basra) reveals another way in which young merchants got started. A number of principals would supply the capital needed for a particular venture; a young merchant would travel, conclude the trade, and keep a percentage (usually one-quarter) of the profits. The rest of the profits went to the principals.[9]

For those lacking good connections there was no alternative to taking high risks. The folklore and poetry of the area is rich with examples that point to a strong work ethic. The following verses from an unknown poet are still popular in Basra:

بقدرِ الكدِ تكتسبُ المعالي   و منْ طلبَ العُلا سهرَ الليالي

يغوصُ البحرَ منْ طلبَ اللآلي   و يحظى بالسيادةِ و النوالِ

و منْ طلبَ العُلا من غيرِ كدِ   اضاعَ العمرَ في طلبِ المحالِ

By means of toil man shall scale the height;
Who to fame aspires mustn't sleep o'night:
Who seeketh pearl in the deep must dive,
Winning weal and wealth by his main and might:
And who seeketh Fame without toil and strife
Th' impossible seeketh and wasteth life.[10]

Young adventurers would borrow some money and try their luck on some promising venture. This was apparently how Ḥajji Rizq began. Ibn Sanad tells us that he started with a loan from the wali, which he invested in the pearl trade. Within a "short time" he had made a great profit.[11] It is likely that the young Rizq traveled to India, encountering several difficulties since he probably had few, if any, contacts. By the end of the century his sons were managing one of the largest family firms, with interests spreading from the Gulf to India.[12]

Long-distance commerce, however, was not for the fainthearted. For each success there must have been numerous failures. The slightest mishap along the way (and there certainly were many) often led to the utter ruin of a young merchant. In 1774, for example, the Kaᶜb fleet seized a ship owned by the shaykh of Bushire laden with a rich cargo of pearls belonging mainly to Basrawi merchants. One of these merchants by the name of Ḥajji ᶜAbdul-Majid lost some five thousand rupees, driving him to near bankruptcy, while other unnamed young merchants were "totally ruined."[13] Should the merchandise arrive safely at its destination, the merchant might then face the danger of a highly unstable market. According to a Dutch report written in 1756, the high risks involved in long-distance trade led most merchants in the Gulf to avoid any venture unless it promised a profit of at least 25 percent.[14] Likewise, a merchant coming to Basra from Istanbul would not be satisfied with a profit margin of less than 50 percent. Should he continue to India, he would look for a profit of at least 100 percent to compensate for the great risks involved.[15]

In addition to pirates, bandits, and an unpredictable market, the threat of shipwrecks, wars, government confiscations, various kinds of swindlers, and many other unforeseen dangers hung, like the sword of Damocles, over all merchants in the area. Ashin Das Gupta's remark that in Surat "it was an existence from one day to the next even for the wealthiest among the merchants"[16] can be equally applied to eighteenth-century Basra. It is no surprise that the narratives of the popular *One Thousand and One Night* stories are rich with tales of the many unforeseen dangers and temptations that could easily lead to the ruin of a merchant.[17] To help limit such losses there were a number of manuals that informed merchants of the various foreign conditions and practices that they might encounter in their voyages. Although most of these texts were written by the Armenians of New Julfa they nevertheless indicate the presence of a well-developed mercantile culture in the area as a whole.[18]

INVESTMENT AND WEALTH

Despite these dangers the prize for those who succeeded was indeed tempting. While Basra never produced a merchant equivalent to the great Mullah ᶜAbdul-Ghafur of Surat,[19] many of Basra's merchants succeeded in accumulating great fortunes. Mir Muḥammad al-Baqir, for example, was considered one of the wealthiest merchants in Basra, worth between 700,000 and 800,000 rupees.[20] There were several merchants who owned their own fleets, which, despite their inferior status when compared to the great fleets of Surat or Masqat, still represented a major investment.[21] Other merchants, like Muhammad "Nubby" [ᶜAbdul-Nabi? al-Nubi?], for example, owned shares in some of the ships of the Masqat fleet.[22] Some merchants commanded enough wealth to regularly provide substantial loans to establishments such as the English East India Company in Basra. In December 1767, Ḥajji ᶜAli, "a reputable merchant of Bussora," provided the English factory with a loan of 797 tumans.[23] The following year the English factory again borrowed as much as 22,290 rupees from Khawjah Buṭrus Malik, Khawjah Elias, and Ḥajji ᶜAli.[24]

The highly risky nature of trade during this period naturally drove Basrawi merchants to diversify their investments and distribute them over the entire region. While most investments were in land, merchants also invested in such trade-related institutions as caravansaries and *khans* (inns). There is little evidence, however, that they invested much in productive economic activities such as the craft industries.[25] A list outlining some of the property of Ḥajji Yusuf ibn Ḥajji Muḥammad, one of the wealthiest merchants during the middle of the century, clearly illustrates this tendency (Table 4.1).[26]

Throughout this study reference has been made to the connections that Basrawi merchants had with the Gulf. The sources, in fact, suggest that their interests were more heavily present in the Gulf than in any

TABLE 4.1
Property of Ḥajji Yusuf ibn Ḥajji Muḥammad in Basra, 1766

Nature of Property	*Value (in tumans)*
Land in "Cust" Shaᶜban, 200 *jaribs*[27]	3,000.00
Land in Thamur, 160 jaribs	2,400.00
Land in "Myrzee," 60 jaribs	720.00
Land in Saraji, Abu al-Khasib, Bani-"Shucker Ehood," the Island of "Buarcen,"[28] the Gate of Mashraq, 251.25 jaribs	4,235.50
Two-thirds interest in the Caravanary near the Roman Church	200.00
The Khan Sansali with its Five Houses	1,125.00
One Coffeehouse in "Seamor"	27.00
One Coffeehouse in Qiblah	47.25
Two Shops in the Silver Smith Bazaar	10.00
Half interest in Five Khans	235.00
Total Value of Property	11,999.75

Source: *MSA*, Bussora Factory Diaries no. 195, entry dated April 4, 1766.

other region. As a result of constant tribal turmoil and tensions with Persia, most Basrawi merchants (with the notable exception of the Jews) generally found it easier to communicate with the different ports of the Gulf than with Baghdad. Ḥajji Ibrahim, for example, preferred to invest his money in the purchase of property in Masqat rather than risk it in Baghdad.[29] During the Persian occupation most Basrawi merchants had to send for their money abroad to satisfy the increasingly heavy taxes imposed upon them. The great majority of them had kept most of their money in India and Masqat.[30] Such economic and social factors meant that most Basrawi merchants generally felt a stronger bond with the Gulf than with any other region, including Baghdad, despite Basra's administrative unity with the latter.

The comparative wealth of Basra's most important communities varied during the century, although the superiority of the Muslim merchants (both Sunni and Shiᶜi) over non-Muslims remained constant. In 1705, Shaykh Mughamis, who was then occupying the city, hastily collected 60,000 *scudos* from the merchants and 500 scudos from the Christian, Jewish, and Sabean communities.[31] The relative wealth of the communities is made clearer by Karim Khan's levy in 1776. Shortly after occupying the city, Karim Khan Zand collected the tribute outlined in Table 4.2.

The apparent equality of the Armenian and Jewish communities in terms of wealth was not evident early in the century. By all accounts the Armenians were, by far, the wealthiest and most influential of the dhimmi communities in Basra. Niebuhr, one of the most perceptive of the eighteenth-century travelers, hardly mentioned the Jewish community of Basra, yet he repeatedly emphasized the importance of the Armenians.[35] Hamilton, in 1721, stated that the Jews were kept "very low."[36] This, however, changed rapidly during the second half of the century, when, under the able leadership of their *nasi*,[37] Yaᶜqub ben Aaron Gabbai, they soon eclipsed the Armenians.

CREDIT AND CONTRACTS

The merchant's most important asset was his reputation as a trustworthy businessman. The nature of Basra's transit trade demanded that much of the merchandise be bought and sold on credit, usually guaranteed by little more than a person's word of honor. Mirza Khan, who visited the city at the end of the century, commented that the people of Basra were "so very punctual in all their commercial dealings, that

TABLE 4.2
Amount (in tumans) Demanded by the Persian Army from the People of Basra, 1776

The Armenian Merchants	17,000[32]
The Jewish Merchants	17,000
Ḥajji Bakr and Ḥajji Ibrahim[33]	13,000
Shaykh Darwish and "His People"[34]	40,000
The Sayyids, Mufti, and Other *Aᶜyan* of Basra	20,000
The Rest of the Inhabitants	18,000

Source: *IOR*, Letters from Basra, G/29/21, letter dated July 2, 1776, folio 223.

they never require bonds from each other."[38] Hala Fattah's argument, that the widespread use of credit in the area should not be seen as a lack of integration within the market but rather as a facilitator of long-distance trade, is certainly correct with respect to Basra.[39] Since the caravans and riverine boats rarely arrived at the same time as the India ships, large amounts of goods had to be purchased, stored, and resold at a later time for export to the hinterland. In a region that suffered from a constant shortage of currency, credit played a significant role in facilitating this type of exchange. The example of the *Salamat Resson*, owned by Ahmad Chalabi of Surat, helps illustrate how this exchange occurred. In July 1726, this ship arrived from Surat with a cargo of various piece goods. It sold half of its merchandise for ready money and half on credit. The owners agreed that payment should be made shortly after the arrival of the merchant boats from Baghdad. The ship sailed back after leaving behind a wakil to collect the debt.[40] It was not unheard of for a wakil to remain for over a year waiting for the merchandise to sell.[41] In another incident, Khawjah Matti Dawud, an Armenian merchant, told the agent that it was normal practice to sell cloth on three to six months' credit. "It was usual," he said, "to deliver the goods at the time of making the bargain and recover the money at or before if possible, the expiration of the contract."[42]

Should a merchant develop a reputation for failing to keep his word, he would certainly find it difficult to maintain his business. This is why, as James Tracy points out, it must surely have been a case of extreme exaggeration on the part of so many contemporary Europeans to claim that Muslims could not be trusted because "they had been taught that promises made to infidels are not binding."[43] Rumors of a merchant unable to repay a loan or fulfill a contract were treated as major catastrophes. In 1764, one Signor Rigo, an Italian shopowner, accused a number of Basra's wealthiest merchants of reneging on promises to supply him with certain goods. Within a few days the "entire town was restless."[44] The accused merchants were so worried that "such a calamny [sic] might have a very bad effect on their credit" that they instigated the people of Basra against the Italian shopowner.[45] The mutasallim, fearing mob action, finally ordered Signor Rigo banished to Aleppo. In an earlier case recorded in 1707, a number of merchants informed the wali, Khalil Pasha, that due to the poor state of the market at that time they were honor-bound to write to the merchants of Baghdad, Aleppo, Mosul, and Diyarbakr advising them not to bring their merchandise to Basra.

While in the short term it would certainly hurt Basra's economy to keep merchants away, in the long term it would preserve a trust, which in the case of some of these merchants (as the document points out), was created through thirty to forty years of fruitful trade.[46] Such evidence lends credence to M. N. Pearson's argument that the early modern states in India and the Middle East lacked the ability or interest to strictly control the commercial activities of merchants. Referring to Mughal India, he adds that "the credit system worked because it depended heavily on a reputation for honesty, rather than on any legal system."[47] While Basra's merchants did, at times, resort to the state's *shariᶜa* courts to settle disputes, this was done only after other informal methods were exhausted.

One method of transferring money, which came increasingly into use by the middle of the century and required a greater role by the state, was the use of what the English called "Bills of Exchange." These documents, usually notarized by the qadi, basically allowed a merchant to take out a loan in one city and pay it off (plus various charges) in another. One such bill worth 20,000 rupees was purchased by Salih Chalabi of Surat from Ḥajji Karim to be payable in Basra upon the arrival of Salih Chalabi.[48] Contracts for the shipment of goods were more numerous. In one of the rare contracts between the English and a Jewish merchant during this period, Khawjah Yaᶜqub Gabbai had some pearls and silk shipped to India on an English vessel. The English agreed to receive payment for the transportation cost three months after the goods were received by Khawjah Yaᶜqub's partners in Bombay.[49]

Similarly, in 1753, the agent at Bandar ᶜAbbas reported that he had signed a contract with Agha ᶜAbdullah, formerly "one of the King of Persia's Eunuchs," to ship his "valuable Bulce of Diamonds" to Basra. The diamonds were to be shipped after the arrival of Agha ᶜAbdullah in Basra. He would then pay the English agent there the sum of 10,000 rupees a few days after his diamonds were received.[50] Most of these money transactions were conducted by a class of native bankers known as the ṣarrafs, who commanded most of the cash. In addition to Bills of Exchange the ṣarrafs also sold "Letters of Credit" which enabled a traveler to deposit his money in one city and collect it from the ṣarraf's partner in another city. The ṣarrafs also benefited from the high number of Istanbuli merchants returning from India. Having usually spent all of their cash purchasing Indian goods, these merchants were desperate enough to borrow cash at an interest rate of 30 percent for their trip home.[51] During the second half of the century, Jewish ṣarrafs like the wealthy Khawjah Dawud came to dominate this important position in Basra.[52]

Notwithstanding this overall dependence on credit, Europeans in general and the English in particular rarely made use of this system. The English East India Company constantly stressed its policy of selling only for ready money. The letters sent by the Basra factors to the board of directors point to their frustration at not being allowed to sell on credit since few merchants at Basra, or indeed in most of the region, used ready cash for large transactions.[53] In the eighteenth century, however, when security was a primary concern for all merchants, the traditional legal institutions did not always seem capable of regulating international trade or guaranteeing contracts and Bills of Exchange. The main guarantee a merchant had was trust, usually in one's relatives or community. Lacking such an indigenous base for most of the century, the caution of the board of directors does not appear misplaced.

MERCHANT COMMUNITIES

Much has been written on the subject of commercial communities of the Indian Ocean in the premodern period. Best known is the work of Philip Curtin, who emphasized their role as "cross-cultural brokers, helping and encouraging trade between the host society and people of their own origin who moved along the trade routes."[54] Because of the "uncertainty of commercial variables"[55] merchants worked within communities usually based on the ties of religion, kinship, tribal affiliation, or ethnic group, and generally free of strict government control. Merchants would, over time, reside within the area of their chief trading interests, creating a network of commercial settlements tied together through the bonds of their particular communal identity. These merchant communities facilitated trade and generally helped bring harmony to a region suffering from chronic instability, particularly in the eighteenth century.[56]

Basra's merchant communities did not differ much from this overall pattern dominant in the early modern Indian Ocean. Unlike the small retail traders, Basra's tujjar did not form their own guilds or separate organizations. In this regard, Basra did not differ from other ports of the time like Venice or Surat, both of which lacked merchant guilds during this period.[57] The institution of the aᶜyan, which certainly included many wealthy tujjar, also included landowners and religious figures, and excluded Shiᶜi and dhimmi merchants for most of the century. There are numerous examples of merchants acting jointly with landowners and other aᶜyan, but no recorded incident of the merchants, as a whole, consciously acting together as a distinct group. Instead, the sources reveal that merchants, outside their family, tended to identify primarily with their religion, place of origin, tribe, or ethnic community. The classical separation of non-Muslims into *millahs* (millets) in the Ottoman Empire does not shed much light on the question of communal identity in Basra, since it leaves out such communities as the Shiᶜi Persians and the Sunni Najdis. The importance of communal affiliation is evident in the nature of merchant partners who conducted some business with the English agent (Table 4.3).

Clearly, partnerships of individuals from separate communities were extremely rare. The two recorded cases of such partnerships included small merchants and appeared only once each in the records, suggesting that they were quite temporary.[58] The majority of these partnerships represented two people, with only a few consisting of three or four individuals. Several, like those of the Armenian "Cuchek" brothers,[59] and Ḥajji Muḥammad ᶜAli ᶜAwad and his son Ḥusayn,[60] represented family partnerships or "firms."[61] Each merchant community tended to succeed in the trade routes with which they had the best contacts and familiarity. Thus, the Persians were mostly active in the raw silk trade with Persia while the Najdis were active in the Gulf and along the desert route to Aleppo.

TABLE 4.3
Merchant Partnerships by Community, 1726–1774

Community	*Number of Partnerships*
Sunnis	16
Armenians	11
Persians (Shiᶜis)	9
Jews	5
Intercommunal	2

Sources: *IOR*, Letters from Basra, nos. G/29/18–20; *MSA*, Gombroon Factory Diaries, nos. 112–118; *MSA*, Bussora Factory Diaries, nos. 193–201.

It is interesting to note here that there is no evidence of sectarian violence in Basra similar to that which afflicted Greek-Turkish relations in Izmir or Muslim-Hindu relations in Surat during the same period.[62] Niebuhr mentions that the Persian Shiʿis of Basra were despised by the general population for their religion.[63] Nevertheless, the numerous conflicts with Persia during this time did not lead to widespread sectarian rioting or violence. A sense of tolerance, more so than in other cities of the region, born of the rather high fluidity of Basrawi society, seems to have dominated intercommunal relations. In fact, the sizable Persian population, which had always existed in Basra, flourished during the height of the Ottoman-Persian wars and the 1689 Ottoman census lists a quarter, Maḥallat Bahbaha'iyya, named after a Persian notable.[64] By the end of the century, with the continuing civil wars in Persia, their numbers seem to have increased noticeably. Mirza Abu Ṭalib Khan, himself a Persian, wrote that Basra had "a number of Persians of good family" who were "agreeable men, much superior to the natives of Bussora."[65] He made no mention of any serious tensions between the Persian community and other Basrawis.

While it is not the goal of this work to deal with the structural details of the European trading communities, a few words are in order. There is little doubt that a trading community, like the English, organized under the English East India Company, enjoyed important advantages at Basra. What they lacked in local contacts they made up for through their large, relatively well-organized companies, which gave them an edge, particularly in cases of long-distance trade.[66] Most important, however, was the support of the English Crown, which avoided absolute control while still providing "a framework for collective discipline" to the English merchants.[67] This support, plus his Company contacts in India, allowed Samuel Manesty to become one of Basra's most successful merchants, eventually owning at least seven trading vessels.[68]

THE JEWISH MERCHANTS

The available sources concerning indigenous communities shed light mostly on the Jewish and Armenian merchants of Basra. Although the Jewish presence in southern Iraq goes back to pre-Islamic times, they did not form an important community in Basra until the Umayyad period of the late seventh century.[69] The fortunes of the Jewish community generally mirrored those of Basra's inhabitants as a whole, flourishing during the Abbasid period and declining after the Mongol invasion of the mid-thirteenth century. They seemed to have been singled out for persecution by Timur Lang, who invaded Iraq in 1393 and destroyed all the city's synagogues.[70] Despite their continued presence, the Jewish community did not regain its importance until the eighteenth century when, according to local tradition, a new migration of Jews from Baghdad increased their numbers and prestige.[71] They must have also benefited from the generally favorable treatment that Jews received in the Ottoman Empire as a whole.

The Jews of Basra were always closely related to those of Baghdad.[72] The strength of the ties between the two was enforced annually during the Feast of Weeks.[73] During this holiday, usually held in May, large numbers of Jews from Baghdad, Basra, and Iran held celebrations at the Tomb of the Prophet Ezra, located to the north of Qurnah on the Tigris River.[74] In addition to the religious and festive nature of the gathering, merchants usually took the opportunity to conclude various business agreements.[75]

Not surprisingly, Jewish merchants were particularly active in the riverine trade with Baghdad. Yaᶜqub ben Aaron Gabbai owned a fleet of boats that transported goods and money between the two cities.[76] Likewise, when the English agent had to send a packet to Baghdad, he usually resorted to a certain "Jew named Aaron Coen" who operated a number of ships on the Euphrates.[77] A strong interest in the riverine trade did not prohibit Jewish merchants from entering into the lucrative India trade. This seems to have occurred quite gradually during the second half of the century. Yaᶜqub Gabbai, for example, began to regularly receive Surat piece goods on Indo-Arab vessels in the 1760s.[78] In the early 1770s, another wealthy merchant, ᶜAbdullah ibn Yusuf, had a regular wakil in Surat by the name of Isḥaq Dawud.[79] The same merchant also acted as a broker in Basra for Tippo Sultan, the ruler of Mysore.[80]

Significantly, Jewish merchants rarely shipped their merchandise on English vessels, despite the latter's growing control of the freight trade with India. The Basra factory diaries usually list the names or communities of the merchants that shipped their goods on English vessels. Throughout the century, there were only three documented cases of Jews shipping pearls to Surat. The cause for this apparent lack of business ties between the English and the Jews is not clear. Hostility between the Jews and the English was not limited to Basra at this time.

Concerning the Jews in Aleppo, Bruce Masters mentions that "the English, in particular, seemed to have been loath to have any business dealings with them," and attributed this to fear of competition and anti-Semitism.[81] Elena Frangakis-Syrett noticed this same hostility at Izmir.[82] In Basra, there is little doubt that the English tended to favor their co-religionists over all other minorities, particularly in the second half of the century. With the entry of the Jews into the India trade, and the rise of Armenian-Jewish rivalry, English support of the Armenians became more pronounced.

THE ARMENIAN MERCHANTS

The presence of the Armenian community in southern Iraq does not date as far back as that of the Jews. Their position in the trade of the region did not become well established until the late sixteenth century. A major turning point in their history occurred in 1604, when the Safavid Shah ᶜAbbas I transferred the entire population of the Armenian city of Julfa, near Tabriz, to the new quarter of New Julfa in Isfahan. Under the protection and generally benevolent treatment of the Safavids, they succeeded in gradually expanding their commercial activities throughout Asia (including Basra) and the Mediterranean.[83] Most historians, in fact, agree that Armenian merchants came to monopolize Iran's foreign trade under the Safavids, with "agents as far afield as Sweden and China."[84] However, with the decline of Isfahan and the fall of the Safavids in 1722, the Armenians lost the patronage of a major power.[85] Nevertheless, thanks to their unmatched sense of communal solidarity, they still managed to persist as one of the important trading communities throughout the eighteenth century.

During the seventeenth and early eighteenth centuries, Armenian participation in Ottoman-Safavid commerce centered mainly on their control of the Persian silk trade.[86] At Basra the Armenian merchants were also active in the India trade. Das Gupta notes that the Armenian merchants of Surat were in the forefront of the trade to Basra and the Gulf.[87] Armenian-owned vessels operated regularly between India and Basra,[88] and in 1729, the English agent reported that they were behind the importation of much of the piece goods from Bengal.[89] By the middle of the century the Armenians were making greater use of English ships. The cargo list of the *Drake*, which sailed from Basra to Surat in September 1763, includes six separate shipments of pearls, five of which belonged to Armenian merchants.[90] There are also numerous accounts, throughout the century, of Armenian merchants traveling between India and Basra on English ships without clear reference to their cargo.[91]

In addition to these connections with India, the Armenians of Basra also had strong commercial links with their co-religionists in Aleppo.[92] Throughout the seventeenth and eighteenth centuries the Armenians of New Julfa represented the most important merchant community in Aleppo, with most of their wealth coming through the lucrative silk trade with Persia.[93] As this trade declined during the eighteenth century, they tended to shift more of their capital to the caravan trade with Basra, which linked Aleppo to India. In the 1768 French report on the trade of Basra, the Armenians are singled out as playing a dominant role in the caravan trade with Aleppo.[94] Not surprisingly, the Armenians of Basra were particularly concerned about ᶜAli Bey al-Kabir's capture of Damascus in 1771, and his possible advance toward Aleppo.[95] There is also evidence that the Armenians, more than others, energetically sought to persuade the wali of Baghdad to allow the Basra caravans to proceed directly to Aleppo without stopping at Baghdad to pay additional taxes.[96]

THE CHALABIS OF BASRA

Of even greater importance than the religious or ethnic community in organizing eighteenth-century trade was the family or clan. Among the most influential merchant families active in Basra's trade with India at this time were the Chalabis.[97] Although their history remains obscure, Ashin Das Gupta suggests that they came to Surat from Iraq in the seventeenth century. By the turn of the century, Muḥammad Saliḥ Chalabi had become one of the wealthiest merchants in western India, with a large and well-organized fleet.[98] The English factory diaries show Chalabi's ships calling at Basra throughout the century. In the 1707 meeting with the wali of Basra, the merchants noted that for the previous two years Aḥmad Chalabi's ships (usually two) were the only vessels from India willing to risk trading at Basra's depressed market.[99]

The records also show that the Chalabis of Basra were certainly related to those of Surat. ᶜAbdul-Qadir, at the end of the eighteenth century, visited the graveyard of the Chalabis of Basra near Zubayr and noted that they had originally come from Surat.[100] Likewise, the close business relations between the Chalabis of Basra and Surat suggest more than just a shared title. ʿUmar Chalabi of Basra, and later his son Murad, were always in charge of receiving the merchandise imported through the Chalabi ships of Surat. They also provided the freight for the voyage back. In 1730, Aḥmad Chalabi, Muḥammad Saliḥ's son, chose Basra as his place of refuge when his life was threatened.[101] Also, when Saliḥ Chalabi, Muḥammad Saliḥ's grandson, arrived in Basra in 1772, he was received by Murad Chalabi and likely stayed at his house.[102]

The Chalabis provide a good example of how merchant families acted as the primary organizations for the conduct of trade. While many merchants relied on wakils, they generally preferred to have members of their family reside in the major cities with which they traded. Trust was certainly one of the most important factors in the trade of the eighteenth century, when unsettled conditions and insecurity were the rule rather than the exception. Most merchants felt that a person of one's own family or clan was less likely to break this trust. Other examples of the same phenomenon abound at this time. During the middle of the century Ḥajji Muḥammad al-Baghdadi, a merchant of some note in Basra, conducted much of his trade with Isfahan. Despite the existence of numerous Persian merchants that were eager to do business with Basra, he preferred to have his son reside in Isfahan and take care of the family's affairs there directly.[103] Likewise, the above-mentioned "Cuchek" brothers had relatives in Surat that handled their business.[104]

The foregoing illustrates two major points. First, the merchants of Basra, like their counterparts in other trading cities of the region, did not develop a clear class identity. While they saw themselves as individuals practicing the same trade, their loyalty remained firmly fixed on their communal affiliation. Normally, the family or clan acted as the primary organizing institution of commercial activities. But merchants also depended on their religious, ethnic, and tribal communities. These traditional institutions were further strengthened by the widespread insecurity of the time and the general decline of law and order. Second, different merchant communities tended to "specialize" in different trade routes. The Jews were heavily involved in the riverine trade with Baghdad, the Armenians in the caravan trade with Aleppo, and the Chalabis in the maritime trade with India. These differences could not but lead to conflicting attitudes with respect to the highly volatile political atmosphere of the time.

The second half of the eighteenth century was an unstable period for the merchants of Basra. The sharp boom of the late 1760s and early 1770s, followed by plague, Persian occupation, tribal revolts, and overall economic decline, must have caused enormous stress and anxiety. This, along with the expansion of the activities of the Jewish merchants seems to have heightened the level of cut-throat competition. The intensifying struggle among merchant communities, particularly between the Armenians and the Jews, tended to express itself in the political issues of the time.

CHAPTER 5

The Merchants and Power

If there is one word that best describes the political situation in Iraq during the eighteenth century it certainly must be "instability." This instability naturally left a deep impression on the relations between the merchants and the mamluk-dominated state. Briefly, the sources for this instability were threefold. First, the decline and collapse of the Safavids during the first two decades of the eighteenth century was followed by a state of almost continuous warfare between the Ottomans and Persians, usually conducted on Iraqi soil. At practically the same time, the main Ottoman army was hard-pressed by Russia and Austria on the European front. This combination forced the Porte to grant the walis of Baghdad a freer hand in organizing the defenses of the province. The autonomy gained led, in turn, to the rise of tensions between Baghdad and Istanbul.[1] Second, the migration of great numbers of nomadic tribes from Najd during the seventeenth and eighteenth centuries resulted in numerous prolonged territorial conflicts. It also allowed for the development of various rural bases of power that constantly challenged government control.[2] Third, the centrifugal forces that gripped the outlying provinces of the Ottoman Empire in the eighteenth century led the Porte to adopt several tactics aimed at preventing their outright secession. In Iraq, where these forces were particularly strong, the Porte tried to limit the tenure of Baghdad's wali, stimulated the rivalry between the local power groups, and, at times, actively encouraged the ambitions of tribal leaders.[3]

Ironically, the walis resorted to some of the same tactics to enhance their bargaining position with the Porte. The Ottomans sought to limit the autonomy of Baghdad by keeping the provincial government weak; they did not, however, wish to see it too weak. The Porte usually acquiesced to demands for greater autonomy if it was convinced that this could prevent a total collapse. Aḥmad Pasha was apparently well accustomed to playing this political balancing game despite its disastrous consequences to the overall health of the province. "As long as Ahmett Basshaw holds these governments," wrote the English agent,

> the country will not be fitt for merchants to sett in, for upon every little disgust that he takes against the Porte he is continually raising the whole country in arms, and at such times his people here take an opportunity of oppressing strangers.[4]

By periodically stirring up trouble within the province he made his removal more problematic and, at times, even succeeded in gaining additional financial and military aid from Istanbul. As a result of these policies some historians have even made the unlikely accusation that he actually encouraged the Persian attack on Basra in 1743.[5] Such tensions were present in various parts of the Ottoman Empire at this time. In nearby Damascus, "the Ottoman state found itself unable to maintain the provincial system except by granting more discretionary powers to the governor."[6] Even in the center of the empire at Izmir, the state was forced to pursue a delicate balancing act to keep the local aᶜyan in the fold.[7] What is peculiar about the situation in Iraq, particularly after 1750, is that the mamluk governors, being of foreign origin, "could not completely operate as indigenous, autonomous elites."[8] Their constant fear of removal added to the general atmosphere of instability.

THE MAMLUKS AND TRADE

Such conditions contributed to an attitude, on the part of the mamluk government, that was not always conducive to the welfare of trade. Generally speaking, Pearson's observation that "merchants were not hindered very much, but neither were they helped"[9] by the state in the great Muslim empires of Asia is certainly correct with respect to Basra. By the middle of the eighteenth century, however, the unstable conditions began to adversely affect this essentially noninterventionist attitude. Nieuwenhuis takes the position that "the state was too weak, too unstable and too entangled with particularistic interests to execute a systematic policy of trade promotion or economic reforms."[10]

The problem is that the Ottoman state, even at its height, never actively executed such a "systematic policy" preferring, instead, to simply provide the basics of stability and some facilities (usually in the form of private endowments) which certainly aided the merchant. While many of Basra's governors owned customs tax-farms (*gumruk muqaṭaᶜat*)[11] and were certainly interested in the port's trade revenues, the pressures of the second half of the eighteenth century were, nevertheless, quite overwhelming. Nieuwenhuis is therefore correct to point out that the need for immediate revenues with which to combat a tribal revolt, a potential uprising by the janissaries, or a new threat from Persia meant that even the strongest walis "took many fiscal and monetary measures that were favorable to their treasuries but disadvantageous for the commercial community."[12]

Nothing exemplifies this attitude better than Baghdad's policy toward the Basra–Aleppo caravan trade. Beginning with Ahmad Pasha in 1739, the walis tried to divert the route, forcing caravans to make a stop near Baghdad before proceeding to Aleppo or Basra.[13] Their success or failure at enforcing this policy depended on the government's strength at that particular time. While the immediate result was to add to the revenues of Baghdad from the additional duties, in the long term it greatly increased the burdens on the merchants and eventually contributed to the decline of this vital trade route. The pressures were so great that even a wali who was consciously aware of the importance of the direct Aleppo–Basra trade link could not avoid adopting such policies.

When Sulayman was still the mutasallim of Basra, he often supported the merchants' demands for permission to use the direct route to Aleppo. After the end of the Persian occupation, he even pressed for the separation of Basra from the province of Baghdad and petitioned the Porte to appoint him as its wali.[14] Shortly after his appointment as the wali of a unified Baghdad and Basra, however, he resumed the policy of his predecessors regarding both the rerouting of the Aleppo caravans and Baghdad's administrative control of Basra.[15] It is also significant to note that despite Sulayman's personal popularity, particularly in Basra, he was unable to stop Basra separatists from continuing to gain strength. His earlier sympathies notwithstanding, he violently suppressed the two major separatist revolts that took place during his governorship.

The mutasallims of Basra were under no less strain. The ease with which they could fall from grace and be replaced or, even worse, lose their lives, must have constantly occupied their thoughts. Thus, they too tended to view merchants simply as an immediate, rather than a strategic asset. The result, particularly in times of acute instability, was repeated demands for payments, confiscation of property, and various forms of expropriation. Some, like the Persian merchants, received more than the usual share of intimidation and property seizures. What happened to Mir Muḥammad al-Baqir was typical of the harassments they endured. In 1769, this noted Persian merchant had thirty-nine bales of Bengal goods confiscated by the mutasallim. When his wakil, Ḥajji Muḥammad ᶜAli (who was also a Persian) went to complain, he was promptly thrown in prison.[16] At his arrival, al-Baqir was worth between seven and eight *lacks*[17] of rupees. After this incident, the last of several others, he was reduced "almost to poverty."[18]

Yet it was with every change in government that the merchants had to truly brace themselves for additional demands usually backed by threats, intimidation, and violence. In December 1768, Basra received a new mutasallim named Ḥajji Sulayman Agha.[19] At first all indications were that he was a sensible mutasallim who moved quickly to root out corrupt officials.[20] Yet as soon as he heard of the decision to remove him from office, he panicked and hastily took measures aimed at milking the merchants for all they were worth prior to the arrival of his replacement.[21] When one Armenian merchant named "Senhar Sherriman" did not produce the amount demanded of him, he was duly beaten in public.[22] The mutasallim's men also broke into several homes and took as much merchandise as they could carry, including ten bales of coffee from the homes of Ḥajji Muḥammad and Ḥajji al-Samiri, both of whom were described as "coffee merchants."[23] Because of his imminent departure, Hajji Sulayman Agha did not hesitate to lock horns with the al-Samiri family, one of the important aᶜyan of Basra, whose members appear periodically in the Ottoman court documents of the century.[24]

Such behavior was not limited to outgoing mutasallims. Newly appointed mutasallims often felt an urgent need to collect large sums of money with which they might purchase the loyalty of their new subordinates. Also, not unlike other cities in the Ottoman Empire and Persia, the mutasallim's post was usually purchased from the wali with money borrowed from the merchants or local ṣarrafs. The need to repay the loan as quickly as possible was an added incentive for forcible collections. This is what happened in November 1748, when the new mutasallim inaugurated his appointment by imprisoning a number of merchants and demanding a considerable payment for their release. As news of this act spread, trade came to a virtual standstill, with ships preferring to unload elsewhere rather than risk confiscation.[25] The sources show that by the end of the century such assaults became progressively more frequent. The overall decline of trade and increasing tribal revolts placed the mutasallims in an unenviable position. Baghdad's constant demands for more from less made the use of force practically unavoidable.

Other than threatening to leave the city altogether, the merchants acted to protect themselves and their properties in two ways. The most common method was by giving "gifts" or paying "protection money" to the various officials. The merchants, however, resorted to such payments when facing almost any type of problem. In 1724, for example, several Armenian merchants paid the mutasallim the equivalent of 2,480 rupees in return for his support of their claims in a contract dispute.[26] Likewise, in a 1763 meeting of the diwan the qaḍi was accused of having been bribed by Ḥajji Yusuf in return for favorable rulings.[27] The other method at the disposal of the merchants was to appeal for help from either the wali of Baghdad or, more likely, the shaykh of the Muntafiq. The incident in 1729 when the aᶜyan succeeded in removing an unpopular mutasallim through the intervention of Shaykh Muḥammad ibn Maniᶜ of the Muntafiq has already been discussed.[28] In 1763 and 1764, similar incidents took place. In the latter year the Muntafiq Shaykh did not bother to appeal to the wali, preferring to take matters into his own hands. After receiving a delegation of the aᶜyan, he surrounded Basra and would have stormed the city had the wali not intervened to depose the mutasallim.[29] By the early 1770s, the merchants were also turning to the English agent, whose stature was rapidly growing. In 1769, the English agent received a delegation of merchants who requested his help in removing the mutasallim. The agent responded by writing several letters to the wali, urging him to change the government.[30] By the end of the year Basra had a new mutasallim.[31]

Such obstacles to the smooth functioning of trade might appear unmanageable when viewed through the lens of the modern world. One might even wonder how merchants could ever make a living. They, however, did and often prospered by carefully managing their informal relations. Arguably, the most merchant-friendly government at Basra in the eighteenth century was that of Sulayman Agha. When oppressions did take place, however, some merchants had an uncanny ability at maintaining good relations even with the most tyrannical governments.

THE CHALABIS AND THE GOVERNMENT

One family that usually enjoyed good relations with most of Basra's mutasallims were the Chalabis. During the two decades prior to the

Persian occupation, Murad Chalabi was a regular member of the city's diwan and his influence on the government was quite apparent. In 1768, he joined a delegation of government officials to negotiate peace with Shaykh Ghanim of the Kaᶜb Arabs. Chalabi was the only merchant among the delegates.[32] Chalabi also played an important role in advising the mutasallim on matters of commerce. In 1768, the mutasallim ordered the seizure of several boats belonging to Mir Muhanna of Kharg Island. Khawajah Yaᶜqub Gabbai, the official ṣarraf, convinced the mutasallim that they should sell the cargo found aboard the boats, mainly coffee, to the English for 100 maḥmudis. As a result of Chalabi's opposition, however, the mutasallim reversed his earlier decision.[33]

Interestingly enough, Chalabi's main worry at this time seems to have been the growing presence of the English. While the evidence is scanty, there is no doubt that the English agent viewed him (as well as his kin in Surat) as a major obstacle to the interests of the East India Company. The causes behind this animosity seem evident enough. As discussed earlier, the English were increasingly successful in achieving a monopoly over the freight trade with India.[34] This "growing control of the English East India Company over [Surat's] carrying trade to the Gulfs made them irrevocable rivals of Muslim ship-owning merchants of the city—the Chellabis in particular."[35] In 1759, when the English were considering their plans to seize the fortress of Surat, John Spenser, EEIC chief at Surat wrote:

> I believe we may expect the family of the Chellabies who have too great interest at present in managing the young Sidi [governor] as they please in their mercantile interests to think that they would act with us besides their jealousy that such an aquisition unto us would have an ill influence on their freight voyages would induce them rather than to wish disappointment than success to us in an undertaking of that sort.[36]

This, however, was not the only cause for growing anti-British feelings among certain merchants.

THE CASES OF MUḤAMMAD AGHA AND ḤAJJI YUSUF

While the Chalabis gained their influence in the government through their long-established local contacts, there were instances where merchants lacking strong local influence would suddenly appear as favorites of the wali or mutasallim. In 1728, Basra received a new wali. Among those who accompanied the new wali was a certain merchant by the name of Muḥammad Agha.[37] The origin of this merchant is unknown, but he apparently gained special favor after agreeing to present the wali with a generous loan. In return, the wali appointed him to the office of shahbandar and gave him additional extraordinary powers in his administration. Muḥammad Agha, eager to make good on his investment, soon proceeded to incur the wrath of Basra's merchant community with his heavy-handed policies aimed at personal enrichment. By June of the following year, the merchants had had enough. After conspiring with the leading shaykhs of the Muntafiq, they successfully kidnapped Muḥammad Agha and then pressured the wali to finally put him to death. While this case shows that it was possible for a merchant to achieve considerable power in the government of the city, it also highlights the importance of local support in maintaining this power.

A much clearer example of the complexity of power relations at Basra can be gathered from the case of the flamboyant Ḥajji Yusuf ibn Ḥajji Muḥammad. Information on Ḥajji Yusuf's background is limited. Early in the century his father apparently held some government post that was concerned with financial and commercial matters.[38] The father's contacts certainly assisted his ambitious young son, and by the middle of the century he was described as a "very considerable merchant . . . worth many lacks of Rupees."[39] One reason for his great wealth was his lucrative contracts for the provisioning of the wali's army. In 1757, he concluded a deal to import large quantities of English woolens for the Baghdad wali's army.[40] By 1763, he had become its main supplier.[41]

Still, the services which he provided the wali of Baghdad and Basra were not limited to commercial matters. Ḥajji Yusuf also played a political role by acting as a forceful representative of the wali's interests at the Basra diwan. His stature as one of the wealthiest merchants in Basra, coupled with the wali's public support, his good relations with the shaykh of the Muntafiq, and his charismatic personality led to his effective leadership of the diwan. The agent reported that Ḥajji Yusuf's behavior in the diwan "intimidated" the mutasallim and his officers.[42] In one meeting, for example, he openly scolded the mutasallim for favoring the English, leaving "the Mussaleem more humble than a slave."[43] Ḥajji Yusuf reached the pinnacle of his power in 1763. The "authority Hodgee Eusoof had," the English agent wrote, was "superior . . . to [that of] the Mussaleem, on account of the great privileges granted him by the Bashaw [of Baghdad], even to the giving him 20 or more sealed orders, with authority to use them as he pleased."[44]

In August of that year, he led the a^cyan in demanding the removal of the mutasallim. That same month he led a delegation of the a^cyan to see Shaykh ^cAbdullah of the Muntafiq. By the end of August, the mutasallim was removed "at the request of the I-ons [a^cyan] and Shaik Abdalla and Hodgee Esoof."[45] The new mutasallim, Aḥmad Agha, was initially nominated by Ḥajji Yusuf.[46] After this incident Ḥajji Yusuf clearly became the most powerful man in Basra. The mutasallim's presence was reduced to that of a mere figurehead, as officers and soldiers began to take orders directly from Ḥajji Yusuf. In September of that year, the English ship, *Swallow*, was ordered to sail up a few miles to collect dates from a certain Shaykh ^cAli. Their request for government troops to support them should they encounter trouble from the Ka^cb Arabs remained unanswered since "the Government of the City was now in the Hands of Hodgee Esoof."[47] The English were unable to receive this assistance until they spoke directly to Ḥajji Yusuf, who "instantly ordered one hundred soldiers" to accompany them.[48]

On the whole, though, Ḥajji Yusuf took a hostile attitude toward the English. In one of his more spirited speeches before the diwan he declared that what the English were really after was no less than the conquest of Basra itself.[49] Unlike Murad Chalabi, however, the cause for the animosity here was debt. As the influence of the English grew in the second half of the century, so too did their financial demands upon the government and an increasing number of merchants. At the time of his death in 1764, Ḥajji Yusuf owed the English over 12,000 tumans.[50] In 1768, the agent reported that the English East India Company's demands on the government of Baghdad and Basra was now well over 15,000 tumans.[51] Most of this debt was a direct result of the government's inability to pay the expenses of the English fleet which protected Basra's maritime trade as stipulated in the 1767 agreement between the two sides.[52] Ḥajji Yusuf's control of Basra's government proved to be short-lived. While the wali wanted him to act as a counterbalance to the mutasallim, he certainly did not wish to see his fellow mamluks so totally stripped of power. Likewise, the a^cyan, who had supported Ḥajji Yusuf's efforts to remove an unpopular mutasallim, soon grew jealous and fearful of his growing powers and overbearing personality. Niebuhr, who arrived in Basra shortly after the conclusion of this affair, referred to the manner in which the aᶜyan turned against Ḥajji Yusuf as an example of the disunity and jealousy common among their ranks.[53] In January 1764, by order of the wali, Ḥajji Yusuf was strangled and his body ignominiously displayed in the market.[54] Shortly thereafter, the wali confiscated his entire estate.

Ḥajji Yusuf's story is interesting on several levels. First, it shows an instance, albeit brief, of a merchant who attained great political powers despite the generally uneasy relationship between the mamluk-dominated state and the tujjar during this period. The basis for this power was, however, inherently unstable. While Ḥajji Yusuf was not as isolated as Muḥammad Agha, his strength still rested on the tensions and evident lack of trust among the wali, the mutasallim, the Muntafiq, and the aᶜyan, and had no stable independent power base of his own. Second, it sheds light on how merchants were often used by the mamluks of Baghdad to limit the powers of the mutasallim. The intense intermamluk rivalries that defined part of the political reality of the time meant that the wali had to keep a close eye on his mutasallim in Basra. Almost without exception, each mutasallim saw his post as a springboard to the office of wali. A merchant, with no power base of his own and dependent on the wali for lucrative contracts, could act as an important ally in the diwan. Apparently, this tactic became particularly widespread by the end of the century as Basra's separatist forces gained strength.

Lastly, this affair, and that of Murad Chalabi, point to the early rise of anti-English feelings among certain sectors of the commercial community. While widespread English penetration of the Iraqi market did not take place until the following century, the first phases of this process were already visible in the eighteenth century.[55] In Basra, this began through English control of the important freight trade with India and their increasing loans to the government and merchants. Despite their general reluctance to sell on credit, the English came to actually view the government debt in a positive light. In a report on the rise of the debt problem, the agent added a suggestion for increase in trade with Basra. The increasing financial dependence on the English, he explained, would result in fewer government barriers to their trade.[56] Government fears of losing control of its finances, coupled with the flagrant involvement of some English representatives in the political affairs of the province, greatly contributed to anti-English feelings.[57]

THE JEWS AND THE MAMLUK ADMINISTRATION

While some minorities like the Shiʿi Persians were at times more vulnerable, the wealthier Jewish merchants had relatively good relations with the mamluk governors. Not until Dawud Pasha's tenure as wali of Baghdad and Basra (1817–31) were they singled out for heavy persecution.[58] Their persecution during that period resulted in a significant emigration of leading merchant families to India, thereby intensifying a process began half a century earlier.[59] Among the most important merchants to leave Baghdad for Bombay during Dawud Pasha's period was Sassoon ben Saliḥ bar David, founder of the celebrated Sassoon family. During most of the eighteenth century, however, Jewish ṣarrafs had particularly close connections with the mamluks in Baghdad.[60] It was not until the second half of the eighteenth century, however, that they began to play a significant role in the political life of Basra. The earliest date we have for a Jewish ṣarraf at the service of the mutasallim is 1763. That year, the English agent reported that the mutasallim's ṣarraf, Khawajah Yaʿqub Gabbai, was asked to testify on some financial matter.[61] It is likely that the Jewish nasi had become the ṣarraf some years earlier.

Gabbai's stature grew gradually and peaked during the thirteen-month Persian siege of 1775–76 for his energetic participation in the defense of the city. Gabbai and the Jews of Iraq in general were particularly wary of the Persians. Under the Safavids Jews and Zoroastrians were often singled out for persecution while Armenians and Gregorians generally enjoyed more benevolent treatment.[62] Gabbai extended several favorable loans to the government, organized the distribution of food and clothing, oversaw defense constructions, and used his contacts to acquire additional arms. News of his deeds reached the sultan who, after the Persian evacuation in 1779, bestowed upon him a special *firman* as a gesture of gratitude. In addition to the great prestige that it brought, the firman also exempted Gabbai from many taxes.[63] The Jews of Basra were so relieved when the Persians evacuated that their rabbi declared that day an annual holiday, Yom Ha-nes, which they continued to observe decades later by refraining from work, reciting special prayers, and exchanging gifts.[64]

It was during the period of Sulayman the Great (1780–1802), however, that the Jews enjoyed the most favorable treatment under the mamluks. Baghdad's Rabbi Jacob Elyashar referred to Sulayman Pasha as "a lover of Israel [and] an upright man."[65] The English resident seemed to concur. "In all Turkish governments," he wrote in 1791,

> the Jews have very considerable influence. Under the Bachas of Bagdat, they have in general had the management of their pecuniary affairs at Bussora. Soliman the present Bacha, has particularly favoured them.[66]

It is perhaps tempting to compare this empowerment of some of the Jews of Iraq during this period to the phenomenon of the so-called alien as a servant of power, observed by Lewis Coser. Referring to the court Jews of baroque Germany, Coser argued that "rulers in absolutist states" often "attract to their court men who have no roots in the society over which these rulers exercise dominion."[67] Since the ghetto Jews of seventeenth-century Germany were generally despised by the population, their resultant insecurity left them "at the mercy of the ruler."[68] Such a group proved to be ideal servants of power because of their inability to develop their own independent power base. While the Jews of Basra, by virtue of their dhimmi status, were not as vulnerable as their counterparts in central Europe, a degree of similarity can certainly be recognized.

By the late 1780s, travelers were reporting that real power in Basra rested with a certain Jewish merchant named Khawjah ᶜAbdullah ibn Yusuf.[69] In a manner similar to that of Ḥajji Yusuf, the wali provided him with the backing needed to become a member of the diwan, the only dhimmi to have had this honor in the eighteenth century.[70] Khawjah ᶜAbdullah was also noted for his staunch opposition to English interests in Basra. During his leadership of the Jewish community, relations between the Jews and the English representatives grew extremely hostile.

THE ARMENIANS AND THE ENGLISH

The strongest allies the English had in Basra were the Armenian merchants. In the seventeenth century, however, Armenian merchants were considered a major obstacle to European commercial penetration of the region. "They were," Gregorian writes, "fierce competitors and detractors of the English and Dutch merchants and companies."[71] As late as 1724, the English agent was still reporting that the Armenians at Basra "do us what prejudice they can everywhere."[72] Shortly after, however, competition had gradually given way to cooperation. With the fall of the Safavids and the loss of their strong protector, the Armenians of Basra sought to compromise with the English in return for protection.

The English seemed just as eager. "It is impossible," wrote the English agent, "to transact business of consequence here without the assistance of the country people."[73] In return for their assistance as consultants, brokers, linguists, and wakils, the English proved to be excellent protectors of Armenian interests. When Khawjah Petrus d'Gregore, "one of the most considerable Armenian merchants in all Bussorah," was imprisoned in 1754 on charges of having a Muslim slave, the English agent helped win his release.[74] This was the first recorded case of successful English intervention in a major internal dispute. By the end of the century nearly all Armenian merchants enjoyed this protection and were increasingly viewed as adjuncts to the English factory.

The lines of demarcation that defined the articulated society of Basra appeared to grow sharper by the end of the century. Communal divisions, separate economic interests, and conflicting political loyalties tended to intensify with the decline of Basra's trade. The city's proud tradition of tolerance, which even withstood repeated Persian invasions, was pushed to the breaking point by the decline of Basra's fortunes. Of all the rivalries that must have flared up at this time, most of the available information centers on the one between the Armenian and Jewish communities. No incident is more revealing of the nature of this conflict and its far-reaching consequences than the bizarre case of the murdered Jew with which this study began.

THE CASE OF THE MURDERED JEW REVISITED

The discovery of the body of the Jewish merchant, Sallum, on March 22, 1791, would soon drive an even wider wedge between the merchants of Basra.[75] As the Jews, led by their fiery leader Khawjah ᶜAbdullah ibn Yusuf, continued to press for the conviction and punishment of the Armenians, whom they accused of this murder, the Armenians increasingly placed their hopes on the protection of the English resident, Samuel Manesty. An extremely intelligent yet arrogant man, Manesty insisted on being at the center of all major events. Several years earlier he had married a local Armenian lady whose family owned several homes and date plantations.[76] He made the most of the immunities granted to British consuls and soon amassed a fortune through the India trade, he was said to have owned at least seven trading vessels. Manesty was also known to be an important horse breeder and dealer.[77]

Although Manesty was allowed to voice his concerns, he was unable to influence the mutasallim's opinion on this case and a number of Armenians were rounded up for interrogation. As Manesty protested the arrests, Khawjah ᶜAbdullah suddenly announced that they had found the murderer four days after the initial discovery of the body. It is unclear whether the accused, an Armenian laborer named Risha, had official British protection or not. Nevertheless, Manesty insisted that he had the right to attend the trial and participate in all the meetings of the diwan relevant to the case. Manesty's demands were reluctantly accepted, and for the first time in the history of the city the English resident was referred to as the "Head of the Christians" of Basra.[78] That evening the Jews held another demonstration where several speeches were made attacking Manesty and demanding the removal of the English factory. The most forceful speaker was none other than Khawjah ᶜAbdullah, who threatened to personally remove the British flag from Basra. Manesty, furious with what he considered to be a grave insult to British pride, responded by ordering that no Jew be allowed inside the factory. As mentioned earlier, even the wali of Baghdad came to express a special interest in the case by sending one of his top officers to help with the investigation.

In Manesty's view the issue was inseparably linked to the commercial rivalry between the Armenians and the Jews. He believed that the Jews wanted to bring "disgrace on the Christians and establish a commercial monopoly."[79] Accordingly, he refused to let the matter rest even after the qaḍi had found Risha innocent and set him free. In several letters to Baghdad and Istanbul, he demanded that the top ten Jewish leaders be imprisoned and later banished from Basra. He also demanded that a "very heavy fine" be placed on the entire Jewish community for their "insults" to the British.[80] In Baghdad, Sulayman the Great not only ignored these demands, but actually made a point of honoring some of the Jewish leaders who had taken part in the demonstrations. Khawjah ᶜAbdullah was promoted to "chief counsellor" of the wali in Baghdad, and became "one of the most prominent members of the informal power structure in the 1790's."[81] Others, like the ṣarraf Sasun ᶜAbdul-Nabi, were given gifts and publicly honored for their services.[82] Sulayman Pasha did, however, require the Jewish leaders to publicly apologize to the British resident. Manesty was so outraged that, on April 30, 1793, he struck the flag and withdrew the residency to Kuwait.[83]

In more than one way, this incident highlights the divisions that tore at Basra's merchant community at the end of the century. As Jewish-Armenian rivalry intensified, so did the tensions between the growing clout of England and Baghdad's attempts at greater central control. Yet, before the underlying factors in this case become clear, there is a need to take a last detour to examine the relevance of Basra's rising separatist inclinations.

THE REBELLIONS OF SHAYKH THUWAYNI AND MUṢṬAFA AGHA

Notwithstanding the unity of Baghdad and Basra in a single province for most of the eighteenth century, separatist feelings remained high in Basra. In addition to the burden that this unity brought to merchants involved in the Aleppo trade, Baghdad's control also meant that the mutasallim was required to send one-half of the customs revenues to the wali, thereby limiting the money available for government officials at Basra.[84] Separatist feelings were further strengthened with memories of flourishing trade and responsible government under the autonomous Afrasiyabs of the seventeenth century.[85] In addition, the English seemed to have had a hand in encouraging any movement toward separation. As early as 1764, the English agent wrote that it would be in the interests of the East India Company "if the two Governments of Bagdat and Bussora could be separated as formerly."[86] This, the agent argued, would improve Basra's commercial position by allowing the government to keep most of its revenues. It would also be much easier to influence the governor of Basra, whose city depended so much on English shipping, than the wali of distant Baghdad.

If in good economic times the burdens of Baghdad's rule were tolerable, then they ceased to be so during the postoccupation decline. Sensing this mood, Shaykh Thuwayni, one of the most celebrated shaykhs of the Muntafiq, seized control of Basra in a bloodless coup on May 6, 1787. With the backing of the shaykhs of the Khazaᶜil and ᶜUbayd as well as many of the aᶜyan and merchants, he petitioned the Porte for his appointment as wali of an autonomous province separate from Baghdad.[87] Shaykh Thuwayni's dreams of reestablishing his family's rule in Basra were shattered when, on October 25, Sulayman the Great routed the tribal army near Qurnah.[88] It is significant that Sulayman found it necessary to punish the merchants of Basra for supporting this uprising by doubling the customs duties for the next year.[89] Sulayman Pasha's decisive victory failed to alter the social and economic foundations of separatist feelings. Barely a year had gone by when Muṣṭafa Agha, Sulayman Pasha's hand-picked mutasallim of Basra, led another attempt at separation. The mutasallim told the English resident that, despite his thirty years of loyal service to Sulayman Pasha, he saw no other way out of Basra's decline than separation from Baghdad.[90] This attempt also failed when Muṣṭafa Agha fled before Sulayman's approaching forces.[91]

In both of these uprisings, the Jewish merchants proved to be among the strongest opponents of separation. Certainly, the primary cause for this must have been their heavy investment in the trade with Baghdad. Unlike the Armenians, they suffered no additional hardships because of Baghdad's diversion of the Aleppo caravan trade. It is more likely, in fact, that the unity with Baghdad was perceived as being beneficial to the Basra–Baghdad trade connection. It is, therefore, no surprise that Khawjah ᶜAbdullah repeatedly tried to dissuade Shaykh Thuwayni from petitioning the Porte for separation.[92] After defeating the two rebellions Sulayman Pasha apparently felt that the Jewish merchants represented a dependable ally against further separatist attempts. In discussing the political influence of the Jews in Basra, Manesty mentioned that the wali greatly increased their powers, particularly following the rebellions of Shaykh Thuwayni and Muṣṭafa Agha. "Coja Abdulla," he wrote, was even

> entrusted with the management of the whole of the receipts and expenditure of the Bussora government, totally independent of the Mussaleem. [The wali] has also vested in him a power of secretly controlling the power of that officer.[93]

While normally such comments by Manesty cannot be taken at face value, particularly because of his hatred for the Jews, his analysis here is in keeping with past practices of the mamluk walis. It is not unlikely that, in addition to their services as ṣarrafs and financial advisors, Sulayman Pasha also empowered some of the Jewish leaders in a manner similar to that observed earlier in the case of Ḥajji Yusuf and for similar reasons. Trade patterns might have also played a role in determining the anti-English feelings shown by the Jewish merchants. It is quite likely that English domination of the freight trade had the same impact on Jewish merchants that it had on the Chalabis. The rising Jewish interest in the India trade, with its dependence on Indo-Arab shipping, was, at this time, certainly threatened by English commercial activities. This, in addition to English support of the Armenians, the main competitors of the Jews, guaranteed a hostile relationship well into the next century.[94]

With this level of social, commercial, and political divisions among the merchants, it is not surprising that they never developed a unified response toward the decline of Basra's trade. Most merchants found it much easier to simply move their operations to other ports in the region, rather than continue to face an unpredictable future. In al-Ḥaydari's discussion of eleven of Basra's most notable families, he mentions that six left for Kuwait, Masqat, and Bombay.[95] Al-Anṣari also laments the departure of so many of Basra's leading merchants. Great merchants like al-Faddagh and ʿAbdul-Razzaq fled to the security of places like Kuwait.[96] Significantly, there is no mention of anyone leaving for Baghdad.

MANESTY'S VICTORY AND THE BEGINNINGS OF BRITISH DOMINANCE

The English remained in Kuwait for nearly two years. Manesty, as obstinate as ever, refused to set foot in Basra until his demands for the punishment of the Jews were met. Desperate to revive the port's trade, Sulayman Pasha finally gave in and on September 4, 1795, Manesty returned to Basra with full honors. The ten Jewish leaders were duly handed over to him "for personal chastisement and imprisonment."[97] Nothing is known of what happened to them after this. Had the great wali waited for only a few more months, he could have realized one of his most precious victories. In April 1795, the Court of Directors for the English East India Company decided to censure Manesty for his conduct, replace him with another resident, and cease pressing for the punishment of the Jews.[98] There was a strong feeling that Manesty had unnecessarily jeopardized their position in one of the most strategic areas of the Gulf at a time when tensions with France were rapidly spinning toward war once again. As it were, though, the board reversed its decision after hearing of Manesty's victory. This victory is indicative of the beginning of a new period in Basra's history. From now on, English political and economic influence developed by leaps and bounds, forever altering the nature of Basra's trade. In 1802, a permanent British resident was appointed in Baghdad. Soon after the appointment of Claudius James Rich to that post in 1808, the *balioz*, as the resident was known, clearly became one of the most powerful political figures in Iraq, perhaps second only to the wali.[99]

The discussion of the relationship between the merchants and political power leads to three broad conclusions. First, it is apparent that the political interests of Basra's merchants were as diverse as their economic interests. The two most important political questions of the time, Basra's unity with Baghdad and rising British influence, failed to create a consensus. The different attitudes that merchants had toward these issues usually reflected their separate, and often conflicting, commercial interests. Second, the decline of Basra's trade tended to intensify these conflicts. Rather than taking a common stand that might have alleviated their commercial difficulties, their divisions actually helped undermine political stability which, in turn, accentuated the decline of Basra's economic fortunes. Third, while the various immunities granted the English consuls provided them with certain advantages, it was the divisions within the merchant community that provided the best path for greater English involvement and eventual incorporation of Basra into the world economy. In other words, England's economic and political penetration of Basra took place through its gradual involvement in the existing internal conflicts, exemplified by the case of the murdered Jewish merchant.

CONCLUSION

The world in which the murder of the Jewish merchant Sallum took place was one undergoing profound transformations. All over the Indian Ocean the "Age of Partnership" between Asians and Europeans was giving way to the decisive domination of the latter. Two events made this coup possible. The first, felt throughout the eighteenth century by the great empires of Asia, was a series of intense crises that provided Europeans with the opportunity to expand their hitherto limited influence. For C. A. Bayly, the hallmarks of these crises in Asia were tendencies toward regional fragmentation followed by widespread tribal invasions.[1]

The second event was the industrial revolution, which armed European merchants and soldiers with the economic and technical weapons needed to take full advantage of the unfolding crisis in Asia. Previous to these transformations, Basra, like all other trading cities, was part of a much larger region tied together by networks of trade. The city had a strategic location at the heart of this region, which stretched from the eastern Mediterranean and Anatolia to India and Yemen. The annual Indian Ocean monsoons facilitated its shipping with India, while the Tigris and Euphrates provided easy access to the hinterland. During the first half of the eighteenth century Basra's trade, typical of premodern commerce, was characterized by an inherent instability, with the volume of trade fluctuating greatly from year to year. By the late 1760s, though, Basra's trade was booming, thanks mainly to an increase in English and Omani shipping.

The broad structural transformations that took place throughout Asia and the Indian Ocean at the end of the century affected the area around Basra in three specific ways. First, the collapse of central authority in Persia and the growing autonomy of Baghdad created a general atmosphere of political instability. Second, the culmination of tribal invasions from Arabia further contributed to insecurity in Basra's hinterland and throughout the Persian Gulf. Lastly, the growing English control of the freight trade with India placed an essential part of Basra's commerce in the hands of Europeans. The first two developments, in particular, were responsible for a profound decline of Basra's trade at the end of the century. The plague of 1773 and the Persian occupation of 1776–79, devastating as they were, merely represented the tip of the iceberg. More important causes appeared much earlier, with their effects lasting well into the next century.

The earliest change occurred in Aleppo. Since the middle of the century Aleppo's fortunes had been waning, and with it, Basra's important caravan trade. The Baghdad wali's policy of forcibly diverting the caravan route through Baghdad accentuated the problem since it increased the financial burdens on the merchants. Around the same time, tribal power, especially in southern Iraq, was reaching its zenith. After more than a century of large migrations from Najd, tribes such as the Khazaʿil, ʿUbayd, and Muntafiq were openly challenging Baghdad's authority and disrupting the caravan and riverine trade. Meanwhile in Persia, the death of Karim Khan Zand in 1779 meant the return of civil war to that country. While such disruptions were not uncommon in Persia, the result of this conflict permanently altered the nature of the country's economy. The eventual victory of the Qajars led to the development of the north at the expense of the south on which part of Basra's trade was dependent. Lastly, tribal migrations from Najd into the Gulf region were culminating in the establishment of new shaykhdoms. Ports such as Kuwait, Bahrayn, and Zubara (Qatar) and confederations like the Wahhabi-backed Qawasim were channeling some of the trade away from Basra. In the process of asserting their independence, these shaykhdoms increased their piratical raids on Basra's shipping, resulting in great loss to the merchants.

The lack of cohesion and solidarity among the merchants of Basra played an important role in determining the extent of the impact of this decline. The manner in which merchants organized their trading operations were, in many ways, directly related to the nature of the city's networks and the instability of the period. The most common method of organization was through family or communal connections, each concentrating on a familiar route. Thus, the Chalabi family traded primarily with Surat, Jewish merchants operated chiefly between Baghdad and Basra, and the Armenians concentrated on the Aleppo and India trade. Such separate specializations led to different political interests. The two most important political questions of the day, the administrative unity with Baghdad and the growing influence of the English, created differences of opinion, usually reflecting conflicting commercial interests. Thus, while some merchants supported separation from Baghdad in order to reduce the flight of tax revenue, others resisted it in the hopes of better riverine trade conditions. Also, while some merchants, such as the Armenians, assisted British penetration in the hopes of receiving better protection, others, like the Jews, resisted the rising powers of the English resident, which threatened to limit their influence.

These differences tended to get more intense with the worsening commercial situation and, in turn, helped create an atmosphere of political instability at a time when the city could ill-afford repeated changes in the government. The reaction that followed the murder of the merchant Sallum is testimony to the intensity of these contradictions. The merchants' strong regional links provided an easy way out of the deteriorating situation in Basra. Rather than remain and ride out the storm, most of Basra's leading merchant families chose to relocate to other ports in the Gulf. By the beginning of the next century, Basrawi merchants were found in Bombay, Masqat, and the newly established Kuwait. The ease with which merchants left Basra also played a role in the decline of the city's trade fortunes.

By the end of the eighteenth century, Basra's trade was but a shadow of its earlier self. It was precisely at this time that the steady incursion of British commercial interests was slowly placing the city under its dominance. Thanks initially to their control of the Indian freight trade and their alliance with the Armenian merchants, English residents were soon regarded as among the most influential people in Basra. Basra's need for British naval protection added greatly to this influence and placed large financial demands on the government. This increase in British influence did not go unchallenged. Sulayman the Great's conflict with Samuel Manesty occurred as a result of the culmination of earlier struggles by some merchants against the British presence. With Manesty's victory over one of the strongest walis of Baghdad, the path was cleared for a qualitative change in the relationship between Iraq and Britain. During the nineteenth century, the British achieved clear dominance over Iraq's foreign trade and a good part of its economy. The process of Iraq's incorporation in the world economy received an additional boost after the enactment of the tanzimat reforms and their vigorous implementation during Midḥat Pasha's governorship (1869–72). In many ways, according to Wallerstein et al., the tanzimat, followed by the Young Turk regime, helped create the conditions which "facilitated the operations of the world-economy."[2]

With the coming of the twentieth century, the British soon found themselves in a position to become masters over Iraq's government as well.

The case of the merchant Sallum, and the political and economic conditions with which it was tied, help reorient our understanding of the roots of European involvement in the Middle East away from the surprisingly still dominant "Eastern Question" paradigm.[3] It shows that the forces affecting the economic and political involvement of European powers in the Middle East were not merely the result of inter-European power rivalries in which Middle Easterners played a passive role. Rather, it highlights the importance of the local struggles and regional transformations that drew in, often reluctantly, greater European involvement. In a word, this case helps to further validate C. A. Bayly's claim that "the origins of the modern World System must be sought in Asia and Africa as much as in Europe."[4]

NOTES

INTRODUCTION

1. The particulars of this case are recorded in *IOR*, Letters from Basra, G/29/22, letters dated April 2, 1791, folios 635–636, April 8, 1791, folios 636–637, and July 5, 1791, folios 663–666.

2. Basra, at the time, was under the jurisdiction of the Ottoman province (wilayah or pashalik) of Baghdad. The provincial governor (wali) based in Baghdad appointed a lieutenant-governor, known as the mutasallim, for the city of Basra.

3. M. N. Pearson, "Introduction" in Blair Kling and M. N. Pearson, eds., *The Age of Partnership: Europeans in Asia Before Dominion* (Honolulu: University Press of Hawaii, 1979), pp. 6 and 11.

4. M. N. Pearson, "Introduction I: The Subject" in Ashin Das Gupta and M. N. Pearson, eds., *India and the Indian Ocean, 1500–1800* (Oxford: Oxford University Press, 1987), pp. 1–24; K. N. Chaudhuri, *Trade and Civilization in the Indian Ocean: An Economic History from the Rise of Islam to 1750* (Cambridge: Cambridge University Press, 1985); S. Arasaratnam, "Recent Trends in the Historiography of the Indian Ocean, 1500 to 1800" in *Journal of World History*, vol. 1, no. 2, 1990, pp. 225–48; Patricia Risso, *Merchants and Faith: Muslim Commerce and Culture in the Indian Ocean* (Boulder: Westview Press, 1995).

5. Andrea Wink, "Review Article: World Trade, Merchant Empires, and the Economy of the Indian Ocean" in *International History Review*, vol. 15, no. 1, February 1993, pp. 112–15.

6. C. A. Bayly, "India and West Asia, c.1700–1830" in *Asian Affairs*, vol. 19, February 1988, p. 4.

7. S. Arasaratnam, "Recent Trends," p. 235.

8. Ibid., p. 236.

9. Ashin Das Gupta, *Indian Merchants and the Decline of Surat, 1700–1740* (Wiesbaden, 1979).

10. Neils Steensgaard, *The Asian Trade Revolution of the Seventeenth Century* (Chicago: University of Chicago Press, 1974).

11. Two volumes edited by James Tracy place this question at the heart of their subject. See James Tracy, ed., *The Rise of Merchant Empires: Long-Distance Trade in the Early Modern World, 1350–1750* (Cambridge: Cam-

bridge University Press, 1990), and *The Political Economy of Merchant Empires* (Cambridge: Cambridge University Press, 1991).

12. The general presentation of Wallerstein's theory can be found in Immanuel Wallerstein, *The Modern World-System: Capitalist Agriculture and the Origins of the European World-Economy in the Sixteenth Century* (New York: Academic Press, 1974), and *The Capitalist World-System: Essays by Immanuel Wallerstein* (Cambridge: Cambridge University Press, 1980). The specific application of the world-systems perspective to India can be found in Immanuel Wallerstein, "The Incorporation of the Indian Subcontinent into the Capitalist World-Economy" in Satish Chandra, ed., *The Indian Ocean: Explorations in History, Commerce and Politics* (New Delhi: Sage Publishers, 1987), pp. 224–53. Its application to the Ottoman Empire can be found in Immanuel Wallerstein, Hale Decdeli, and Rasat Kasaba, "The Incorporation of the Ottoman Empire into the World-Economy" in Huri Islamoglu-Inan, ed., *The Ottoman Empire and the World Economy* (Cambridge: Cambridge University Press, 1988), pp. 88–97.

13. M. N. Pearson, *Before Colonialism: Theories on Asian-European Relations 1500–1750* (Delhi: Oxford University Press, 1988), p. 50.

14. Eric Wolf, *Europe and the People Without History* (Berkeley: University of California Press, 1982), pp. 85–86.

15. M. N. Pearson, "Introduction," p. 5.

16. Huri Islamoglu-Inan, "Introduction: 'Oriental Despotism' in World-System Perspective" in Huri Islamoglu-Inan, ed., *The Ottoman Empire and the World Economy*, p. 12.

17. Ibid.

18. Ibid.

19. Certainly his most influential work on this subject is Andre Raymond, *Artisans et commerçants au Caire au XVIIIe siecle*, 2 vols. (Damascus: Institut francais de Damas, 1973–74).

20. Dina Khoury, *State and Provincial Society in the Ottoman Empire: Mosul, 1540–1834* (Cambridge: Cambridge University Press, 1997); Elena Frangakis-Syrett, *The Commerce of Smyrna in the Eighteenth Century, 1700–1820* (Athens: Center for Asia Minor Studies, 1992); Bruce Masters, *The Origins of Western Economic Dominance in the Middle East: Mercantilism and the Islamic Economy in Aleppo, 1600–1750* (New York: New York University Press, 1988); Abraham Marcus, *The Middle East on the Eve of Modernity: Aleppo in the Eighteenth Century* (New York: Columbia University Press, 1989).

21. See, for example, ^{c}Ali Shakir ^{c}Ali, *Tarikh al-^{c}Iraq fi al-^{c}Ahd al-^{c}Uthmani, 1638–1750: Dirasah fi Aḥwalihi al-Siyasiyyah* (Naynawa, 1985); Tom Nieuwenhuis, *Politics and Society in Early Modern Iraq: Mamluk Pashas, Tribal Shaykhs and Local Rule Between 1802 and 1831* (The Hague: Martinus Nijhoff Publishers, 1982); ^{c}Abbas al-^{c}Azawi, *Tarikh al-^{c}Iraq Bayn*

Iḥtilalayn, vol. VI (Baghdad, 1954); ʿAla' Musa Kazim Nawras, *Ḥukm al-Mamalik fi al-ʿIraq, 1750–1831* (Baghdad, 1975).

22. Two still highly influential works which utilize this argument are: Halil Inalcik, *The Ottoman Empire: The Classical Age, 1300–1600* (New York, 1973); and Stanford Shaw, *History of the Ottoman Empire and Modern Turkey*, vol. I: *Empire of the Gazis: The Rise and Decline of the Ottoman Empire, 1280–1808* (Cambridge: Cambridge University Press, 1976).

23. Halil Inalcik and Donald Quataert, eds., *An Economic and Social History of the Ottoman Empire, 1300–1914* (New York: Cambridge University Press, 1994). The problem is particularly evident in the volume's treatment of the eighteenth century ("The Age of the Ayans, 1699–1812") by Bruce McGowan.

24. Daniel Panzac, "International and Domestic Maritime Trade in the Ottoman Empire During the 18th Century" in *International Journal of Middle East Studies*, March 1992, pp. 189–206.

25. Serap Yılmaz, "Osmanlı Imparatorlugu'nun Dogu Ile Ekonomik Iliskileri: XVIII. Yuzyilin Ikinci Yarisinda Osmanlı-Hint Ticareti Ile Ilgili Bir Arastirma Fransiz Arsivlerinden" in *Belleten*, vol. 61, April 1992, pp. 33–68.

26. Dina Khoury, "Merchants and Trade in Early Modern Iraq" in *New Perspectives on Turkey*, Fall 1991, pp. 53–86.

27. Fredric Lane, *Profit From Power: Readings in Protection Rent and Violence Controlling Enterprises* (Albany: State University of New York Press, 1979); and Niels Steensgaard, *Carracks, Caravans and Companies: The Structural Crisis in European Asian Trade in the Early Seventeenth Century* (Denmark: Andelsbogtrykkereit I Odense, 1973).

28. Dina Khoury, "Merchants and Trade," p. 82.

29. Hala Fattah, *The Politics of Regional Trade in Iraq, Arabia and the Gulf, 1745–1900* (Albany: State University of New York Press, 1997).

30. Ibid., p. 1.

31. Ibid.

32. Ibid., p. 208.

CHAPTER 1. AL-BAṢRAH AL-FAYḤA'

1. *Al-Fayḥa'* was the word used by the Arabs to describe Basra and it is still in use today. Roughly, it translates as "Spacious, Fruitful, and Exhilirating."

2. Yaʿqub Sarkis, *Mabaḥith ʿIraqiyyah*, vol. III (Baghdad, 1981), pp. 111–22.

3. "Mesene" in *The New Encyclopaedia Britannica*, vol. 8 (Chicago: Encyclopaedia Britannica Inc., 1990), p. 46; Ahmad Kamal Zaki, *al-Ḥayat al-Adabiyyah fi al-Baṣrah ila Nihayat al-Qirn al-Thani al-Hijri* (Damascus: al-Fikr Publishers, 1961), p. 21.

4. Richard D. Sullivan, *Near Eastern Royalty and Rome, 100–30 B.C.* (Toronto: University of Toronto Press, 1990), pp. 109–10.

5. Fred Donner, "Basra" in *Encyclopaedia Iranica*, vol. 2 (London: Routledge & Kegan Paul, 1989), p. 851.

6. For a brief history of Basra in the Islamic period, see Fred Donner, *The Early Islamic Conquests* (Princeton: Princeton University Press, 1981), pp. 239–45; ᶜAbdul-Ḥusayn al-Mubarak and ᶜAbdul-Jabbar Naji al-Yasiri, *Min Mashahir Aᶜlam al-Baṣrah* (Basra: Publication of the Center for Arabian Gulf Studies in Basra University, 1983); Stephen Hemsley Longrigg, "al-Basra" in *The Encyclopaedia of Islam*, vol. II (London: Luzac & Co., 1960), pp. 1085–87; Aḥmad Kamal Zaki, *al-Ḥayat al-Adabiyyah*; Ibn al-Ghimlas, *Wilat al-Baṣrah wa Mutasallimuha* (Baghdad: al-Baṣri Publishers, 1962), pp. 1–63; ᶜAbdul-Qadir Bash Aᶜyan al-ᶜAbbasi, *al-Baṣrah fi Adwariha al-Tarikhiyyah* (Baghdad: al-Baṣri Publishers, 1961), pp. 1–55.

7. Ḥamid al-Bazi, "Min Turathiyyat Ma Shamalathu Makramat al-Sayyid al-Ra'is al-Qa'id fi Ḥamlat 'Iᶜmar al-Baṣrah" in *al-Turath al-Shaᶜbi*, no. 3, Summer 1989, p. 163.

8. Although dated, George W. Stripling's *The Ottoman Turks and the Arabs, 1511–1574* (Urbana: University of Illinois Press, 1942), pp. 78–85, still contains some useful information on the political history of the early Ottoman period in Iraq. For Ottoman policy in the Persian Gulf, see Ahmet Tabakoglu, "The Economic Importance of the Gulf in the Ottoman Era" in *Studies on Turkish-Arab Relations*, vol. 3, 1988, p. 159.

9. ᶜAli Shakir ᶜAli, *Tarikh al-ᶜIraq*, pp. 123–27; ᶜImad Ra'uf, "al-Madinah al-ᶜIraqiyyah" in *Ḥadarat al-ᶜIraq*, vol. 10 (Baghdad: Dar al-Ḥurriyyah, 1985), pp. 163–65.

10. For information on the Afrasiyabs, see Fathallah ibn ᶜAlwan, *Zad al-Musafir*, British Museum MS. Add. 23,450; Stephen Hemsley Longrigg, *Four Centuries of Modern Iraq* (Oxford: Clarendon Press, 1925), pp. 99–123; J. G. Lorimer, *Gazetteer of the Persian Gulf, ᶜOman and Central Arabia*, vol. I, part 1B (Calcutta, 1915); ᶜAli Shakir ᶜAli, *Tarikh al-ᶜIraq*, pp. 123–53; P. M. Holt, *Egypt and the Fertile Crescent, 1516–1922: A Political History* (Ithaca: Cornell University Press, 1966), pp. 134–43; and Muḥammad al-Khal, *Tarikh al-Imarah al-Afrasiybiyyah* (Baghdad: Maṭbaᶜat al-Majmaᶜ al-ᶜIlmi al-ᶜIraqi, 1961).

11. ᶜAli Shakir ᶜAli, *Tarikh al-ᶜIraq*, p. 128. For the practice of selling posts throughout the Ottoman Empire during this period, see P. M. Holt, *Egypt and the Fertile Crescent*, p. 64.

12. Ahmet Tabakoglu, "The Economic Importance of the Gulf," p. 162.

13. According to ᶜAli, Basra became a dependency of Baghdad in 1706. Longrigg, on the other hand, cites 1709 as the year of Basra's incorporation. See ᶜAli Shakir ᶜAli, *Tarikh al-ᶜIraq*, pp. 109 and 149; and Stephen Hemsley Longrigg, *Four Centuries*, p. 126.

14. For the history of the mamluk period, see Stephen Hemsley Longrigg, *Four Centuries*, pp. 123–276; Tom Nieuwenhuis, *Politics and Society*; ᶜAbbas al-ᶜAzzawi, *Tarikh al-ᶜIraq Bayn Iḥtilalayn*; Yusuf ᶜIzz al-Din, *Dawud Basha wa Nihayat al-Mamalik fi al-ᶜIraq* (Baghdad: al-Shaᶜb Printers, 1976); ᶜAla' Musa Kazim Nawras, *Ḥukm al-Mamalik*; ᶜImad Ra'uf, "al-Qiwa wa al-Mu'assasat al-ᶜAskariyyah" in *Ḥadarat al-ᶜIraq*, vol. 10 (Baghdad: Dar al-Ḥurriyyah, 1985), pp. 44–47.

15. For a good discussion of the nature of the mamluks and the mamluk sultanate in Egypt, see P. M. Holt, *The Age of the Crusades* (New York: Longman, 1987).

16. Saliḥ Muḥammad al-ᶜAbid, "al-Niḍam al-'Idari" in *Ḥaḍarat al-ᶜIraq*, vol. 10 (Baghdad: Dar al-Ḥurriyyah, 1985), p. 21.

17. Stephen Hemsley Longrigg, *Four Centuries*, p. 126.

18. These figures were taken from J. B. Kelly, *Britain and the Persian Gulf, 1795–1880* (London: Oxford University Press, 1968), p. 34. The exact length of the river cannot be determined with precision since it is known to have varied over the years. A contemporary estimate of the location of Basra can be found in Samuel Manesty and Harvard Jones, *Report on the British Trade With Persia and Arabia*, India Office Records G/29/25, 1791, folio 227. In this report, the authors state that the length of Shaṭṭ al-ᶜArab is 160 miles. This is certainly an exaggeration.

19. Samuel Manesty and Harvard Jones, *Report on the British Trade*, folio 227.

20. The Iraqis refer to these pools as *ma' al-mawḥ*. They often stretch for miles at a depth of several inches to over a yard. See ᶜImad Ra'uf's commentary in ᶜAbdul-Raḥman ibn ᶜAbdullah al-Suwaydi, *Tarikh Ḥawadith Baghdad wa al-Baṣrah min 1186 ila 1192 H.* (Iraq: Wizarat al-Thaqafah wa al-Funun, 1978), p. 50.

21. Sir Hermann Gollancz, *Chronicle of Events Between the Years 1623 and 1733 Relating to the Settlement of the Order of Carmelites in Mesopotamia* (London: Oxford University Press, 1927), p. 624.

22. Ibid.

23. Mirza Abu Taleb Khan, *The Travels of Mirza Abu Taleb Khan in Asia, Africa, and Europe During the Years 1799, 1800, 1801, 1802 and 1803*, vol. II, translated by Charles Stewart (London, 1810), p. 365.

24. The Muntafiq Arabs used this tactic during their conflict with the mutasallim in 1769. See *MSA*, Bussora Factory Diaries, no. 200, folio 72.

25. *MSA*, Gombroon Factory Diaries, no. 7/118, entry dated April 28, 1757.

26. Khwaja Abdul Qadir, *Waqai-i Manazil-i Rum: Diary of a Journal to Constantinople*, edited by Mohibbul Hasan (New York: Asian Publishing House, 1968), p. 35.

27. K. N. Chaudhuri, *Trade and Civilization*, p. 161.

28. *MSA*, Bussora Factory Diaries, no. 199, folios 189, 212.

29. *MSA*, Gombroon Factory Diaries, no. 117, entries dated January 2, 1754 and July 17, 1754.

30. For an account of the difficulties encountered by the Persian army in 1743, see *MSA*, Gombroon Factory Inward Letter Book, no. 40, entry dated December 7, 1743; and on those encountered by Karim Khan's army in 1775, see *MSA*, Bussora Factory Diaries, no. 203, folio 46.

31. For the sociological impact of Ottoman-Persian rivalry for Iraq, see ᶜAli al-Wardi, *Lamaḥat Ijtimaᶜiyyah min Tarikh al-ᶜIraq al-Ḥadith*, vol. 1 (Baghdad: al-Irshad Publishers, 1969). For an overall view of the Ottoman-Persian wars in Iraq, see Stephen Hemsley Longrigg, *Four Centuries*, pp. 123–63 and 187–95.

32. For a discussion of early Wahhabi raids on Basra, see Stephen Hemsley Longrigg, *Four Centuries*, pp. 229–30. The Persian traveler Mirza Khan also speaks of the Wahhabis and the attacks of "Wandering Arabs" in Mirza Abu Talib Khan, *The Travels*, pp. 359, 365.

33. The following account of the weather conditions around Basra is taken mainly from the British Naval Intelligence Division Handbook entitled *Iraq and the Persian Gulf*, September 1944, pp. 166–81.

34. Ibid., p. 172.

35. A discussion of the nature of sandstorms in the Iraqi desert can be found in ibid., pp. 177–80.

36. Ibid., p. 177.

37. On the role that the monsoons played in the history of the Indian Ocean, see K. N. Chaudhuri, *Trade and Civilization*, p. 127.

38. For wind patterns over Iraq and the Persian Gulf, see Naval Intelligence Division, *Iraq*, pp. 169–70.

39. ᶜAbd al-Laṭif al-Dilayshi, "Kalimah fi al-Adab al-Shaᶜbi fi al-Baṣrah" in *al-Turath al-Shaᶜbi*, no. 3, Summer 1989, p. 195.

40. William Beawes, "Remarks and Occurrences in a Journey from Aleppo to Bussora by the Way of the Desert" in Douglas Carruthers, ed., *The Desert Route to India, Being the Journals of Four Travellers by the Great Desert Caravan Route Between Aleppo and Bussora, 1745–1751* (London, 1929), p. 34; and M. Otter, *Voyage en Turquie et en Perse, Avec une Relation des Expeditions de Tahmas Kouli-Khan* (Paris, 1748), p. 76.

41. *MSA*, Bussora Factory Diaries, no. 199, folio 152.

42. J. G. Lorimer, *Gazetteer of the Persian Gulf*, p. 278.

43. Fatḥallah Ibn ᶜAlwan, *Zad al-Musafir*, folios 43–44. For the material used to build the wall, see M. Otter, *Voyage en Turquie*, p. 57; and Edward Ives, *A Voyage from England to India in the Year MDCCLIV* (London, 1773), p. 231.

44. For the towers, see Khwaja Abdul Qadir, *Waqai-i Manazil-i Rum*, p. 51. For the gates, see Carsten Niebuhr, *Voyage en Arabie & en Autre Pays Circonvoisins*, vol. II (Amsterdam, 1780), p. 172.

45. William Heude, *A Voyage Up the Persian Gulf and a Journey Overland from India to England in 1817* (London: Longman, 1819), p. 49; and George Kepple, *Personal Narrative of a Journey from India to England, By Bassorah, Bagdad, the Ruins of Babylon, Curdistan, the Court of Persia, the Western Shore of the Caspian Sea, Astrakhan, Nishney, Novogorod, Moscow, and St. Petersburgh, in the Year 1824*, vol. 1 (London, 1827), p. 69.

46. Today Nahr al-Khandaq and Nahr al-Khawrah, on the northern and southern sides of the city respectively, are the remnants of the old dike. Compare the map of Basra city in Government of Iraq, *Maps of Iraq with Notes for Visitors* (Baghdad, 1929), map no. 7, with Niebuhr's map (Map 1.6).

47. Ḥamid al-Bazi, "Min Turathiyyat," p. 175.

48. Sir Hermann Gollancz, *Chronicle of Events*, p. 621.

49. Khwaja Abdul Qadir, *Waqai-i Manazil-i Rum*, p. 51.

50. See, for example, *BA*, MM, no. 10231, folio 269.

51. William Heude, *A Voyage Up the Persian Gulf*, p. 49.

52. Ibid.; and Aḥmad Nur al-Anṣari, *al-Naṣrah fi Akhbar al-Baṣrah* (Baghdad: al-Shaᶜb Printers, 1976), p. 25.

53. See in this regard Andre Raymond, *al-Mudun al-ᶜArabiyyah al-Kubra fi al-ᶜAṣr al-ᶜUthmani* (Les Grand Villes Arabes a l'Epoque Ottoman), translated by Latif Faraj (Cairo: Dar al-Fikr, 1991), p. 36.

54. *BA*, MM, no. 5461.

55. Carsten Niebuhr, *Voyage en Arabie*, p. 173.

56. Ibid.; and *BA*, MM, no. 5461, folio 33.

57. Dina Khoury, "Merchants and Trade," p. 55.

58. Edward Ives, *A Voyage from England*, p. 231; and George Keppel, *Personal Narrative*, p. 70.

59. Aḥmad Kamal Zaki, *al-Ḥayat al-Adabiyyah*, p. 38.

60. The report was written by the then governor of Basra, Maᶜshuq Pasha, and dealt with the question of reviving Basra's trade. See Mahdi al-Bustani, "Watha'iq ᶜUthmaniyyah Ghayr Manshurah ᶜan al-Baṣrah wa 'Usṭuliha wa Ṣilatiha b-il-Khalij al-ᶜArabi 'Awasiṭ al-Qirn al-Tasiᶜ ᶜAshar" in *al-Wathiqah*, no. 17, July 1990, p. 109.

61. Ḥamid al-Bazi, "Min Turathiyyat," p. 171.

62. John Carmichael, "Narrative of a Journey from Aleppo to Basra in 1751" in Douglas Carruthers, ed., *The Desert Route to India*, p. 178.

63. Bartholomew Plaisted, "Narrative of a Journey from Basra to Aleppo in 1750" in Douglas Carruthers, ed., *The Desert Route to India*, p. 59.

64. Mirza Abu Taleb Khan, *The Travels*, p. 304.

65. Aḥmad Nur al-Anṣari, *al-Naṣrah fi Akhbar al-Baṣrah*, p. 25.

66. Khwaja Abdul Qadir, *Waqai-i Manazil-i Rum*, pp. 54–55.

67. George Keppel, *Personal Narrative*, p. 52.

68. Khwaja Abdul Qadir, *Waqai-i Manazil-i Rum*, p. 55; Carsten

Niebuhr, *Voyage en Arabie*, p. 172; and Alexander Hamilton, *A New Account of the East Indies* (London: Argonaut Press, 1930), p. 56.

69. ᶜAli Shakir ᶜAli, *Tarikh al-ᶜIraq*, p. 129.

70. Khwaja Abdul Qadir, *Waqai-i Manazil-i Rum*, p. 52.

71. Ibid.

72. Tariq al-Janabi, "al-ᶜImarah al-ᶜIraqiyyah" in *Ḥaḍarat al-ᶜIraq*, vol. 10 (Baghdad: Dar al-Ḥurriyyah lil-Ṭibaᶜah, 1985), p. 270.

73. Gavin Young, *Iraq: Land of Two Rivers* (London: Collins, 1980), p. 163.

74. Edward Ives, *A Voyage from England*, p. 232.

75. Khwaja Abdul Qadir, *Waqai-i Manazil-i Rum*, pp. 52 and 54.

76. Pelly, *Report on the Tribes &c., Around the Shores of the Persian Gulf* (Calcutta, 1874), p. 34.

77. Frangakis-Syrett's observation concerning the impact of the plague on the population fluctuations of Izmir (Smyrna), or Andre Raymond's concerning Cairo, in the eighteenth century is equally valid for Basra. See Elena Frangakis-Syrett, *The Commerce of Smyrna*, p. 46; and Andre Raymond, *al-Mudun al-ᶜArabiyyah*, p. 47.

78. These outbreaks occurred in 1690, 1691, 1704, 1727, 1741, and 1773. For information on each in turn see *BA*, DBŞM, BSH, Sıra nos. 2 and 25; Sir Hermann Gollancz, *Chronicle of Events*, pp. 409, 410, 495, 624–26; and ᶜAbdul-Raḥman al-Suwaydi, *Tarikh Ḥawadith*, pp. 41–47.

79. Samuel Manesty and Harvard Jones, *Report on the British Trade*, folio 236.

80. *BA*, MM, no. 5461, folios 1–93.

81. Edward Ives, *A Voyage from England*, p. 231.

82. Carsten Niebuhr, *Voyage en Arabie*, p. 179.

83. ᶜAbdul-Qadir Bash Aᶜyan al-ᶜAbbasi, *al-Baṣrah fi Adwariha*, p. 57.

84. Serap Yılmaz, "Osmanlı Imparatorlugu'nun Dogu," p. 33.

85. Dina Khoury, "Merchants and Trade," p. 55.

86. Quoted in ᶜAli Shakir ᶜAli, *Tarikh al-ᶜIraq*, p. 91.

87. Ibid.

88. J. B. Kelly, *Britain and the Persian Gulf*, p. 35.

89. Andre Raymond, *Al-Mudun al-ᶜArabiyyah*, p. 46.

90. The following description of the nature of Basra's population is based on the accounts of William Heude, *A Voyage Up the Persian Gulf*, p. 48; Khwaja Abdul Qadir, *Waqai-i Manazil-i Rum*, pp. 52–54; Carsten Niebuhr, *Voyage en Arabie*, p. 180; George Keppel, *Personal Narrative*, p. 71; Mirza Abu Taleb Khan, *The Travels*, pp. 362–64; Ibrahim Faṣiḥ al-Ḥaydari, *Aḥwal al-Baṣrah* (Baghdad: al-Basra Publishers, 1961), pp. 6–7; Sir Hermann Gollancz, *Chronicle of Events*, *passim*; Joseph Emin, *The Life and Adventures of Joseph Emin, 1726–1809* (Calcutta, 1918); Mir ᶜAbdul-Laṭif al-Shustari, *Tuḥfat al-ᶜAlam*, manuscript at the National Museum of India.

91. William Heude, *A Voyage Up the Persian Gulf*, p. 49.

92. Mirza Abu Taleb Khan, *The Travels*, p. 364.

93. George Keppel, *Personal Narrative*, p. 71.

94. A derogatory term meaning "rejectionists" used by Sunnis in reference to the Shiᶜis. See Ibrahim Faṣiḥ al-Ḥaydari, *ᶜUnwan al-Majd fi Bayan Aḥwal Baghdad wa al-Baṣrah wa Nadj* (Baghdad: al-Baṣri Publishers, 1962), p. 6.

95. Carsten Niebuhr, *Voyage en Arabie*, p. 180.

96. The distinctive way in which members of the Tamim tribe were known to pronounce the " ج " with the "y" sound is still evident in the Basrawi dialect. See Aḥmad Kamal Zaki, *al-Ḥayat al-Adabiyyah*, p. 23.

97. Aḥmad Nur al-Anṣari, *al-Naṣrah fi Akhbar al-Baṣrah*, p. 58.

98. The incident took place in 1820. See J. G. Lorimer, *Gazetteer of the Persian Gulf*, pp. 1312–13.

99. Ibid.

100. Alexander Hamilton, *A New Account*, p. 57.

101. *MSA*, Bussora Factory Dairies, no. 202, folio 167.

102. Joseph Emin, *The Life and Adventures*, pp. 417–18.

103. For references to the Armenians of Basra and their professions, see ibid., p. 426; and Sir Hermann Gollancz, *Chronicle of Events*, p. 350 and *passim*.

104. Sir Hermann Gollancz, *Chronicle of Events*, pp. 391, 507–8.

105. Alexander Hamilton, *A New Account*, p. 55; and Mir ᶜAbdul-Laṭif al-Shustari, *Tuḥfat al-ᶜAlam*, pp. 210–12.

106. Subramanian states that the term banyan refers to "a community of Hindu and Jaina merchants engaged in trade and banking, brokerage and money-lending." See Lakshmi Subramanian, "Capital and Crowd in a Declining Asian Port City: The Anglo-Bania Order and the Surat Riots of 1795" in *Modern Asian Studies*, vol. 19, no. 2, 1985, p. 206.

107. M. Otter, *Voyage en Turquie*, p. 77.

108. Calvin H. Allen, "The Indian Merchant Community of Masqat" in *Bulletin of the School of Oriental and African Studies*, vol. 44, part 1, 1981, p. 41.

109. Sir Hermann Gollancz, *Chronicle of Events*, pp. 357–69 and *passim*; Carsten Niebuhr, *Voyage en Arabie*, p. 180.

110. Very little has been written on the Mandaeans, or Sabeans, of Iraq. Despite its dated research, Lady Ethel Drower's *The Mandaeans of Iraq and Iran: Their Cults, Customs, Magic, Legends, and Folklore* (London, 1962) remains a good introduction to the history and beliefs of this community. The recent book by ᶜAziz Sbahi, *'Uṣul al-Sabi'ah (al-Manda'iyyin) wa Muᶜtaqadatihim al-Diniyyah* (Damascus: Dar al-Mada, 1996), is also an excellent source.

111. Dina Khoury, "Merchants and Trade," p. 77.

112. Sir Herman Gollancz, *Chronicle of Events*, pp. 337–40.

113. For a brief yet concise discussion of the history of the English East India Company's presence in Basra, see Penelope Tuson, "British Representation in Turkish Arabia and Iraq, 1635–1932" in *The Records of the British Residency and Agencies in the Persian Gulf* (London: India Office Records, 1979), pp. 175–79.

114. Ibid., p. 175.

115. P. J. Marshall, *Problems of Empire: Britain and India, 1757–1813* (London: George Allen & Unwin Ltd., 1968), p. 18.

116. Willem Floor, "The Bahrain Project of 1754" in *Persica*, vol. 11, 1984, p. 129.

117. Willem Floor, "Dutch Trade With Masqat in the Second Half of the Eighteenth Century" in *Asian and African Studies*, vol. 16, 1982, p. 213.

118. J. B. Kelly, *Britain and the Persian Gulf*, p. 54.

119. Abdul Aziz M. Awad, "The Gulf in the Seventeenth Century" in *British Society for Middle Eastern Studies Bulletin*, vol. 12, no. 2, 1985, p. 129.

120. Salih Ozbaran, "Some Notes on the Salyane System in the Ottoman Empire as Organized in Arabia in the Sixteenth Century" in *The Journal of Ottoman Studies*, vol. 6, 1986, p. 39.

121. For a description of the iltizam system as it operated in the eighteenth century, see Amon Cohen, *Palestine in the Eighteenth Century: Patterns of Government and Administration* (Jerusalem: The Magnes Press, 1973), pp. 179–203.

122. ᶜAli Shakir ᶜAli, *Tarikh al-ᶜIraq*, p. 88.

123. Also known as the *katukhda* or the *kakhya*. Originally a Persian word meaning the head of the village, quarter, or guild. In Baghdad the kahyah acted as the chief assistant to the wali in all administrative, military, and financial matters. He was sometimes referred to as the "second wali." See Yusuf ᶜIzz al-Din, *Dawud Basha*, pp. 18–19.

124. Ibn al-Ghimlas, *Wilat al-Baṣrah*, pp. 66–69.

125. *IOR*, OC, E/3/65, Bussora letter dated December 22, 1702.

126. Sir Hermann Gollancz, *Chronicle of Events*, p. 446.

127. See, for example, the list of tax-farms (muqaṭaᶜat) for Basra for the year 1710 in *BA*, DBŞM, no. 16791, folios 10–12.

128. *BA*, DBŞM, BSH-2, Sıra 12.

129. Ibid.

130. Carsten Niebuhr, *Voyage en Arabie*, p. 175.

131. Ibid.; and Khwaja Abdul Qadir, *Waqai-i Manazil-i Rum*, p. 53.

132. Khwaja Abdul Qadir, *Waqai-i Manazil-i Rum*, p. 53.

133. Sir Hermann Gollancz, *Chronicle of Events*, pp. 343–44.

134. *IOR*, Letters from Basra, G/29/18, letter dated June 2, 1726.

135. Alexander Hamilton, *A New Account*, p. 53. The town of Qurnah

was located at the intersection of the Tigris and Euphrates rivers. In the early seventeenth century, ᶜAli Pasha Afrisayab constructed a fort there which was later expanded by his son Husayn Pasha. It had a custom house for the collection of duties on articles coming down the rivers to Basra. By the end of the eighteenth century, it seemed to have suffered from the general decline that afflicted the area. See ᶜImad Ra'uf's comment in ᶜAbdul-Raḥman al-Suwaydi, *Tarikh Ḥawadith*, p. 47.

136. On the differences between the two, see Andre Raymond, *al-Mudun al-ᶜArabiyyah*, p. 58.

137. Carsten Niebuhr, *Voyage en Arabie*, p. 177.

138. A Janissary regiment. In Basra each 'urṭa had about two hundred men. See ᶜAbdul-Raḥman al-Suwaydi, *Tarikh Ḥawadith*, p. 47.

139. Carsten Niebuhr, *Voyage en Arabie*, p. 177.

140. ᶜImad Ra'uf, "al-Qiwa wa al-Mu'assasat," p. 46.

141. Originally a Turkish word meaning "lazy person." It later came to designate the local militia who were composed mostly of landless peasants. See ᶜAli Shakir ᶜAli, *Tarikh al-ᶜIraq*, p. 99.

142. Carsten Niebuhr, *Voyage en Arabie*, p. 177.

143. The classic work dealing with this subject with particular reference to the Arab provinces of the Ottoman Empire is Albert Hourani, "Ottoman Reform and the Politics of Notables" in W. Polk and R. Chambers, eds., *Beginnings of Modernization in the Middle East* (Chicago: University of Chicago Press, 1968), pp. 41–68. For a brief discussion of their characteristics and role in the eighteenth century, see Malcolm Yapp, *The Making of the Modern Near East, 1792–1923* (New York: Longman, 1987), pp. 8–9; and P. M. Holt, *Egypt and the Fertile Crescent*, pp. 69–70.

144. Margaret L. Meriwether, "Urban Notables and Rural Resources in Aleppo, 1770–1830" in *International Journal of Turkish Studies*, vol. 4, no. 1, Summer 1987, p. 55. See also H. Bowen, "Aᶜyan" in *The Encyclopaedia of Islam*, vol. 1 (Leiden: E. J. Brill, 1960), p. 778.

145. Ibid.

146. Niebuhr refers to the aᶜyan as *ajals*. I have not seen this term used by any other source and certainly all the local sources use the term aᶜyan. See Carsten Niebuhr, *Voyage en Arabie*, p. 177.

147. See, for example, the case recorded in Sir Hermann Gollancz, *Chronicle of Events*, pp. 438–39.

148. This is what happened in 1704 after the death of the wali Muhammad Pasha. See ibid., pp. 480–81.

149. *MSA*, Bassora Factory Diaries, no. 203, folio 68.

150. *MSA*, Bassora Factory Diaries, no. 201, folio 379.

151. Those who claim to be descendants of the Prophet Muhammad.

152. Or "Head of the Aᶜyan of Basra." See Yusuf ᶜIzz al-Din's comments in Aḥmad Nur al-Anṣari, *al-Naṣrah fi Akhbar al-Baṣrah*, p. 58.

153. *MSA*, Bassora Factory Diaries, no. 200, folios 132 and 151.

154. ᶜImad Ra'uf, "al-Tanẓimat al-Ijtimaᶜiyyah" in *Ḥaḍarat al-ᶜIraq*, vol. 10 (Baghdad: Dar al-Hurriyyah, 1985), p. 130.

155. Ibid., pp. 130 and 140; and "al-Rifaᶜi" in H. A. R. Gibb and J. H. Kramers, eds., *Shorter Encyclopaedia of Islam* (Leiden: E. J. Brill, 1961), pp. 475–76.

156. ᶜImad Ra'uf, "al-Tanẓimat al-Ijtimaᶜiyyah," p. 132.

157. Ibid., p. 151.

158. A zawiyah is usually a small mosque or room that sufi shaykhs and their followers use for their prayers and practices. See ibid., p. 140.

159. Carsten Niebuhr, *Voyage en Arabie*, p. 176.

160. See, for example, *IOR*, Factory Records: Persia, G/29/22, vol. IV, folios 635–636.

161. Yusuf ᶜIzz al-Din, *Dawud Basha*, pp. 20–21.

162. Carsten Niebuhr, *Voyage en Arabie*, p. 176.

163. ᶜAbdul-Raḥman al-Suwaydi, *Tarikh Ḥawadith*, p. 50.

164. Ibrahim Faṣiḥ al-Ḥaydari, *Aḥwal al-Baṣrah* (Baghdad: al-Baṣri Publishers, 1961), p. 10; and Carsten Niebuhr, *Voyage en Arabie*, p. 176.

165. Carsten Niebuhr, *Voyage en Arabie*, p. 176.

166. ᶜAli al-Wardi, *Lamaḥat Ijtimaᶜiyyah*, p. 21.

167. Robert G. Landen, "The Changing Pattern of Political Relations Between the Arab Gulf and the Arab Provinces of the Ottoman Empire" in B. R. Pridham, ed., *The Arab Gulf and the Arab World* (London: Croom Helm, 1988), pp. 46–47.

168. G. Vida and P. Sluglett, "al-Muntafiq" in *The Encyclopaedia of Islam*, vol. 7 (Leiden: E. J. Brill, 1993), p. 582.

169. Ḥusayn al-Qahwati, "al-Tarkib al-'Ijtimaᶜi" in *Ḥaḍarat al-ᶜIraq*, vol. 10 (Baghdad: Dar al-Ḥurriyyah, 1985), p. 115.

170. ᶜAli Shakir ᶜAli, *Tarikh al-ᶜIraq*, p. 109; and Stephen Hemsley Longrigg, *Four Centuries*, p. 78.

171. ᶜImad Ra'uf, "al-Madinah al-ᶜIraqiyyah," p. 164.

172. See, for example, *BA*, DBŞM, BSH-1, sıra 29.

173. See *IOR*, Letters from Basra, G/29/18, letter dated August 14, 1729.

174. Ibid.

175. Khwaja Abdul Qadir, *Waqai-i Manazil-i Rum*, p. 53.

176. *IOR*, Factory Diaries: Persia, G/29/22, vol. 2, folios 304–10 and 445.

177. Mirza Abu Taleb Khan, *The Travels*, p. 367.

178. Samuel Manesty successfully employed this tactic in 1793 in a conflict with the mutasallim. See *IOR*, Factory Records: Persia, G/29/22, vol. 4, folios 737–41.

179. In 1765, the English sent a fleet of six large ships and several smaller ones to aid the wali in a campaign against Kaᶜb. Several of these ships

remained to patrol Shaṭṭ al-ᶜArab for most of the remainder of the century. See *IOR*, Miscellaneous Correspondence, G/29/25, folios 38–40.

180. J. B. Kelly, *Britain and the Persian Gulf*, p. 57; and Edward Ingram, "From Trade to Empire in the Near East—III: The Uses of the Residency at Baghdad, 1794–1804" in *Middle East Studies*, vol. 14, no. 3, October 1978, p. 281.

181. *IOR*, Factory Records: Persia, G/29/22, vol. 4, folio 635.

182. Mirza Abu Taleb Khan, *The Travels*, p. 376.

CHAPTER 2. THE SHIFTING FORTUNES OF TRADE

1. For information on ancient trade routes in Iraq, see *The Cambridge Ancient History*, vol. I, part II (Cambridge: Cambridge University Press, 1971), pp. 132–33 and 452–53; and Georges Roux, *Ancient Iraq* (London: Penguin Books, 1992), pp. 12–16 and *passim*.

2. Fred Donner, "Basra," p. 853.

3. Quoted in A. J. Naji and Y. N. Ali, "The Suqs of Basrah: Commercial Organization and Activity in a Medieval Islamic City" in *Journal of the Economic and Social History of the Orient*, vol. 24, part 3, p. 301.

4. This account is given in *MSA*, Bussora Factory Diaries, no. 197, entry dated October 9, 1767.

5. Imports from each region will be discussed separately in the following chapter.

6. Serap Yılmaz, "Osmanlı Imparatorlugu'nun Dogu," p. 33.

7. For a discussion of Iraq's horse trade in the nineteenth century, see Hala Fattah, *The Politics of Regional Trade*, particularly chapter 5. For information on its limited scale in the eighteenth century, see Stephen R. Grummon, "The Rise and Fall of the Arab Shaykhdom of Bushire: 1750–1850" (unpublished Ph.D. dissertation, Johns Hopkins University, 1985), p. 196. For comments on its nature in the sixteenth century, see Dina Khoury, "Merchants and Trade," p. 67.

8. Basrawi literature is full of admiration for the date tree. In one of his poems, for example, the celebrated Basrawi poet, Abu Nuwas (d. 803), likens the date tree to a beautiful bride. See ᶜAbdul-Qadir Bash Aᶜyan al-ᶜAbbasi, *al-Nakhlah: Sayyidat al-Shajar* (Baghdad: al-Baṣri Publishers, 1964), pp. 18–19.

9. Carsten Niebuhr, *Voyage en Arabie*, p. 173.

10. ᶜAbdul-Qadir Bash Aᶜyan al-ᶜAbbasi, *al-Nakhlah*, pp. 67–68.

11. Ibid.

12. Hamid al-Bazi, "Min Turathiyyat," p. 164.

13. Alexander Hamilton, *A New Account*, p. 52.

14. J. B. Kelly, *Britain and the Persian Gulf*, p. 37.

15. *BA*, DBŞM, BSH-2, sıra 82.

16. M. Otter, *Voyage en Turquie*, p. 66.

17. *BA*, DBŞM, BSH-1, sıra 25.

18. In one popular story told in Iraq for many generations, the wise man, given the choice of dates or meat for his meal, chose the dates, enabling him to travel much farther than his companion, who foolishly chose to eat meat. See ᶜAbdul-Qadir Bash Aᶜyan al-ᶜAbbasi, *al-Nakhlah*, pp. 115–18.

19. K. N. Chaudhuri, *Trade and Civilization*, p. 184.

20. Hamilton stated that dates "support and sustain many millions of people." Although this is certainly an exaggeration, it does capture the importance of this fruit to the people of the Shaṭṭ al-ᶜArab region. See Alexander Hamilton, *A New Account*, p. 52.

21. For a discussion of the different stages involved in the production of dates, see ᶜAbdul-Qadir Bash Aᶜyan al-ᶜAbbasi, *al-Nakhlah*, pp. 57–58, 74–76, and *passim*.

22. See, for example, the record of ships sailing from Basra to India in *MSA*, Bussora Factory Outward Letter Book, no. 30, entry dated December, 1724.

23. ᶜAbdul-Qadir Bash Aᶜyan al-ᶜAbbasi, *al-Nakhlah*, pp. 108–11.

24. Otter gives several examples of these uses in 1734 and they are still largely unchanged today. See M. Otter, *Voyage en Turquie*, pp. 64–66; and ᶜAbdul-Qadir Bash Aᶜyan al-ᶜAbbasi, *al-Nakhlah*, p. 39.

25. ᶜImad Ra'uf, in ᶜAbd-al-Raḥman al-Suwaydi, *Tarikh Ḥawadith*, pp. 47–48.

26. Sir Hermann Gollancz, *Chronicle of Events*, p. 619.

27. Khwaja Abdul Qadir, *Waqai-i Manazil-i Rum*, p. 52.

28. Aḥmad Nur al-Anṣari, *al-Naṣrah fi Akhbar al-Baṣrah*, p. 26.

29. J. G. Lorimer, *Gazetteer of the Persian Gulf*, p. 1276.

30. Sir Hermann Gollancz, *Chronicle of Events*, p. 466.

31. The Capitulations were commercial treaties that the Ottoman Empire signed with a number of European powers. In addition to tariff limitations, they also created a system of extraterritorial jurisdiction for Europeans and some of their local associates. See P. M. Holt, *Egypt and the Fertile Crescent*, p. 197.

32. J. B. Kelly, *Britain and the Persian Gulf*, p. 37.

33. French sources mention the slightly different figures of 7% on imports and 5% on exports. See Serap Yılmaz, "Osmanlı Imparatorlugu'nun Dogu," pp. 45–46.

34. Samuel Manesty and Harvard Jones, *Report on the British Trade*, folios 234–235; and J. G. Lorimer, *Gazetteer of the Persian Gulf*, pp. 1276–78.

35. *MSA*, Gombroon Factory Diaries, no. 7/118, entry dated October 20, 1756.

36. Samuel Manesty and Harvard Jones, *Report on the Persian Gulf*, folios 231–32.

37. *BA*, DBŞM, BSH-1, sıra 23, folios 13, 15.

38. Salih Ozbaran, *The Ottoman Response to European Expansion: Studies on Ottoman-Portuguese Relations in the Indian Ocean and Ottoman Administration in the Arab Lands During the Sixteenth Century* (Istanbul: The Isis Press, 1994), p. 45.

39. *BA*, DBŞM, BSH-1, sıra 27.

40. Mehmet Genc, "A Study of the Feasibility of Using Eighteenth-Century Ottoman Financial Records as an Indicator of Economic Activity" in Huri Islamoglu-Inan, ed., *The Ottoman Empire and the World Economy* (Cambridge: Cambridge University Press, 1987), p. 347.

41. A copy of this case can be found in *BA*, DBŞM, BSH-1, sıra 22.

42. Pierre-Yves Manguin, "Late Mediaeval Asian Shipbuilding in the Indian Ocean: A Reappraisal" in *Moyen Orient & Ocean Indien / Middle East & Indian Ocean, XVIe–XIXe s.*, vol. 2, no. 2, 1985, p. 2.

43. A. H. J. Prins, "The Persian Gulf Dhows: Two Variants in Maritime Enterprise" in *Persica*, no. 2, 1966, pp. 1–2.

44. Pierre-Yves Manguin, "Late Mediaeval," pp. 3–4; and George Hourani, *Arab Seafaring in the Indian Ocean in Ancient and Early Medieval Times* (Princeton: Princeton University Press, 1951), pp. 89–91.

45. Pierre-Yves Manguin, "Late Mediaeval," p. 6; and M. N. Pearson, *Merchants and Rulers in Gujarat: The Response to the Portuguese in the Sixteenth Century* (Berkeley: University of California Press, 1976), p. 8.

46. George Hourani, *Arab Seafaring*, pp. 90–91; and Abdul-Aziz El-Ashban, "The Formation of the Omani Trading Empire Under the Yaᶜaribah Dynasty (1624–1719)" in *Arab Studies Quarterly*, vol. 1, no. 4, 1979, p. 365.

47. Ahmad Mustafa Abu Hakima, *History of Eastern Arabia, 1750–1800: The Rise and Development of Bahrain and Kuwait* (Beirut: Khayats, 1965), pp. 167–68; and ᶜAbdul-Amir Amin, *al-Qiwa al-Baḥriyyah fi al-Khalij al-ᶜArabi* (Baghdad: Asᶜad Printers, 1966), pp. 31 and 40.

48. Ahmad Mustafa Abu Hakima, *History of Eastern Arabia*, p. 167.

49. ᶜAbdul-Amir Amin, *al-Qiwa al-Baḥriyyah*, pp. 31, 40; and Willem Floor, "Dutch Trade With Masqat in the Second Half of the Eighteenth Century" in *Asian and African Studies*, vol. 16, 1982, p. 205.

50. Quoted in Ahmad Mustafa Abu Hakima, *History of Eastern Arabia*, p. 167.

51. Quoted in ibid.

52. Ibid.

53. Ibid., p. 168.

54. Quoted in ibid., p. 167.

55. *NAI*, Home Department, Public Branch, OC no. 21, dated December 2, 1796.

56. See Ashin Das Gupta, *Indian Merchants*, p. 13.

57. William Heude, *A Voyage Up the Persian Gulf*, p. 47.

58. K. N. Chaudhuri, *Trade and Civilization*, p. 143.

59. This word is probably derived from the Arabic *ᶜaskar*, meaning "soldier." It later came to mean a native sailor employed on a European vessel. See Henry Yule and A. C. Burnell, *Hobson-Jobson: A Glossary of Colloquial Anglo-Indian Words and Phrases, and of Kindered Terms, Etymological, Historical, Geographical and Discursive* (New York: Humanities Press, 1968), pp. 507–8.

60. *MSA*, Gombroon Factory Inward Letter Book, no. 40, December 7, 1743.

61. For Basra's revenue figures in the eighteenth century, see *BA*, MM, nos. 10306, 10148, 10147, 10145, 10151, 10150, 10166, 10172, 10174, 10173, 10171, 10219, 4879, 10205, 10168, 10231, 10226, 10234, 10211, 10224, 10199, 3392, 10164, 10149, 10157, 10231, 10152, 10222, 10307, 10160, 10145.

62. Sir Hermann Gollancz, *Chronicle of Events*, pp. 418–20.

63. For a record of this meeting, see *BA*, DBŞM, BSH-1, sıra 25.

64. See, for example, *BA*, DBŞM, BSH-1, sıra 29.

65. Willem Floor, "The Decline of the Dutch East Indies Company in Bandar ᶜAbbas (1747–1759)" in *Moyen Orient & Ocean Indien*, vol. 6, 1989, p. 45.

66. Referred to in contemporary English records as "Gombroon."

67. *IOR*, Letters from Basra, G/29/18, letter dated August 14, 1729.

68. *MSA*, Bussora Factory Diaries, no. 194, entry dated May 5, 1765.

69. For a detailed description of the military campaigns, see Stephen Hemsley Longrigg, *Four Centuries*, pp. 134–62; and ᶜAli Shakir ᶜAli, *Tarikh al-ᶜIraq*, pp. 181–206.

70. *IOR*, Letters from Basra, G/29/19, letter dated February 22, 1736.

71. *IOR*, Letters from Basra, G/29/19, letter dated April 7, 1744.

72. *IOR*, Letters from Basra, G/29/19, letter dated September 7, 1744.

73. Sir Hermann Gollancz, *Chronicle of Events*, pp. 625–26.

74. See Samuel Manesty and Harvard Jones, *Report on the British Trade*, folio 236. Some forty years earlier, the Dutch gave an identical estimation. See Willem Floor, "A Description of the Persian Gulf and Its Inhabitants in 1756" in *Persica*, no. 8, 1979, p. 167.

75. *BA*, DBŞM, BSH-1, sıra 25.

76. For a description of these events, see ᶜAbdul-Amir Amin, *al-Qiwa al-Baḥriyyah*, pp. 38–39.

77. *MSA*, Bussora Factory Diaries, no. 199, entries dated February 5 and March 25, 1769.

78. See ᶜAbdul-Amir Amin, *al-Qiwa al-Baḥriyyah*, pp. 40–42; ᶜAla' Nawras and ᶜImad Ra'uf, *'Imarat Kaᶜb al-ᶜArabiyyah fi al-Qirn al-Thamin ᶜAshar* (Baghdad: al-Rashid Publishers, 1982); and J. B. Kelly, *Britain and the Persian Gulf*, pp. 38–39.

79. *IOR*, Miscellaneous Correspondence, G/29/25, letter dated March 17, 1769, folios 38–40.

80. This treaty was signed by Sulayman Agha, then the mutasallim of Basra, and the English agent on January 25, 1767. For the English description of the treaty, see *MSA*, Bussora Factory Diaries, no. 199, entry dated August 3, 1768, folio 6; for the Ottoman description, see *BA*, DBŞM, BSH-3, sıra 106.

81. Stephen Hemsley Longrigg, *Four Centuries*, p. 187.

82. J. G. Lorimer, *Gazetteer of the Persian Gulf*, p. 1285.

83. *MSA*, Bussora Factory Diaries, no. 196, entry dated June 29, 1767.

84. Ibid.

85. See, for example, ʿAbdul-Raḥman al-Suwaydi, *Tarikh Ḥawadith*, p. 52.

86. See ʿImad Ra'uf's comment in ibid., p. 41.

87. Chafchir, in the local Iraqi dialect, means "sieve." The reference here is to the scars that the disease left on victims' faces.

88. *MSA*, Bussora Factory Diaries, no. 201, entry dated April 2, 1773, folio 336 and no. 202, entry dated January 10, 1774, folio 4.

89. ʿAbdul-Raḥman al-Suwaydi, *Tarikh Ḥawadith*, p. 47.

90. *MSA*, Bussora Factory Diaries, no. 201, entry dated May 22, 1773, folio 356.

91. Ibid.

92. Ibid.

93. *MSA*, Bussora Factory Diaries, no. 202, entry dated January 10, 1774, folio 5.

94. Samuel Manesty and Harvard Jones, *Report on the British Trade*, folio 236.

95. *MSA*, Bussora Factory Diaries, no. 202, entry dated January 10, 1774, folio 5.

96. See, for example, *MSA*, Bussora Factory Diaries, no. 202, entry dated November 3, 1774, folio 299.

97. Mentioned in J. G. Lorimer, *Gazetteer of the Persian Gulf*, p. 1243.

98. Elena Frangakis-Syrett, *The Commerce of Smyrna*, p. 131.

99. For a full discussion of the causes and consequences of Karim Khan's occupation of Basra, see John R. Perry, *Karim Khan Zand: A History of Iran, 1747–1779* (Chicago: University of Chicago Press, 1979), pp. 167–201; and Stephen Hemsley Longrigg, *Four Centuries*, pp. 187–95.

100. John R. Perry, *Karim Khan Zand*, p. 173.

101. Ibid.

102. *MSA*, Bussora Factory Diaries, no. 203, entry dated March 8, 1775, folio 37.

103. Many believe that the popular Iraqi saying, "بعد خراب البصره" (after the destruction of Basra), originated as a result of this siege. The sar-

castic expression, which recalls Baghdad's inaction, is used when one speaks of taking action when it is already too late.

104. See *MSA*, Bussora Factory Diaries, no. 203, entry dated January 17, 1777, folio 306; Stephen Hemsley Longrigg, *Four Centuries*, p. 193; and John R. Perry, *Karim Khan Zand*, pp. 194–96.

105. ʿImad Ra'uf, "al-Qiwa wa al-Mu'asasat," pp. 49–50.

106. Samuel Manesty and Harvard Jones, *Report on the British Trade*, folio 237. For the causes behind the Persian evacuation, see John R. Perry, *Karim Khan Zand*, pp. 198–99.

107. *IOR*, Letters from Basra, G/29/22, letter dated May 25, 1785, folios 149–150.

108. Serap Yılmaz, "Osmanlı Imparatorlugu'nun Dogu," pp. 50, 57, 58.

109. Samuel Manesty and Harvard Jones, *Report on the British Trade*, folios 235 and 237.

110. Hala Fattah, *The Politics of Regional Trade*, p. 69.

111. Mohammad S. Hasan, "The Role of Foreign Trade in the Economic Development of Iraq, 1864–1964: A Study in the Growth of a Dependent Economy" in M. A. Cook, ed., *Studies in the Economic History of the Middle East* (Oxford: Oxford University Press, 1970), p. 348. On this point, see also Ahmet Tabakoglu, "The Economic Importance of the Gulf," p. 162.

112. Panzac mentions that the empire's trade with Europe "grew appreciably" at the end of the century. Frangakis-Syrett reaches a similar conclusion with respect to the trade of Smyrna (Izmir). See Daniel Panzac, "International and Domestic Maritime Trade," p. 192; and Elena Frangakis-Syrett, *The Commerce of Smyrna*, p. 120 and *passim.*

113. Samuel Manesty and Harvard Jones, *Report on the British Trade*, folio 236.

114. See, for example, J. B. Kelly, *Britain and the Persian Gulf*, p. 37.

115. Daniel Panzac, "International and Domestic Maritime Trade," p. 190.

116. Charles Issawi, *The Economic History of the Middle East, 1800–1914* (Chicago: University of Chicago Press, 1966), p. 127; and Roger Owen, *The Middle East in the World Economy, 1800–1914* (London: Methuen, 1981), pp. 82, 180, 273.

CHAPTER 3. NETWORKS OF TRADE

1. On the concept of boundaries during this period, see Hala Fattah, *The Politics of Regional Trade*, particularly Chapter 1.

2. Neils Steensgaard, "The Indian Ocean Network and the Emerging World-Economy, c. 1500–1750" in Satish Chandra, ed., *The Indian Ocean*, pp. 130–31, 144.

3. Ibid., pp. 144–45.

4. Ibid., pp. 145–46.

5. Serap Yılmaz, "Osmanlı Imparatorlugu'nun Dogu," p. 40.

6. Ibid., p. 59.

7. Daniel Panzac, "International and Domestic Maritime Trade," p. 191.

8. Serap Yılmaz, "Osmanlı Imparatorlugu'nun Dogu," p. 36.

9. These bales varied in weight from three hundred to four hundred pounds each. See Samuel Manesty and Harvard Jones, *Report on the British Trade*, folio 229.

10. See, for example, the list of the *Albion*'s cargo in *MSA*, Bussora Factory Diaries, no. 198, entry dated July 5, 1768.

11. Samuel Manesty and Harvard Jones, *Report on the British Trade*, folio 232.

12. *BA*, DBŞM, BSH-1, sıra 20.

13. Samuel Manesty and Harvard Jones, *Report on the British Trade*, folios 228–229.

14. Serap Yılmaz, "Osmanlı Imparatorlugu'nun Dogu," p. 58 and Daniel Panzac, "International and Domestic Maritime Trade," pp. 191, 192.

15. K. N. Chaudhuri, *Trade and Civilization*, p. 92.

16. In Figures 3.1 and 3.2, the total number of arrivals appears larger than that of the departures because some of the ships that arrived from India chose to depart to another destination. The arrivals were also usually better recorded than the departures.

17. *BA*, DBŞM, BSH-1, sıra 25.

18. Ibid.

19. Sir Hermann Gollancz, *Chronicle of Events*, p. 568.

20. Ashin Das Gupta argues that the backbone of this boom was a "vigorous merchant class" taking advantage of "feudal fragmentation" which ensured an atmosphere of commercial freedom. See Ashin Das Gupta, *Malabar in Asian Trade, 1740–1800* (Cambridge: Cambridge University Press, 1967), pp. 4, 19.

21. The Turkish word *chalabi* (çelebi) was a title given to some of the wealthier merchants in the Ottoman Empire. The Chalabis of Surat, however, formed a single clan or extended family. For information on the title of chalabi in Iraq, see Hana Batatu, *The Old Social Classes and the Revolutionary Movements of Iraq: A Study of Iraq's Old Landed and Commercial Classes and of its Communists, Ba^cthists, and Free Officers* (Princeton: Princeton University Press, 1978), pp. 124–25. For information on the Chalabis of Surat, see Ashin Das Gupta, *Indian Merchants*, pp. 76–77 and *passim*.

22. *BA*, DBŞM, BSH-1, sıra 25.

23. See *IOR*, Letters from Basra, G/29/19, letter dated August 29, 1739; and *MSA*, Bussora Factory Diaries, no. 201, folio 203.

24. For a full discussion of this episode, although favoring the Dutch

view, see Edward Ives, *A Voyage from England*, pp. 209–15; and *MSA*, Gombroon Factory Diaries, no. 117, entry dated July 17, 1754.

25. Ashin Das Gupta, *Malabar in Asian Trade*, pp. 89–100, 102–23, and *passim*.

26. Catherine Manning, "French Interest in East Asian Trade, 1719–1748" in *Moyen Orient & Ocean Indien*, vol. 7, 1990, p. 155.

27. Holden Furber, *Rival Empires of Trade in the Orient, 1600–1800* (Minneapolis: University of Minnesota Press, 1976), p. 282.

28. Elena Frangakis-Syrett, *The Commerce of Smyrna*, pp. 85–86.

29. Ashin Das Gupta, *Malabar in Asian Trade*, p. 33.

30. On this point, see Ashin Das Gupta, "India and the Indian Ocean in the Eighteenth Century" in Ashin Das Gupta and M. Pearson, eds., *India and the Indian Ocean, 1500–1800* (Calcutta: Oxford University Press, 1987), pp. 131–61.

31. Lakshmi Subramanian, "The Eighteenth-Century Social Order in Surat: A Reply and an Excursus on the Riots of 1788 and 1795" in *Modern Asian Studies*, vol. 25, no. 2, 1991, pp. 344–45.

32. As early as the middle of the century, the Dutch resident, von Kniphausen, wrote that profits from the India freight trade was the main factor keeping other European companies in the Gulf. See Willem Floor, "The Dutch on Khark Island: A Commercial Mishap" in *International Journal of Middle East Studies*, vol. 24, no. 3, August 1992, p. 450.

33. An example of the first case can be found in a statement by sixty-two merchants from Surat to the city's qaḍi in 1764. A copy of this is at *IOR*, Miscellaneous Correspondence with Agents in Turkish Arabia, G/29/25, folio 30. An example of the second case can be found in a 1768 letter of twelve Basrawi merchants to the English agent in *MSA*, Bussora Factory Diaries, no. 199, folio 113.

34. Serap Yılmaz, "Osmanlı Imparatorlugu'nun Dogu," p. 33.

35. For a discussion of the extent of European control of Ottoman trade in the Mediterranean, see Daniel Panzac, "International and Domestic Maritime Trade," pp. 195–97.

36. For a brief yet concise history of Oman, see G. P. Badger's introduction to Hamid ibn Muhammad Ibn Ruzayq, *History of the Imams and Seyyids of ʿOman by Salilibn-Razik, from A.D. 661–1856* (London: Hakluyt Society, no. 43, 1871). For the history of Oman in the seventeenth and eighteenth centuries, see Abdul Aziz El-Ashban, "The Formation of the Omani Trading Empire Under the Yaʿaribah Dynasty (1624–1719)" in *Arab Studies Quarterly*, vol. 1, no. 4, 1979, pp. 354–71; Patricia Risso, *Oman and Muscat: An Early Modern History* (London: Croom Helm, 1986); Willem Floor, "Dutch Trade With Masqat in the Second Half of the Eighteenth Century" in *Asian and African Studies*, vol. 16, 1982, pp. 197–213.

37. Ashin Das Gupta, *Indian Merchants*, p. 71; Abdul Aziz El-Ashban, "The Formation of the Omani Trading Empire," pp. 360–61.

38. Abdul Aziz El-Ashban, "The Formation of the Omani Trading Empire," p. 368.

39. *BA*, DBŞM, BSH-1, sıra 25.

40. Samuel Manesty and Harvard Jones, *Report on the British Trade*, folio 219.

41. Murray Gordon, *Slavery in the Arab World* (New York: New Amsterdam Books, 1989), pp. 141–43; and Abdul Sheriff, *Slaves, Spices and Ivory in Zanzibar: Integration of an African Commercial Empire into the World Economy, 1770–1873* (Athens: Ohio University Press, 1987), *passim.*

42. Ehud Toledano, *The Ottoman Slave Trade and Its Suppression: 1840–1890* (Princeton: Princeton University Press, 1982), pp. 34–35.

43. M. Otter, *Voyage en Turquie*, p. 73.

44. Dina Khoury, "Merchants and Trade," pp. 66–67.

45. Ehud Toledano, *The Ottoman Slave Trade*, p. 33.

46. Ralph A. Austen, "The 19th Century Islamic Slave Trade From East Africa (Swahili and Red Sea Coasts): A Tentative Census" in *Slavery & Abolition*, vol. 9, no. 3, December 1988, p. 29.

47. Ehud Toledano, *The Ottoman Slave Trade*, p. 82.

48. Thomas M. Ricks, "Slaves and Slave Traders in the Persian Gulf, 18th and 19th Centuries: An Assessment" in *Slavery & Abolition*, vol. 9, no. 3, December 1988, pp. 64–65.

49. Albertine Jwaideh and J. W. Cox, "The Black Slaves of Turkish Arabia During the 19th Century" in *Slavery & Abolition*, vol. 9, no. 3, December 1988, pp. 51–52.

50. Ibid., pp. 52–53.

51. Patricia Risso, *Oman and Muscat*, pp. 77–80.

52. Samuel Manesty and Harvard Jones, *Report on the British Trade*, folio 219.

53. Ibid., folios 219–20.

54. Ibid.

55. Mentioned in Kristof Glamann, *Dutch-Asiatic Trade, 1620–1740* (The Hague: Martinus Nijhoff, 1958), p. 206.

56. *BA*, DBŞM, BSH-1, sıra 25.

57. Ashin Das Gupta, "Gujarati Merchants and the Red Sea Trade, 1700–1725" in Blair King and M. N. Pearson, eds., *The Age of Partnership: Europeans in Asia Before Dominion* (Honolulu: University of Hawaii, 1979), p. 130.

58. Paul Dresch, *Tribes, Government, and History in Yemen* (Oxford: Clarendon Press, 1989), p. 206. Dresch estimates that Mukha's export of coffee in the first half of the century peaked in 1730.

59. Carsten Niebuhr, *Voyage en Arabie*, p. 192.

60. *MSA*, Bussora Factory Diaries, no. 198, folios 84–85.

61. Calvin H. Allen, "The State of Masqat in the Gulf and East Africa,

1785–1829" in *International Journal of Middle East Studies*, no. 2, vol. 14, May 1982, pp. 117–18.

62. For Ibn Saᶜud's raids on southern Iraq, see Stephen Hemsley Longrigg, *Four Centuries*, pp. 212–17; and ᶜAli al-Wardi, *Lamaḥat Ijtimaᶜiyyah*, pp. 183–206.

63. Hala Fattah, *The Politics of Regional Trade*, p. 56.

64. J. B. Kelly, "Kursan" in *The Encyclopaedia of Islam*, vol. 5 (Leiden: E. J. Brill, 1986), p. 507.

65. Ibid., pp. 120–22.

66. Patricia R. Dubuisson, "Qasimi Piracy," pp. 52–53.

67. Paul Dresch, *Tribes, Government and History*, p. 200.

68. Mohammed al-Zulfa, "Omani-Ottoman Relations During the Reign of Imam Ahmad b. Saᶜid, 1741–83, in the Light of a Recently Discovered Exchange of Letters Between the Imam and the Ottoman Sultan" in *Arabian Studies*, vol. 8, 1990, pp. 95–96.

69. Ibid., p. 96.

70. Ibid., p. 100.

71. Calvin H. Allen, "The State of Masqat," p. 121.

72. ᶜAbdul-Malik al-Tamimi, *Tarikh al-ᶜIlaqat al-Tijariyyah Bayn al-Hind wa Manṭaqat al-Khalij al-ᶜArabi fi al-ᶜAṣr al-Ḥadith*, vol. 8, 48th monograph (Baghdad: al-Adab College, 1986), p. 21.

73. See Willem Floor, "A Description of the Persian Gulf and Its Inhabitants in 1756" in *Persica*, no. 8, 1979, p. 164.

74. Ibid., p. 165.

75. For the history of Bushire in the eighteenth and early nineteenth centuries, see Stephen R. Grummon, "The Rise and Fall of the Arab Shaykhdom of Bushire."

76. J. B. Kelly, *Britain and the Persian Gulf*, p. 44.

77. The pearl fisheries of Bahrayn brought in an estimated 500,000 rupees annually in the 1770s. See Holden Furber, *Rival Empires of Trade*, p. 293.

78. Rosemarie Said Zahlan, *The Creation of Qatar* (London: Croom Helm, 1979), pp. 27–28; Willem Floor, "The Iranian Navy in the Gulf During the Eighteenth Century" in *Iranian Studies*, vol. 20, no. 1, 1987, pp. 34–36.

79. Hala Fattah, *The Politics of Regional Trade*, pp. 67–68.

80. Ahmad Mustafa Abu Hakima, *History of Eastern Arabia*, pp. 175–77 and *passim*.

81. Rosemarie Said Zahlan, *The Creation of Qatar*, p. 28.

82. G. Rentz, "al-Kawasim" in *The Encyclopaedia of Islam*, vol. 6 (Leiden: E. J. Brill, 1978), p. 777.

83. *MSA*, Bussora Factory Diaries, no. 197, entry dated August 22, 1767.

84. For a contemporary description of pearl fishing in the Gulf, see the

report by the head of the Dutch factory at Kharg, Baron von Kniphausen, in Willem Floor, "Pearl Fishing in the Persian Gulf in 1757" in *Persica*, no. 10, 1982, pp. 209–22.

85. ᶜAli al-Wardi, *Lamaḥat Ijtimaᶜiyyah*, p. 192.

86. Ahmad Mustafa Abu Hakima, *History of Eastern Arabia*, pp. 176–77.

87. Patricia R. Dubuisson, "Qasimi Piracy," p. 48.

88. Rosmarie Said Zahlan, *The Creation of Qatar*, pp. 29–30.

89. Charles Belgrave, *The Pirate Coast* (Beirut: Libraire du Liban, 1972), pp. 28–36.

90. Patricia R. Dubuisson, "Qasimi Piracy," p. 49.

91. Rosemarie Said Zahlan, *The Creation of Qatar*, p. 32.

92. Charles Issawi, ed., *The Economic History of Iran, 1800–1914* (Chicago: University of Chicago Press, 1971), p. 82.

93. Samuel Manesty and Harvard Jones, *Report on the British Trade*, folio 235.

94. See Ahmad Mustafa Abu Hakima, *History of Eastern Arabia*, pp. 45–63.

95. Samuel Manesty and Harvard Jones, *Report on the British Trade*, folio 213.

96. Ahmad Mustafa Abu Hakima, *History of Eastern Arabia*, pp. 96–97.

97. Samuel Manesty and Harvard Jones, *Report on the British Trade*, folio 235.

98. See the summary of Maᶜshuq Pasha's report to the Porte in Mahdi al-Bustani, "Watha'iq ᶜUthmaniyyah," p. 110.

99. J. B. Kelly, *Britain and the Persian Gulf*, p. 29; Rosemarie Said Zahlan, *The Creation of Qatar*, p. 28; and Hala Fattah, *The Politics of Regional Trade*, p. 59.

100. See Mir ᶜAbdul-Laṭif al-Shustari, *Tuḥfat al-ᶜAlam, passim.*

101. *IOR*, Letters from Basra, G/29/18, letter dated August 14, 1729.

102. *MSA*, Bussora Factory Diaries, no. 199, entry dated May 1, 1768, folio 140.

103. Gavin Hambly, "An Introduction to the Economic Organization of Early Qajar Iran" in *Iran*, vol. 2, 1964, p. 74.

104. Hala Fattah, *The Politics of Regional Trade*, p. 65.

105. Ibid.

106. Samuel Manesty and Harvard Jones, *Report on the British Trade*, folios 242–243; Gavin Hambly, "An Introduction," p. 78; Charles Issawi, *The Economic History of Iran*, p. 88; J. B. Kelly, *Britain and the Persian Gulf*, p. 36; and Ann K. S. Lambton, *Qajar Persia* (London: I. B. Tauris & Co. Ltd., 1987), pp. 115–16.

107. Charles Issawi, *The Economic History of Iran*, p. 11.

108. Ahmad Seyf, "Despotism and the Disintegration of the Iranian Economy, 1500–1800" in Elie Kedourie and Sylvia Haim, eds., *Essays on the*

Economic History of the Middle East (London: Frank Cass, 1988), p. 15; Thomas M. Ricks, "Slaves and Slave Traders," pp. 62–63; John Perry, *Karim Khan Zand, passim.*

109. In Charles Issawi, *The Economic History of Iran*, p. 86.

110. *MSA*, Bussora Factory Diaries, nos. 199–203.

111. See, for example, *BA*, DBŞM, BSH-3, sıra 106.

112. Ahmad Mustafa Abu-Hakima, "Banu Ka^cb" in *The Encyclopaedia of Islam*, vol. 6 (Leiden: E. J. Brill, 1978), p. 314.

113. For more on the Ka^cb tribe, see ^cAbdul-Amir Amin, *al-Qiwa al-Baḥriyyah*; and ^cAla' Nawras and ^cImad Ra'uf, *'Imarat Ka^cb.*

114. *BA*, DBŞM, BSH-3, sıra 106.

115. Stephen R. Grummon, "The Rise and Fall," p. 120.

116. Ann Lambton, *Qajar Persia*, pp. 111–12.

117. The shaykhas were ships of around thirty-five tons and the takanahs were smaller ships distinguished by their flat hull. For the former, see *NAI*, Home Department, Public Branch, OC, July 31, 1797, no. 2. For the latter, see ^cAbdul-Amir Amin, *al-Qiwa al-Baḥriyyah*, p. 31.

118. ^cAli Shakir ^cAli, *Tarikh al-^cIraq*, pp. 147–53.

119. Serap Yılmaz, "Osmanlı Imparatorlugu'nun Dogu," p. 33.

120. *IOR*, Letters from Basra, G/29/18, letter dated July 21, 1725.

121. Khwaja Abdul Qadir, *Waqai-i Manazil-i Rum*, p. 45; and Joseph Emin, *The Life and Adventures*, pp. 415–20.

122. *MSA*, Bussora Factory Diaries, no. 202, entry dated March 7, 1774, folio 146.

123. Information on the copper trade was taken from two independent reports in 1797 by W. Page, "Custom Master at Bombay," and Samuel Manesty, the English resident at Basra. For the former, see *NAI*, Home Department, Public Branch, OC, February 24, 1797, no. 3. For the latter, see *NAI*, Home Department, Public Branch, OC, July 31, 1797, no. 2.

124. The attaree maund or *man-i attar* was the most common unit of weight prevalent in the West Indian Ocean and can be traced back as far as the Babylonian *mana*. Although its value varied over time and place, in eighteenth-century Basra it equaled some twenty-eight pounds. For its origins, see Henry Yule and A. C. Burnell, *Hobson-Jobson*, pp. 563–65. For its value at Basra in the late eighteenth century, see *NAI*, Home Department, Public Branch, OC, February 24, 1797, no. 3.

125. *NAI*, Home Department, Public Branch, OC, July 31, 1797, no. 2. These figures should not be taken literally since the English resident had no way of knowing the exact amount being exported. They do, however, point to a significant increase in the export of copper to India.

126. ^cImad Ra'uf, "al-Madinah al-^cIraqiyyah," pp. 174–75.

127. *IOR*, Letters from Basra, G/29/22, letter dated October 17, 1787, folio 401.

128. *IOR*, Letters from Basra, G/29/22, letter dated December 16, 1787, folios 417–22. For information on Shaykh Ḥamad al-Ḥumud, see Ḥumud al-Saᶜidi, *Dirasat ᶜan ᶜAsha'ir al-ᶜIraq al-Khazaᶜil* (Najaf: Maṭbaᶜat al-Adab, 1974), pp. 35–60.

129. For references to the problems caused by the Khazaᶜil to the riverine trade, see Khwaja Abdul Qadir, *Waqai-i Manazil-i Rum*, p. 45; and Samuel Manesty and Harvard Jones, *Report on the British Trade*, folio 230.

130. For information on al-Shawi's rebellion, see Stephen Hemsley Longrigg, *Four Centuries*, pp. 203–4; and ᶜAbdul-Raḥman al-Suwaydi, *Tarikh Ḥawadith*, pp. 131–38, and *passim*.

131. Willem Floor, "La Revolte des Muntafiqs en 1787—une Nouvelle Source" in *Zeitschrift der Deutschen Morgenlandischen Gesellschaft*, vol. 135, no. 1, 1985, p. 56.

132. Abraham Marcus, *The Middle East on the Eve of Modernity*, pp. 338–39.

133. *BA*, DBŞM, BSH-3, sıra 106; and *IOR*, Letters from Basra, G/29/21, letter dated January 23, 1781, folios 396–97.

134. Samuel Manesty and Harvard Jones, *Report on the British Trade*, folio 230.

135. Serap Yılmaz, "Osmanlı Imparatorlugu'nun Dogu," p. 48.

136. The following description of the caravans is based on Christina P. Grant, *The Syrian Desert, Caravans, Travel and Exploration* (London: A. & C. Black Ltd., 1937), pp. 125–56; Ahmad Mustafa Abu Hakima, *History of Eastern Arabia*, pp. 169–75; and the travelers' accounts printed in Douglas Carruthers, ed., *The Desert Route to India, Being the Journals of Four Travellers by the Great Desert Caravan Route Between Aleppo and Basra, 1745–1751* (London, 1929).

137. Ahmad Mustafa Abu Hakima, *History of Eastern Arabia*, p. 172.

138. Bartholomew Plaisted, "Narrative of a Journey," pp. 98–99.

139. Christina P. Grant, *The Syrian Desert*, p. 134.

140. Ahmad Mustafa Abu Hakima, *History of Eastern Arabia*, p. 170.

141. Yılmaz mentions that in the 1760s merchants usually paid a total of 80 ghurush (about 80 rupees) for each camel-load. See Serap Yılmaz, "Osmanlı Imparatorlugu'nun Dogu," p. 43.

142. One who calls the Muslims to prayer.

143. William Beawes, "Remarks and Occurrences," p. 38; Bartholomew Plaisted, "Narrative of a Journey," p. 62.

144. William Beawes, "Remarks and Occurrences," p. 33.

145. *IOR*, Letters from Basra, G/29/19, letter dated October 20, 1739.

146. *MSA*, Bussora Factory Diaries, no. 200, entry dated November 23, 1769, folio 126.

147. *MSA*, Bussora Factory Diaries, no. 202, entries dated January 12 and February 15, 1774, folios 10 and 115.

148. For a full discussion of the causes behind this economic decline, see Bruce Masters, *The Origins of Western Economic Dominance*, *passim*; and Abraham Marcus, *The Middle East*, *passim*.

149. Mentioned by Bruce Masters, *The Origins of Western Economic Dominance*, p. 86.

150. ᶜAli al-Wardi, *Lamaḥat Ijtimaᶜiyyah*, p. 204.

151. Murphey, using Ottoman sources, mentions that the volume of trade from the Aleppo–Basra route declined after the second half of the eighteenth century, but he attributes this solely to the conflict with Persia. See R. Murphey, "Conditions of Trade in the Eastern Mediterranean: An Appraisal of Eighteenth Century Ottoman Documents from Aleppo" in *Journal of the Economic and Social History of the Orient*, vol. 33, 1990, p. 46.

152. For a discussion of the causes behind the decline of Aleppo's caravan trade and the rise of Damascus, see Bruce Masters, *The Origins of Western Economic Dominance*, pp. 30–33 and *passim*.

153. Mahdi al-Bustani, "Watha'iq ᶜUthmaniyyah," p. 110.

CHAPTER 4. THE MERCHANTS (TUJJAR) AND TRADE

1. Hana Batatu, *The Old Social Classes*, p. 233.

2. ᶜUthman Ibn Sanad, *Saba'ik al-ᶜAsjad fi Akhbar Aḥmad Najl Rizq al-Asᶜad*, British Museum MS. Or. 7565, folio 11.

3. Hala Fattah, *The Politics of Regional Trade*, p. 27.

4. Bruce Masters encountered a similar problem when dealing with the merchants of Aleppo. See Bruce Masters, *The Origins of Western Economic Dominance*, pp. 48–49.

5. In most of these traits Basrawi merchants were not unlike their counterparts in other cities of the region. For Aleppo, see ibid.; for Cairo, see Andre Raymond, *Artisants et commerçants*; for Surat, see Ashin Das Gupta, *Indian Merchants*; for Iran, see Willem Floor, "The Merchants (*tujjar*) in Qajjar Iran" in *Zeitschrift der Deutschen Morgenlandischen Gesellschaft*, vol. 126, no. 1, 1976, pp. 101–35.

6. Hala Fattah, *The Politics of Regional Trade*, p. 79.

7. *MSA*, Bussora Factory Diaries, nos. 198–203.

8. Meir Benayahu, *Rabbi Yaakob Elyichar and His Megillat Paras* (Jerusalem: Tzur-Ot Press, 1975), pp. 59–60.

9. Philip D. Curtin, *Cross Cultural Trade in World History* (Cambridge: Cambridge University Press, 1984), pp. 193–94.

10. The English translation can be found in Richard F. Burton, trans., *The Book of the Thousand Nights and a Night: A Plain and Literal Translation of the Arabian Nights Entertainments*, vol. 6 (The Burton Club, n.d.), p. 5.

11. ᶜUthman Ibn Sanad, *Saba'ik al-ᶜAsjad*, folio 9.

12. Today branches of the Rizq family can be found in Basra, Kuwait, and Bombay.

13. *MSA*, Bussora Factory Diaries, no. 202, entry dated October 2, 1774, folio 279.

14. Mentioned in a report by the Dutch residents Tido von Kniphausen and Jan van der Hulst. See Willem Floor, "A Description of the Persian Gulf and Its Inhabitants in 1756" in *Persica*, no. 8, 1979, p. 179.

15. Serap Yılmaz, "Osmanlı Imparatorlugu'nun Dogu," p. 50.

16. Ashin Das Gupta, *Indian Merchants*, p. 92.

17. A complete translation of these tales can be found in Richard F. Burton, trans., *The Book of the Thousand Nights and a Night*.

18. Philip D. Curtin, *Cross-Cultural Trade*, pp. 192–93.

19. For information on this important Surati merchant, see Ashin Das Gupta, *Indian Merchants*, particularly Chapter 2.

20. *MSA*, Bussora Factory Diaries, no. 200, entry dated October 18, 1769, folio 112.

21. See, for example, the English agent's remarks concerning the importance of ibn Zayd's fleet to the internal trade of the Gulf in *MSA*, Bussora Factory Diaries, no. 195, entries dated January 12, 1766, and November 2, 1766.

22. See reference to Muḥammad "Nubby's" part ownership of the two Masqat ships, *al-Manṣuri* and *Safinat al-Nabi*, in *NAI*, Home Department, Public Branch, OC, no. 53, dated February 8, 1799.

23. *MSA*, Bussora Factory Diaries, no. 197, entry dated December 26, 1767.

24. *MSA*, Bussora Factory Diaries, no. 198, entry dated May 23, 1768, folio 257.

25. Similar observations were made by Andre Raymond in his study of eighteenth-century Cairo, and Ashin Das Gupta in his study of eighteenth-century Malabar. See Andre Raymond, "Les Sources de la Richesse Urbaine au Caire au Dix-huitieme Siecle" in Thomas Naff and Roger Owen, eds., *Studies in Eighteenth Century Islamic History* (Carbondale: Southern Illinois University Press, 1977), pp. 196–99; and Ashin Das Gupta, *Malabar in Asian Trade, 1740–1800* (Cambridge: Cambridge University Press, 1967), p. 106.

26. This list does not include Ḥajji Yusuf's substantial properties in Baghdad, the Gulf, and India.

27. A jarib was a unit of measurement for land usually used for date plantations. In Basra it was equivalent to 3,967 square meters. See Yusuf ᶜIzz al-Din's comment in Aḥmad Nur al-Anṣari, *al-Naṣrah fi Akhbar al-Baṣrah*, p. 50.

28. Probably one of the islands in Shaṭṭ al-ᶜArab.

29. *MSA*, Bussora Factory Diaries, no. 202, entry dated February 10, 1774, folio 106.

30. *IOR*, Letters from Basra, G/29/21, letter dated July 24, 1776, folio 237.

31. Sir Hermann Gollancz, *Chronicle of Events*, p. 523.

32. According to Rabbi Yaᶜqub Elyichar, who was an eyewitness to the occupation, the Armenians had to pay 18,000 tumans. See Meir Benayahu, *Rabbi Yaakob*, p. 47.

33. Both Ḥajji Bakr and Ḥajji Ibrahim were Sunni Arabs and members of the diwan. Prior to the Persian invasion they were considered among the wealthiest Muslim merchants in Basra. For members of the diwan in 1775 see *MSA*, Bussora Factory Diaries, no. 203, entry dated March 27, 1775, folio 68.

34. This refers to Shaykh Darwish al-Kawazi, the *Bash Aᶜyan* of Basra (see Chapter 1). "His people" probably means his many dependents, including peasants.

35. Carsten Niebuhr, *Voyage en Arabie*, p. 180.

36. Alexander Hamilton, *A New Account*, p. 55.

37. The nasi was the leader of the Jewish community. In eighteenth-century Iraq there were two nasis, one in Baghdad, the other in Basra. For the meaning and history of the title, see "Nasi" in *Encyclopaedia Judaica*, vol. 12 (Jerusalem: Keter Publishing House Ltd., 1971), pp. 834–35. For information on the nasis of Iraq, see David Sassoon, "The History of the Jews in Basra" in *The Jewish Quarterly Review*, vol. 17, 1926–27, p. 418; and Nissim Rejwan, *The Jews of Iraq: 3000 Years of History and Culture* (Boulder: Westview Press, 1985), pp. 177–85.

38. Mirza Abu Taleb Khan, *The Travels*, p. 364.

39. Hala Fattah, *The Politics of Regional Trade*, p. 87.

40. *IOR*, Letters from Basra, G/29/18, letter dated April 25, 1726.

41. Sir Hermann Gollancz, *Chronicle of Events*, p. 614.

42. *MSA*, Bussora Factory Records, no. 193, entry dated November 14, 1763.

43. James Tracy, "Introduction" in James Tracy, ed., *The Political Economy of Merchant Empires*, p. 10.

44. *MSA*, Bussora Factory Diaries, no. 193, entry dated May 1, 1764.

45. Ibid.

46. *BA*, DBŞM, BSH-1, sıra 25.

47. M. N. Pearson, "Merchants and States" in James Tracy, ed., *The Political Economy*, p. 57.

48. Michelgugliemo Torri, "Trapped Inside the Colonial Order: The Hindu Bankers of Surat and Their Business World During the Second Half of the Eighteenth Century" in *Modern Asian Studies*, vol. 25, no. 2, 1991, p. 371.

49. *MSA*, Bussora Factory Diaries, no. 203, entry dated December 22, 1777, folio 399.

50. *MSA*, Gombroon Factory Diaries, no. 116, entry dated April 13, 1753.

51. Serap Yılmaz, "Osmanlı Imparatorlugu'nun Dogu," p. 50.

52. Khawjah Dawud appears repeatedly in the sources. See, for example, *MSA*, Bussora Factory Diaries, no. 200, entries dated September 8, 1769, folio

47; January 19, 1770, folio 202; and April 3, 1770, folio 232.

53. The Dutch faced a similar problem in India, where the practice of selling on credit was the norm. See Ashin Das Gupta, *Malabar in Asian Trade*, p. 12.

54. Philip D. Curtin, *Cross-Cultural Trade*, p. 2.

55. Patricia Risso, *Merchants and Faith*, p. 71

56. On this question of the creation of harmony, although with broader reference, see Fredric Mauro's interesting conclusion to his article entitled "Merchant Communities, 1350–1750" in James Tracy, ed., *The Rise of Merchant Empires*, p. 286.

57. For the lack of merchant guilds in Venice, see ibid., p. 259. For Surat, see Ashin Das Gupta, *Indian Merchants*, pp. 86–87.

58. *IOR*, Letters from Basra, G/29/18, letter dated September 25, 1726; and *MSA*, Bussora Factory Diaries, no. 199, entry dated April 23, 1768, folio 141.

59. *MSA*, Gombroon Factory Diaries, no. 112, entry dated September 19, 1741.

60. *IOR*, Letters from Basra, G/29/19, letter dated May 11, 1747.

61. C. A. Bayly uses this term to describe the merchant family organizations of nineteenth-century northern India. See C. A. Bayly, *Rulers, Townsmen and Bazaars: North Indian Society in the Age of British Expansion, 1770–1870* (Cambridge: Cambridge University Press, 1983), pp. 369–427.

62. For the role that sectarianism played in Izmir (Smyrna) during this time, see Elena Frangakis-Syrett, *The Commerce of Smyrna*, p. 74. On the tensions between Hindus and Muslims in Surat, see Lakshmi Subramanian, "Capital and Crowd," pp. 205–37, and Michelgugliemo Torri, "Trapped Inside the Colonial Order," pp. 367–401.

63. Carsten Niebuhr, *Voyage en Arabie*, p. 180.

64. F. M. Donner, "Basra," pp. 851–55. For the Ottoman census of 1689, see *BA*, MM 5461, folio 51.

65. Mirza Abu Taleb Khan, *The Travels*, pp. 363–64.

66. For a good discussion of the debates concerning the organizational strengths of the European trading companies see Niels Steensgaard, *The Asian Trade Revolution*, pp. 114–53.

67. M. N. Pearson, "Merchants and States," p. 88.

68. Sir Denis Wright, "Samuel Manesty and His Unauthorised Embassy to the Court of Fath ʿAli Shah" in *Iran*, vol. 24, 1986, p. 153.

69. "Basra" in *Encyclopaedia Judaica*, vol. 4 (Jerusalem: Keter Publishing House Ltd., 1971), p. 310.

70. Ibid., p. 311.

71. "Bassora" in *The Jewish Encyclopedia*, vol. 2 (New York: KTAV Publishing House, n.d.), p. 586.

72. For the religious and political relations between the Jews of Baghdad

and Basra, see David Sassoon, *A History of the Jews of Baghdad* (Letchworth, 1949), pp. 129–32.

73. This holiday, also called "Shavuot," commemorates the giving of the Ten Commandments to Moses.

74. This tomb, referred to by the Arabs as al-ʿUzayr, is considered sacred by both Muslims and Jews. See Naval Intelligence Division, *Iraq and the Persian Gulf*, p. 332.

75. David Sassoon, "The History of the Jews in Basra," p. 442.

76. *MSA*, Bussora Factory Diaries, no. 197, entry dated February 2, 1768.

77. *MSA*, Bussora Factory Diaries, no. 194, entry dated April 4, 1764.

78. *MSA*, Bussora Factory Diaries, no. 198, entry dated June 21, 1768, folio 359.

79. *MSA*, Bussora Factory Diaries, no. 202, entry dated March 23, 1774, folio 149.

80. See Mohibbul Hasan's introduction in Khwaja Abdul Qadir, *Waqai-i Manazil-i*, p. 14.

81. Bruce Masters, *The Origins of Western Economic Dominance*, pp. 89–90.

82. Elena Frangakis-Syrett, *The Commerce of Smyrna*, pp. 80, 106.

83. Vatran Gregorian, "Minorities of Isfahan: The Armenian Community of Isfahan, 1587–1722" in *Iranian Studies*, vol. 7, part II, nos. 3–4, Summer–Autumn 1974, p. 670; R. W. Ferrier, "The Armenians and the East Indian Company in Persia in the Seventeenth and Early Eighteenth Centuries" in *The Economic History Review*, vol. 26, no. 1, February 1973, pp. 38–39; Vera B. Moreen, "The Status of Religious Minorities in Safavid Iran, 1617–61" in *Journal of Near Eastern Studies*, vol. 40, no. 2, April 1981, p. 129.

84. Charles Issawi, ed., *The Economic History of Iran, 1800–1914* (Chicago: University of Chicago Press, 1971), p. 12.

85. It is odd that Fredric Mauro fails to make any mention of the loss of Safavid patronage as a contributing cause to the decline of Armenian trade. See Fredric Mauro, "Merchant Communities," p. 274.

86. Elena Frangakis-Syrett, *The Commerce of Smyrna*, pp. 107–8.

87. Ashin Das Gupta, *Indian Merchants*, p. 136.

88. See, for example, the reference made in Sir Hermann Gollancz, *Chronicle of Events*, p. 346.

89. *IOR*, Letters from Basra, G/29/18, letter dated August 14, 1729.

90. *MSA*, Bussora Factory Diaries, no. 193, entry dated September 30, 1763.

91. See, for example, the entry concerning Sulayman ibn Dawud in *MSA*, Bussora Factory Diaries, no. 196, entry dated July 17, 1767.

92. This was also true with respect to the Armenian control of the trade between Baghdad and Aleppo. See Tom Nieuwenhuis, *Politics and Society*, p. 72.

93. See Bruce Masters, *The Origins of Western Economic Dominance*, pp. 84–85.

94. Serap Yılmaz, "Osmanlı Imparatorlugu'nun Dogu," p. 36.

95. For ᶜAli Bey's expedition to Syria, see P. M. Holt, *Egypt and the Fertile Crescent*, p. 97. For the reaction of the Armenians of Basra, see *MSA*, Bussora Factory Diaries, no. 201, entry dated August 9, 1771, folio 9.

96. See, for example, *MSA*, Bussora Factory Diaries, no. 200, entry dated November 23, 1769, folio 126.

97. See Chapter 3, p. 000.

98. Ashin Das Gupta, *Indian Merchants*, p. 76.

99. *BA*, DBŞM, BSH-1, sıra 25.

100. Khwaja Abdul Qadir, *Waqai-i Manazil-i*, pp. 51–52.

101. Ashin Das Gupta, *Indian Merchants*, p. 214.

102. *MSA*, Bussora Factory Diaries, no. 201, entry dated September 17, 1772, folio 231.

103. *MSA*, Gombroon Factory Diaries, no. 114, entries dated December 24, 1748, and January 24, 1749.

104. *MSA*, Gombroon Factory Diaries, no. 112, entry dated September 19, 1741.

CHAPTER 5. THE MERCHANTS AND POWER

1. It is not clear why Tom Nieuwenhuis, *Politics and Society*, refers to the Ottoman-Persian conflict only in passing when discussing the contradictions that affected the nature of mamluk rule in Iraq. Most historians, on the other hand, consider this conflict essential for understanding the mamluk period. See, for example, Stephen Hemsley Longrigg, *Four Centuries*; ᶜAli al-Wardi, *Lamaḥat Ijtimaᶜiyyah*; ᶜAbbas al-ᶜAzawi, *Tarikh al-ᶜIraq Bayn 'Iḥtilalayn*; ᶜAli Shakir ᶜAli, *Tarikh al-ᶜIraq fi al-ᶜAhd al-ᶜUthmani*.

2. ᶜAli al-Wardi, *Lamahat Ijtimaᶜiyyah*, pp. 17–21, in particular, believes this to be the single most important feature of Iraqi society in the eighteenth century.

3. Tom Nieuwenhuis, *Politics and Society*, p. 169.

4. *MSA*, Gombroon Factory Inward Letter Book, no. 40, letter dated December 7, 1743.

5. ᶜAli Shakir ᶜAli, *Tarikh al-ᶜIraq fi al-ᶜAḥd al-ᶜUthmani*, p. 115.

6. Karl Barbir, *Ottoman Rule in Damascus, 1708–1758* (Princeton: Princeton University Press, 1980), p. 179.

7. Elena Frangakis-Syrett, *The Commerce of Smyrna*, p. 61.

8. Hala Fattah, *The Politics of Regional Trade*, p. 40.

9. M. N. Pearson, "Merchants and States," p. 97.

10. Tom Nieuwenhuis, *Politics and Society*, p. 47.

11. See, for example, the numerous gumruk muqaṭaᶜat held by Mustafa Pasha and his officials at Basra in 1710 in *BA*, DBŞM, no. 16791.

12. Tom Nieuwenhuis, *Politics and Society*, p. 47.

13. In this regard, see *IOR*, Letters from Basra, G/29/19, letter dated October 20, 1739.

14. *IOR*, Letters from Basra, G/29/21, letters dated October 14, 1779, folios 364–365, and December 5, 1779, folios 368–369.

15. *MSA*, Secret & Political Department, no. 36, entry dated September 16, 1787.

16. *MSA*, Bussora Factory Diaries, no. 200, entry dated October 10, 1769, folio 91.

17. A lack is a Hindi word meaning one hundred thousand. See Henry Yule and A. C. Burnell, *Hobson-Jobson*, p. 500.

18. *MSA*, Bussora Factory Diaries, no. 200, entry dated October 18, 1769, folio 112.

19. Not to be confused with Sulayman Agha, who later became the wali of Baghdad. See Chapter 2, pp. 000–000.

20. *MSA*, Bussora Factory Diaries, no. 199, entry dated December 3, 1768, folio 214.

21. *MSA*, Bussora Factory Diaries, no. 199, entry dated July 31, 1769, folio 459.

22. *MSA*, Bussora Factory Diaries, no. 199, entry dated April 12, 1769, folio 337.

23. See *MSA*, Bussora Factory Diaries, no. 200, entry dated October 16, 1769, folio 104.

24. The names, for example, of Ḥajji Qasim al-Samiri and his son, Ḥajji Muṣṭafa, appear at the head of a list of prominent aᶜyan called in by the qaḍi, in 1707, to act as witnesses in a case relating to customs collection. See *BA*, DBŞM, BSH-1, sıra 22.

25. *IOR*, Letters from Basra, G/29/19, letter dated March 6, 1749.

26. *MSA*, Bussora Factory Outward Letter Book, no. 30, letter dated September 22, 1724.

27. *MSA*, Bussora Factory Diaries, no. 193, entry dated June 16, 1763.

28. See Chapter 1, pp. 000–000.

29. *MSA*, Bussora Factory Diaries, no. 193, entries dated July 26 and 28, 1764.

30. See, for example, *MSA*, Bussora Factory Diaries, no. 199, entries dated April 11, 1769, folio 334, April 12, 1769, folio 337 and June 22, 1769, folio 367.

31. *MSA*, Bussora Factory Diaries, no. 200, entry dated December 19, 1769, folio 165.

32. *MSA*, Bussora Factory Diaries, no. 199, entry dated August 21, 1768, folio 47.

33. *MSA*, Bussora Factory Diaries, no. 198, entry dated March 30, 1768, folios 84–85.

34. See Chapter 3, pp. 000–000.

35. Lakshmi Subramanian, "Capital and Crowd," p. 210.

36. Quoted in Lakshmi Subramanian, "The Eighteenth-Century Social Order in Surat," p. 339.

37. Information on the case of Muḥammad Agha can be found in Sir Hermann Gollancz, *Chronicle of Events*, pp. 629–33.

38. *MSA*, Bussora Factory Diaries, no. 193, entry dated July 13, 1763.

39. *MSA*, Gombroon Factory Diaries, no. 118, entry dated May 25, 1757.

40. Ibid. English woolens, at this time, were in great demand by armies all over the region. There are many references to Persian merchants concluding similar deals with the English to supply Karim Khan's forces. See, for example, *MSA*, Bussora Factory Diaries, no. 198, entries dated June 5 and July 9, 1768, folios 295 and 363.

41. *MSA*, Bussora Factory Diaries, no. 193, entry dated August 15, 1763.

42. *MSA*, Bussora Factory Diaries, no. 193, entry dated June 26, 1763.

43. *MSA*, Bussora Factory Diaries, no. 193, entry dated August 15, 1763.

44. *MSA*, Bussora Factory Diaries, no. 193, entry dated May 24, 1763.

45. *MSA*, Bussora Factory Diaries, no. 193, entry dated August 26, 1763.

46. *MSA*, Bussora Factory Diaries, no. 193, entries dated August 11, 17, and 26, 1763.

47. *MSA*, Bussora Factory Diaries, no. 193, entry dated September 17, 1763.

48. Ibid.

49. *MSA*, Bussora Factory Diaries, no. 193, entry dated August 11, 1763.

50. *MSA*, Bussora Factory Diaries, no. 198, entry dated May 17, 1768, folio 244.

51. *MSA*, Bussora Factory Diaries, no. 198, entry dated May 17, 1768, folio 243; and no. 199, entry dated August 3, 1768.

52. See Chapter 2, pp. 000–000.

53. See Carsten Niebuhr, *Voyage en Arabie*, pp. 178–79.

54. *MSA*, Bussora Factory Diaries, no. 193, entry dated January 15, 1764.

55. For the effects of British economic penetration in the nineteenth century, see Muḥammad Salman Ḥasan, *al-Taṭawwur al-'Iqtiṣadi fi al-ᶜIraq: al-Tijarah al-Kharijiyyah wa al-Taṭawwur al-'Iqtiṣadi, 1864–1958* (Sidon, 1965); Roger Owen, *The Middle East*, Chapters 7 and 11; and Charles Issawi, *The Economic History of the Middle East*, part III.

56. *MSA*, Bussora Factory Diaries, no. 198, entry dated May 17, 1768, folio 243.

57. The two English representatives most notorious for their political involvement were Samuel Manesty at Basra and James Claudius Rich at Baghdad. The first was prominent during the end of Sulayman the Great's

government (1780–1802), and the second was active during Dawud Pasha's time (1817–31). Both repeatedly clashed with the wali. We deal with Manesty's role shortly. For J. C. Rich, see Tom Nieuwenhuis, *Politics and Society*, p. 82.

58. Nissim Rejwan, *The Jews of Iraq*, p. 167; and "Basra," p. 311.

59. See Nissim Rejwan, *The Jews of Iraq*, p. 168; and David Sassoon, "The History of the Jews in Basra," p. 422.

60. Tom Nieuwenhuis, *Politics and Society*, p. 73.

61. *MSA*, Bussora Factory Diaries, no. 193, entry dated June 10, 1763.

62. See Vatran Gregorian, *Minorities of Isfahan*, pp. 654–56.

63. For an account of Gabbai's role during the siege, see *IOR*, Letters from Basra, G/29/21, letter dated October 28, 1776, folio 239; and Meir Benayahu, *Rabbi Yaakob Elyichar*, pp. 39–53.

64. Meir Benayahu, *Rabbi Yaakob Elyichar*, p. 72; David Sassoon, "The History of the Jews in Basra," p. 435; and "Basra," p. 311.

65. David Sassoon, "The History of the Jews in Basra," p. 434.

66. *IOR*, Letters from Basra, G/29/22, letter dated July 5, 1791, folio 663.

67. Lewis A. Coser, "The Alien as a Servant of Power: Court Jews and Christian Renegades" in *American Sociological Review*, vol. 37, October 1972, p. 574.

68. Ibid., p. 576.

69. Mir ᶜAbdul-Laṭif al-Shustari, *Tuhfat al-ᶜAlam*, p. 211; and Khwaja Abdul Qadir, *Waqai-i Manazil-i Rum*, p. 55.

70. *IOR*, Letters from Basra, G/29/22, letter dated April 2, 1791, folios 635–636 and *passim*.

71. Vatran Gregorian, "Minorities of Isfahan," p. 671.

72. *MSA*, Bussora Factory Outward Letter Book, no. 30, letter dated September 22, 1724.

73. *IOR*, Letters from Basra, G/29/21, letter dated August 31, 1783, folio 527.

74. *MSA*, Gombroon Factory Diaries, no. 117, entry dated July 17, 1754.

75. As mentioned earlier, the particulars of this case are recorded in *IOR*, Letters from Basra, G/29/22, letters dated April 2, 1791, folios 635–636, April 8, 1791, folios 636–637, and July 5, 1791, folios 663–666.

76. Sir Denis Wright, "Samuel Manesty and His Unauthorised Embassy to the Court of Fath ᶜAli Shah" in *Iran*, vol. 24, 1986, p. 153.

77. Ibid.

78. *IOR*, Letters from Basra, G/29/22, letter dated July 5, 1791, folio 664.

79. Ibid.

80. *IOR*, Letters from Basra, G/29/22, letter dated February 7, 1792, folio 680.

81. Tom Nieuwenhuis, *Politics and Society*, p. 74.

82. *IOR*, Letters from Basra, G/29/22, January 31, 1793, folio 739.

83. J. G. Lorimer, *Gazetteer of the Persian Gulf*, p. 1289.

84. *MSA*, Bussora Factory Diaries, no. 199, entry dated July 22, 1769, folio 445.

85. *MSA*, Secret and Political Department, no. 36, entry dated September 16, 1787.

86. *MSA*, Bussora Factory Diaries, no. 193, entry dated April 23, 1764.

87. *MSA*, Secret and Political Department, no. 36, entry dated September 16, 1787. The French consul's remarks on this event, which corroborate those of the English, can be found in Willem Floor, "La Revolte des Muntafiqs en 1787—une Nouvelle Source" in *Zeitschrift der Deutschen Morgenlandischen Gesellschaft*, vol. 135, no. 1, 1985, p. 56.

88. J. G. Lorimer, *Gazetteer of the Persian Gulf*, p. 1275.

89. Ibid.

90. *IOR*, Letters from Basra, G/29/22, letter dated October 23, 1788, folios 491–493.

91. *IOR*, Letters from Basra, G/29/22, letter dated January 24, 1789.

92. *MSA*, Secret and Political Department, no. 36, entry dated September 16, 1787, folio 426.

93. *IOR*, Letters from Basra, G/29/22, letter dated July 5, 1791, folio 663.

94. The competitive relationship between the Jews and the British which Hanna Batatu observed in the nineteenth and early twentieth centuries might have had part of its roots in this conflict. See Hanna Batatu, *The Old Social Classes*, pp. 247–49.

95. Ibrahim Faṣiḥ al-Ḥaydari. *ʿUnwan al-Majd*, pp. 164–69.

96. Aḥmad Nur al-Anṣari, *al-Naṣrah fi Akhbar al-Baṣrah*, pp. 36–39.

97. J. G. Lorimer, *Gazetteer of the Persian Gulf*, p. 1290.

98. Ibid., p. 1289.

99. Stephen Hemsley Longrigg, *Four Centuries*, pp. 254–57.

CONCLUSION

1. C. A. Bayly, *Imperial Meridian*, pp. 54, 55.

2. Immanuel Wallerstein, Hale Decdeli, and Resat Kasaba, "The Incorporation of the Ottoman Empire," p. 95.

3. For a good review and critique of the Eastern Question paradigm, see M. E. Yapp, *The Making of the Modern Near East*, Chapter 2.

4. C. A. Bayly, "India and West Asia," p. 19.

BIBLIOGRAPHY

ARCHIVAL SOURCES

1. India Office Records, London

Original Correspondence: E/3/64, E/3/65.

Persia Factory Records, Letters from Basra: G/29/18, G/29/19, G/29/20, G/29/21, G/29/22.

Miscellaneous Correspondence with Agents in Turkish Arabia: G/29/25, 1769–81.

Manesty, Samuel, and Harvard Jones. *Report on the British Trade with Persia and Arabia*, G/29/25, 1791.

2. National Archives of India, New Delhi

Public Records Department, Consultations dated: May 5, 1755, no. 531; June 13, 1757, no. 851; March 3, 1758, no. 1003; June 16, 1768, no. L; December 6, 1773, no. 14.

Foreign Department, Consultations dated: November 26, 1773, no. 3; March 8, 1775, no. 3; July 10, 1775, no. 8; March 13, 1781, no. 7; April 8, 1782, nos. 1–3.

Home Department, Public Branch, Consultations dated: June 7, 1773, nos. 4–7; June 9, 1773, no. 2; December 18, 1775, no. 9; October 4, 1779, no. 1; April 28, 1783, nos. 8, 19; October 19, 1784, no. 8; November 8, 1784, no. 1; April 25, 1785, no. 17; August 3, 1785, no. 5; October 31, 1787, no. 1; May 2, 1788, no. 18; May 26, 1788, no. 3; April 22, 1789, no. 28.

3. Maharashtra State Archives, Bombay

Bussora Factory Outward Letter Book: no. 30.

Secretariat Inward Letter Book: nos. 3, 4, 5.

Gombroon Factory Outward Letter Book: no.4 0.

Gombroon Factory Diaries: nos. 112, 113, 114, 115, 116, 117, 118.

Bussora Factory Diaries: nos. 193, 194, 195, 196, 197, 198, 199, 200, 201, 202, 203, 204.

Secret and Political Department: nos. 15, 31, 36, 38, 45, 49.

4. Başbakanlık Arşivi, Istanbul

Maliyeden Müdevver: nos. 3392, 4879, 5461, 10145, 10147, 10148, 10149, 10150, 10151, 10152, 10157, 10160, 10164, 10166, 10168, 10171, 10172, 10173, 10174, 10199, 10205, 10211, 10219, 10222, 10224, 10226, 10231, 10234, 10306, 10307.

Bab-ı Defteri, Başmuhasebe Kalemi, no. 16791,
Basra Hazinesi-1, Gömlek Sıra, nos. 2, 20, 22, 23, 25, 27, 29.
Basra Hazinesi-2, Gömlek Sıra, nos. 12, 82.
Basra Hazinesi-3, Gömlek Sıra, no. 106.

UNPUBLISHED MANUSCRIPTS

Ibn ᶜAlwan, Fatḥallah. *Zad al-Musafir*. British Museum, Add. 23, 450.
Al-Baṣri, ᶜUthman Ibn Sanad. *Kitab Saba'ik al-ᶜAsjad fi Akhbar Aḥmad Najl Rizq al-Asᶜad*. British Museum, Or.7565.
al-Shustari, Mir ᶜAbdul-Laṭif. *Tuḥfat al-ᶜAlam*. National Museum of India.

PUBLISHED WORKS

Aba Ḥusayn, ᶜAli. "al-ᶜIlaqat al-Tarikhiyyah Bayn al-Baḥrayn wa al-Hind." In *al-Wathiqah*, no. 17, July 1990, pp. 70–103.
al-ᶜAbbasi, ᶜAbdul-Qadir Bash Aᶜyan. *al-Nakhlah, Sayyidat al-Shajar*. Baghdad: al-Baṣri Publishers, 1964.
———. *al-Baṣrah fi Adwariha al-Tarikhiyyah*. Baghdad: al-Baṣri Publishers, 1961.
al-ᶜAbid, Saliḥ Muḥammad. "al-Niḍam al-'Idari." In *Ḥaḍarat al-ᶜIraq*. vol. 10. Baghdad: Dar al-Ḥurriyyah, 1985, pp. 7–36.
Abu Hakima, Ahmad Mustafa. *History of Eastern Arabia 1750–1800: The Rise and Development of Bahrain and Kuwait*. Beirut: Khayats, 1965.
———. *The Modern History of Kuwait, 1750–1965*. London: Luzac & Co. Ltd., 1983.
———. "Banu Kaᶜb." In *The Encyclopaedia of Islam*. Vol. 6. Leiden: E. J. Brill, 1978, p. 314.
Adamov, Alexander. *Wilayat al-Baṣrah fi Maḍiha wa Ḥaḍiriha*. Vol. 1. Translated by Hashim Ṣaliḥ al-Tikriti. Publication of the Center for Arabian Gulf Studies in Basra University, 1982.
ᶜAli, ᶜAli Shakir. *Tarikh al-ᶜIraq fi al-ᶜAhd al-ᶜUthmani, 1638–1750: Dirasah fi Aḥwalihi al-Siyasiyyah*. Naynawa: 30 Tamuz Publishers, 1984.
Allen, Calvin H. "The Indian Merchant Community of Masqat." In *Bulletin of the School of Oriental and African Studies*, vol. 44, part 1, 1981, pp. 39–53.

———. "The State of Masqat in the Gulf and East Africa, 1785–1829." In *International Journal of Middle East Studies*, no. 2, vol. 14, May 1982, pp. 117–27.

Amin, ᶜAbdul-Amir. *al-Qiwa al-Baḥriyyah fi al-Khalij al-ᶜArabi*. Baghdad: Asᶜad Printers, 1966.

al-Anṣari, Aḥmad Nur. *al-Naṣrah fi Akhbar al-Baṣrah*. Baghdad: al-Shaᶜb Press, 1976.

Arasaratnam, S. "Recent Trends in the Historiography of the Indian Ocean, 1500 to 1800." In *Journal of World History*, vol. 1, no. 2, 1990, pp. 225–48.

———. "India and the Indian Ocean in the Seventeenth Century." In Ashin Das Gupta and M. N. Pearson, eds. *India and the Indian Ocean, 1500–1800*. Oxford: Oxford University Press, 1987, pp. 94–130.

Austen, Ralph A. "The 19th Century Islamic Slave Trade From East Africa (Swahili and Red Sea Coasts): A Tentative Census." In *Slavery & Abolition*, vol. 9, no. 3, December 1988, pp. 21–44.

Awad, Abdul Aziz M. "The Gulf in the Seventeenth Century." In *British Society for Middle Eastern Studies Bulletin*, vol. 12, no. 2, 1985, pp. 123–35.

al-ᶜAzzawi, ᶜAbbas. *Tarikh al-ᶜIraq Bayn 'Iḥtilalayn, al-Juz' al-Sadis: Ḥukumat al-Mamalik*. Baghdad: al-Tijarah wa al-Ṭibaᶜah Ltd., 1954.

Barbir, Karl. *Ottoman Rule in Damascus, 1708–1758*. Princeton: Princeton University Press, 1980.

Barendse, Rene J. "The East India Companies in the Indian Ocean, XVIth–XVIIIth Century Some General Problems." In *Moyen Orient & Ocean Indien*, vol. 7, 1990, pp. 13–26.

"Basra." In *Encyclopaedia Judaica*. Vol. 4. Jerusalem: Keter Publishing House Ltd., 1971, pp. 310–11.

"Bassora." In *The Jewish Encyclopedia*. Vol. 2. New York: KTAV Publishing House, n.d., p. 586.

Batatu, Hanna. *The Old Social Classes and the Revolutionary Movements of Iraq: A Study of Iraq's Old Landed and Commercial Classes and of its Communists, Baᶜthists, and Free Officers*. Princeton: Princeton University Press, 1978.

Bayly, C. A. *Rulers, Townsmen and Bazaars: North Indian Society in the Age of British Expansion, 1770–1870*. Cambridge: Cambridge University Press, 1983.

———. *Imperial Meridian: The British Empire and the World, 1780–1830*. New York: Longman Press, 1989.

———. "India and West Asia, c.1700–1830." In *Asian Affairs*, vol. 19, February 1988, pp. 3–19.

al-Bazi, Ḥamid. "Min Turathiyat Ma Shamalathu Makramat al-Sayyid al-Ra'is al-Qa'id fi Ḥamlat 'Iᶜmar al-Baṣrah." In *al-Turath al-Shaᶜbi*, no. 3, Summer 1989, pp. 160–76.

Beawes, William. "Remarks and Occurrences in a Journey from Aleppo to Bassora by the Way of the Desert." In Douglas Carruthers, ed. *The Desert Route to India, Being the Journals of Four Travellers by the Great Desert Caravan Route Between Aleppo and Basra, 1745–1751.* London, 1929, pp. 5–40.

Belgrave, Charles. *The Pirate Coast.* Beirut: Libraire du Liban, 1972.

Benayahu, Meir. *Rabbi Yaakob Elyichar and His Megillat Paras.* Jerusalem: Tzur-Ot Press, 1975.

Boxhall, Peter. "The Diary of a Mocha Coffee Agent." In R. B. Serjeant and R. L. Bidwell, eds. *Arabian Studies*, vol. 1, 1974, pp. 102–15.

Burton, Richard F. *The Book of the Thousand Nights and a Night: A Plain and Literal Translation of the Arabian Nights Entertainments.* Vol. 6. Translated and annotated by Richard F. Burton. The Burton Club, n.d.

al-Bustani, Mahdi. "Watha'iq ᶜUthmaniyyah Ghayr Manshurah ᶜan al-Baṣrah wa 'Usṭuliha wa Ṣilatiha b-il-Khalij al-ᶜArabi 'Awasiṭ al-Qirn al-Tasiᶜ ᶜAshar." In *al-Wathiqah*, no. 17, July, 1990.

The Cambridge Ancient History. Vol. I, part II. Cambridge: Cambridge University Press, 1971.

Carmichael, John. "Narrative of a Journey From Aleppo to Basra in 1751." In Douglas Carruthers, ed. *The Desert Route to India, Being the Journals of Four Travellers by the Great Desert Caravan Route Between Aleppo and Basra, 1745–1751.* London, 1929, pp. 135–79.

Carruthers, Douglas, ed. *The Desert Route to India, Being the Journals of Four Travellers by the Great Desert Caravan Route Between Aleppo and Basra, 1745–1751.* London, 1929.

Chandra, Satish, ed. *The Indian Ocean: Explorations in History, Commerce and Politics.* New Delhi: Sage Publishers, 1987.

Chaudhuri, K. N. *Trade and Civilization in the Indian Ocean: An Economic History from the Rise of Islam to 1750.* New Delhi: Munshiram Manoharlal Publications, 1985.

———. *Asia Before Europe: Economy and Civilization of the Indian Ocean from the Rise of Islam to 1750.* Cambridge: Cambridge University Press, 1990.

———. "India's International Economy in the Nineteenth Century: An Historical Survey." In *Modern Asia Studies*, vol. 2, 1968, pp. 31–50.

Clarence-Smith, William Gervase. "The Economics of the Indian Ocean Slave Trades in the 19th Century: An Overview." In *Slavery & Abolition*, vol. 9, no. 3, December 1988, pp. 1–20.

Cohen, Amon. *Palestine in the Eighteenth Century: Patterns of Government and Administration.* Jerusalem: The Magnes Press, 1973.

Coser, Lewis A. "The Alien as a Servant of Power: Court Jews and Christian Renegades." In *American Sociological Review*, vol. 37, October 1972, pp. 574–81.

Curtin, Philip D. *Cross-Cultural Trade in World History*. Cambridge: Cambridge University Press, 1984.

Das Gupta, Ashin. *Malabar in Asian Trade, 1740–1800*. Cambridge: Cambridge University Press, 1967.

———. *Indian Merchants and the Decline of Surat, c. 1700–1750*. Wiesbaden: Franz Steiner Verlag, 1979.

———. "India and the Indian Ocean in the Eighteenth Century." In Ashin Das Gupta and M. N. Pearson, eds. *India and the Indian Ocean, 1500–1800*. Oxford: Oxford University Press, 1987, pp. 131–61.

———. "Gujarati Merchants and the Red Sea Trade, 1700–1725." In Blair King and M. N. Pearson, eds. *The Age of Partnership: Europeans in Asia Before Dominion*. Honolulu: University of Hawaii, 1979, pp. 123–58.

Davis, Ralph. *Aleppo and Devonshire Square, English Traders in the Levant in the Eighteenth Century*. London: Macmillan, 1967.

al-Dilayshi, ᶜAbd al-Laṭif. "Kalimah fi al-Adab al-Shaᶜbi fi al-Baṣrah." In *al-Turath al-Shaᶜbi*, no. 3, Summer 1989, pp. 185–201.

Donner, Fred. *The Early Islamic Conquests*. Princeton: Princeton University Press, 1981.

———. "Basra." In *Encyclopaedia Iranica*. London: Routledge & Kegan Paul, 1989, pp. 851–55.

Dresch, Paul. *Tribes, Government, and History in Yemen*. Oxford: Clarendon Press, 1989.

Drower, Lady Ethel. *The Mandaeans of Iraq and Iran: Their Cults, Customs, Magic, Legends, and Folklore*. London, 1962.

Dubuisson, Patricia R. "Qasimi Piracy and the General Treaty of Peace (1820)." In *Arabian Studies*, no. 4, 1978, pp. 47–57.

El-Ashban, Abdul Aziz. "The Formation of the Omani Trading Empire Under the Yaᶜaribah Dynasty (1624–1719)." In *Arab Studies Quarterly*, vol. 1, no. 4, 1979, pp. 354–71.

Emin, Joseph. *The Life and Adventures of Joseph Emin, 1726–1809*. London, 1792.

Fattah, Hala. *The Politics of Regional Trade in Iraq, Arabia and the Gulf, 1745–1900*. Albany: State University of New York Press, 1997.

Ferrier, R. W. "The Armenians and the East India Company in Persia in the Seventeenth and Early Eighteenth Centuries." In *Economic History Review*, vol. 26, no. 1, February 1973, pp. 38–62.

Floor, Willem. "Dutch Trade With Masqat in the Second Half of the Eighteenth Century." In *Asian and African Studies*, vol. 16, 1982, pp. 197–213.

———. "The Decline of the Dutch East Indies Company in Bandar 'Abbas (1747–1759)." In *Moyen Orient & Ocean Indien*, vol. 6, 1989, pp. 45–80.

———. "The Customs in Qajar Iran." In *Zeitschrift der Deutschen Morgenlandischen Gesellschaft*, vol. 126, no. 2, 1976, pp. 281–311.

———. "The Iranian Navy in the Gulf During the Eighteenth Century." In *Iranian Studies*, vol. 20, no. 1, 1987, pp. 31–53.

———. "Pearl Fishing in the Persian Gulf in 1757." In *Persica*, no. 10, 1982, pp. 209–22.

———. "Dutch Trade With Masqat in the Second Half of the Eighteenth Century." In *Asian and African Studies*, vol. 16, 1982, pp. 197–213.

———. "The Bahrain Project of 1754." In *Persica*, vol. 11, 1984, pp. 129–48.

———. "The Merchants (*tujjar*) in Qajjar Iran." In *Zeitschrift der Deutschen Morgenlandischen Gesellschaft*, vol. 126, no. 1, 1976, pp. 101–35.

———. "A Description of the Persian Gulf and Its Inhabitants in 1756." In *Persica*, no. 8, 1979, pp. 163–85.

———. "Pearl Fishing in the Persian Gulf in 1757." In *Persica*, no. 10, 1982, pp. 209–22.

———. "The Dutch East India Company's Trade With Sind in the 17th and 18th Centuries." In *Moyen Orient & Ocean Indien / Middle East & Indian Ocean, XVIe–XIXe s.*, vol. 2, no. 1, 1985, pp. 111–44.

———. "A Report on the Trade in Jedda in the 1730s: Introduction and Translation." In *Moyen Orient et Ocean Indien*, vol. 5, 1988, pp. 161–73.

———. "La Revolte des Muntafiqs en 1787—une Nouvelle Source." In *Zeitschrift der Deutschen Morgenlandischen Gesellschaft*, vol. 135, no. 1, 1985, pp. 55–59.

———. "The Dutch on Khark Island: A Commercial Mishap." In *IJMES*, vol. 24, no. 3, August 1992, pp. 441–60.

Frangakis-Syrett, Elena. *The Commerce of Smyrna in the Eighteenth Century, 1700–1820*. Athens: Centre for Asia Minor Studies, 1992.

Furber, Holden. *Rival Empires of Trade in the Orient, 1600–1800*. Minneapolis: University of Minnesota Press, 1976.

Genc, Mehmet. "A Study of the Feasibility of Using Eighteenth-Century Ottoman Financial Records as an Indicator of Economic Activity." In Huri Islamoglu-Inan, ed. *The Ottoman Empire and the World Economy*. Cambridge: Cambridge University Press, 1987, pp. 345–73.

Ghumaymah, Yusuf Rizq Allah. *Nuzhat al-Mushtaq fi Tarikh Yahud al-ᶜIraq*. London: Al-Warrak Publishing, 1997.

Glamann, Kristof. *Dutch-Asiatic Trade, 1620–1740*. The Hague: Martinus Nijhoff, 1958.

Gollancz, Sir Hermann. *Chronicle of Events Between the Years 1623 and 1733 Relating to the Settlement of the Order of Carmelites in Mesopotamia*. London: Oxford University Press, 1927.

Gordon, Murray. *Slavery in the Arab World*. New York: New Amsterdam Books, 1989.

Government of Iraq. *Maps of Iraq with Notes for Visitors*. Baghdad, 1929.

Grant, Christina P. *The Syrian Desert, Caravans, Travel and Exploration*. London: A&C Black Ltd., 1937.

Gregorian, Vartan. "Minorities of Isfahan: The Armenian Community of Isfahan, 1587–1722." In *Iranian Studies*, vol. 7, part 2, nos. 3–4, Summer–Autumn 1974, pp. 652–80.

Grummon, Stephen R. "The Rise and Fall of the Arab Shaykhdom of Bushire: 1750–1850." Unpublished Ph.D. dissertation, Johns Hopkins University, 1985.

Hambly, Gavin. "An Introduction to the Economic Organization of Early Qajar Iran." In *Iran*, vol. 2, 1964, pp. 69–81.

Hamilton, Alexander. *A New Account of the East Indies*. London: Argonaut Press, 1930.

Ḥasan, Muḥammad Salman. *al-Taṭawwur al-'Iqtiṣadi fi al-ᶜIraq: al-Tijarah al-Kharijiyyah wa al-Taṭawwur al-'Iqtiṣadi, 1864–1958*. Sidon, 1965.

———. "The Role of Foreign Trade in the Economic Development of Iraq, 1864–1964: A Study in the Growth of a Dependent Economy." In M. A. Cook, ed. *Studies in the Economic History of the Middle East, from the Rise of Islam to the Present Day*. London: Oxford University Press, 1970, pp. 346–72.

al-Ḥaydari, Ibrahim Faṣiḥ. *ᶜUnwan al-Majd fi Bayan Aḥwal Baghdad wa al-Baṣrah wa Nadj*. Baghdad: al-Baṣri Publishers, 1962.

———. *Aḥwal al-Baṣrah*. Baghdad: al-Baṣrah Publishers, 1961.

Heude, William. *A Voyage Up the Persian Gulf and a Journey Overland From India to England in 1817*. London: Longman, 1819.

Hodgson, Marshall G. S. *The Venture of Islam, Conscience and History in a World Civilization*. Volume 3: *The Gunpowder Empires and Modern Times*. Chicago: University of Chicago Press, 1974.

Holt, P. M. *Egypt and the Fertile Crescent 1516–1922: A Political History*. Ithaca: Cornell University Press, 1966.

———. *The Age of the Crusades: The Near East from the Eleventh Century to 1517*. New York: Longman, 1987.

Hourani, Albert. "Ottoman Reform and the Politics of Notables." In W. Polk and R. Chambers, eds. *Beginnings of Modernization in the Middle East*. Chicago, 1968, pp. 41–68.

Hourani, George. *Arab Seafaring in the Indian Ocean in Ancient and Early Medieval Times*. Princeton: Princeton University Press, 1951.

Ibn al-Ghimlas. *Wilat al-Baṣrah wa Mutasallimuha*. Baghdad: al-Baṣri Publishers, 1962.

Ibn Ruzayq, Ḥamid ibn Muḥammad. *History of the Imams and Seyyids of ᶜOman by Salilibn-Razik, from A.D. 661–1856*. London: Hakluyt Society, no. 43, 1871.

Inalcik, Halil. *The Ottoman Empire: The Classical Age, 1300–1600*. New York: Weidenfeld & Nicolson, 1973.

———, and Donald Quataert, eds. *An Economic and Social History of the Ottoman Empire, 1300–1914*. New York: Cambridge University Press, 1994.

Ingram, Edward. "From Trade to Empire in the Near East—III: The Uses of the Residency at Baghdad, 1794–1804." *Middle East Studies*, vol. 14, no. 3, October 1978, pp. 278–306.

Islamoglu-Inan, Huri, ed. *The Ottoman Empire and the World Economy*. Cambridge: Cambridge University Press, 1988.

———. "Introduction: 'Oriental Despotism' in World-System Perspective." In Huri Islamoglu-Inan, ed. *The Ottoman Empire and the World Economy*. Cambridge: Cambridge University Press, 1988, pp. 1–24.

Issawi, Charles, ed. *The Economic History of the Middle East, 1800–1914*. Chicago: University of Chicago Press, 1966.

———, ed. *The Fertile Crescent, 1800–1914: A Documentary Economic History*. Oxford: Oxford University Press, 1988.

———, ed. *The Economic History of Iran, 1800–1914*. Chicago: University of Chicago Press, 1971.

Ives, Edward. *A Voyage from England to India in the Year MDCCLIV*. London, 1773.

ᶜIzz al-Din, Yusuf. *Dawud Basha wa Nihayat al-Mamalik fi al-ᶜIraq*. Baghdad: al-Shaᶜb Press, 1976.

al-Janabi, Ṭariq. "al-ᶜImarah al-ᶜIraqiyyah." In *Ḥaḍarat al-ᶜIraq*. Vol. 10. Baghdad: Dar al-Ḥurriyyah lil-Ṭibaᶜah, 1985, pp. 243–370.

Jwaideh, Albertine, and J. W. Cox. "The Black Slaves of Turkish Arabia During the 19th Century." In *Slavery & Abolition*, vol. 9, no. 3, December 1988, pp. 45–59.

al-Karkukli, Rasul. *Dawḥat al-Wizara' fi Tarikh Waqa'iᶜ Baghdad al-Zawra'*. Beirut: al-Katib al-ᶜArabi Publishers, n.d.

Kelly, J. B. *Britain and the Persian Gulf, 1795–1880*. Oxford: Oxford University Press, 1968.

———. "Kursan." In *The Encyclopaedia of Islam*. Vol. 5. Leiden: E. J. Brill, 1986, pp. 507–9.

Kepple, George. *Personal Narrative of a Journey from India to England, By Bassorah, Bagdad, the Ruins of Babylon, Curdistan, the Court of Persia, the Western Shore of the Caspian Sea, Astrakhan, Nishney, Novogorod, Moscow, and St. Petersburgh, in the Year 1824*. Vol. 1. London: Henery Colburn, 1827.

al-Khal, Muḥammad. *Tarikh al-Imarah al-Afrasiyabiyyah*. Baghdad: Maṭbaᶜat al-Majmaᶜ al-ᶜIlmi al-ᶜIraqi, 1961.

Khan, Mirza Abu Taleb. *The Travels of Mirza Abu Taleb Khan in Asia, Africa, and Europe During the Years 1799, 1800, 1801, 1802 and 1803*. Translated by Charles Stewart (Esq). Vol. II. London: Watts, Broxbourn, Herts, 1810.

Khoury, Dina. "Merchants and Trade in Early Modern Iraq." In *New Perspectives on Turkey*, Fall 1991, pp. 53–86.

———. *State and Provincial Society in the Ottoman Empire: Mosul, 1540–1834*. Cambridge: Cambridge University Press, 1997.

Kling, Blair, and M. N. Pearson, eds. *The Age of Partnership: Europeans in Asia Before Dominion*. Honolulu: University Press of Hawaii, 1979.

Lambton, Ann K. S. *Qajar Persia*. London: I. B. Tauris & Co. Ltd., 1987.

Landen, Robert G. "The Changing Pattern of Political Relations Between the Arab Gulf and the Arab Provinces of the Ottoman Empire." In B. R. Pridham, ed. *The Arab Gulf and the Arab World*. London: Croom Helm, 1988, pp. 41–64.

Lane, Fredric. *Profit From Power: Readings in Protection Rent and Violence Controlling Enterprises*. Albany: State University of New York Press, 1979.

Longrigg, Stephen Hemsley. *Four Centuries of Modern Iraq*. Oxford: Clarendon Press, 1925.

———. "al-Basra." In *The Encyclopaedia of Islam*. Vol. II. London: Luzac & Co., 1960.

Lorimer, J. G. *Gazetteer of the Persian Gulf, ʿUman and Central Arabia*. 2 vols. Calcutta, 1915.

McGowan, Bruce. "The Age of the Ayans, 1699–1812." In Halil Inalcik and Donald Quataert. *An Economic and Social History of the Ottoman Empire, 1300–1914*. Cambridge: Cambridge University Press, 1994, pp. 639–758.

Manguin, Pierre-Yves. "Late Mediaeval Asian Shipbuilding in the Indian Ocean: A Reappraisal." In *Moyen Orient & Ocean Indien / Middle East & Indian Ocean, XVIe–XIXe s.*, vol. 2, no. 2, 1985, pp. 1–30.

Manning, Catherine. "French Interest in East Asian Trade, 1719–1748." In *Moyen Orient & Ocean Indien*, vol. 7, 1990, pp. 145–56.

Marcus, Abraham. *The Middle East on the Eve of Modernity: Aleppo in the Eighteenth Century*. New York: Columbia University Press, 1989.

Marshall, P. J. *Problems of Empire: Britain and India, 1757–1813*. London: George Allen & Unwin Ltd., 1968.

Masters, Bruce. *The Origins of Western Economic Dominance in the Middle East: Mercantilism and the Islamic Economy in Aleppo, 1600–1750*. New York: New York University Press, 1988.

———. "Patterns of Migration to Ottoman Aleppo in the 17th and 18th Centuries." *International Journal of Turkish Studies*, vol. 4, no. 1, Summer 1987, pp. 75–89.

Mauro, Fredric. "Merchant Communities, 1350–1750." In James Tracy, ed. *The Rise of Merchant Empires: Long-Distance Trade in the Early Modern World, 1350–1750*. Cambridge: Cambridge University Press, 1990, pp. 255–86.

Meriwether, Margaret L. "Urban Notables and Rural Resources in Aleppo, 1770–1830." In *International Journal of Turkish Studies*, vol. 4, no. 1, Summer 1987, pp. 55–73.

Moreen, Vera B. "The Status of Religious Minorities in Safavid Iran, 1617–61." In *Journal of Near Eastern Studies*, vol. 40, no. 2, April 1981, pp. 119–35.

al-Mubarak, ᶜAbdul-Ḥusayn, and ᶜAbdul-Jabbar Naji al-Yasiri. *Min Mashahir 'Aᶜlam al-Baṣrah*. Basra: Center for Arabian Gulf Studies in Basra University, 1983.

Murphey, R. "Conditions of Trade in the Eastern Mediterranean: An Appraisal of Eighteenth Century Ottoman Documents from Aleppo." In *Journal of the Economic and Social History of the Orient*, vol. 33, 1990, pp. 35–50.

Naji, A. J., and Y. N. Ali. "The Suqs of Basrah: Commercial Organization and Activity in a Medieval Islamic City." In *Journal of the Economic and Social History of the Orient*, vol. 24, part 3, pp. 298–309.

"Nasi." In *Encyclopaedia Judaica*. Vol. 12. Jerusalem: Keter Publishing House Ltd., 1971, pp. 834–35.

Naval Intelligence Division of Great Britain. *Iraq and the Persian Gulf*. 1944.

Nawras, ᶜAla' Musa Kaẓim. *Ḥukm al-Mamalik fi al-ᶜIraq, 1750–1831*. Baghdad, 1975.

Nawras, ᶜAla' Musa Kaẓim, and ᶜImad ᶜAbdul-Salam Ra'uf. *'Imarat Kaᶜb al-ᶜArabiyyah fi al-Qirn al-Thamin ᶜAshar ᶜAla Ḍaw' al-Watha'iq al-Biriṭaniyyah*. Baghdad: al-Rashid Publishers, 1982.

Niebuhr, Carsten. *Voyage en Arabie & en Autre Pays Circonvoisins*. Vol. II. Amsterdam, 1780.

Nieuwenhuis, Tom. *Politics and Society in Early Modern Iraq: Mamluk Pashas, Tribal Shaykhs and Local Rule Between 1802 and 1831*. The Hague: Martinus Nijhoff Publishers, 1982.

Otter, M. *Voyage en Turquie et en Perse, Avec une Relation des Expeditions de Tahmas Kouli-Khan*. Paris, 1748.

Owen, Roger. *The Middle East in the World Economy, 1800–1914*. London: Methuen, 1981.

Ozbaran, Salih. "Some Notes on the Salyane System in the Ottoman Empire as Organized in Arabia in the Sixteenth Century." In *The Journal of Ottoman Studies*, vol. 6, 1986, pp. 39–45.

———. *The Ottoman Response to European Expansion: Studies on Ottoman-Portuguese Relations in the Indian Ocean and Ottoman Administration in the Arab Lands During the Sixteenth Century*. Istanbul: The Isis Press, 1994.

Panzac, Daniel. "International and Domestic Maritime Trade in the Ottoman Empire During the Eighteenth Century." In *International Journal of Middle East Studies*, vol. 24, March 1992, pp. 189–206.

Pearson, M. N. *Merchants and Rulers in Gujarat: The Response to the Portuguese in the Sixteenth Century*. Berkeley: University of California Press, 1976.

———. *Before Colonialism: Theories on Asian-European Relations 1500–1750*. Delhi: Oxford University Press, 1988.

———. "Introduction." In Blair Kling and M. N. Pearson, eds. *The Age of Partnership: Europeans in Asia Before Dominion*. Honolulu: University Press of Hawaii, 1979, pp. 1–14.

———. "India and the Indian Ocean in the Sixteenth Century." In Ashin Das Gupta and M. N. Pearson, eds. *India and the Indian Ocean, 1500–1800.* Oxford: Oxford University Press, 1987.

———. "Merchants and States." In James Tracy, ed. *The Political Economy of Merchant Empires.* Cambridge: Cambridge University Press, 1991, pp. 41–116.

Pelly, Lieutenant-Colonel. *Reports on the Tribes etc., Around the Shores of the Persian Gulf.* Calcutta: Foreign Department Press, 1874.

Perry, John R. *Karim Khan Zand: A History of Iran, 1747–1779.* Chicago: University of Chicago Press, 1979.

Phillips, Wendell. *Oman: A History.* London: Reynal & Co., 1967.

Plaisted, Bartholomew. "Narrative of a Journey From Basra to Aleppo in 1750." In Douglas Carruthers, ed. *The Desert Route to India, Being the Journals of Four Travellers by the Great Desert Caravan Route Between Aleppo and Basra, 1745–1751.* London, 1929, pp. 59–128.

Prins, A. H. J. "The Persian Gulf Dhows: Two Variants in Maritime Enterprise." In *Persica,* no. 2, 1966, pp. 1–18.

Qadir, Khwaja Abdul. *Waqai-i Manazil-i Rum: Diary of a Journey to Constantinople.* Edited by Mohibbul Hassan, New York: Asia Publishing House, 1968.

al-Qahwati, Ḥusayn. "al-Tarkib al-'Ijtimaᶜi." In *Ḥaḍarat al-ᶜIraq.* Vol. 10. Baghdad: Dar al-Ḥurriyyah, 1985, pp. 111–28.

Ra'uf, ᶜImad. "al-Qiwa wa al-Mu'asasat al-ᶜAskariyyah." In *Ḥaḍarat al-ᶜIraq.* Vol. 10. Baghdad: Dar al-Ḥurriyyah, 1985, pp. 37–52.

———. "al-Madinah al-ᶜIraqiyyah." In *Ḥaḍarat al-ᶜIraq.* Vol. 10. Baghdad: Dar al-Ḥurriyyah, 1985, pp. 161–98.

———. "al-Tanẓimat al-Ijtimaᶜiyyah." In *Ḥaḍarat al-ᶜIraq.* Vol. 10. Baghdad: Dar al-Ḥurriyyah, 1985, pp. 129–60.

Raymond, Andre. *Artisans et commerçants au Caire au XVIIIᵉ siecle.* 2 vols. Damascus: Institut français de Damas, 1973–74.

———. "Les Sources de la Richesse Urbaine au Caire au Dix-huitieme Siecle." In Tom Naff and Roger Owen, eds. *Studies in Eighteenth Century Islamic History.* Carbondale: Southern Illinois University Press, 1977, pp. 184–204.

———. *al-Mudun al-ᶜArabiyyah al-Kubra fi al-ᶜAṣr al-ᶜUthmani.*(Les Grand Villes Arabes a l'Epoque Ottoman). Translated by Laṭif Faraj. Cairo: Dar al-Fikr, 1991.

Rejwan, Nissim. *The Jews of Iraq: 3000 Years of History and Culture.* Boulder: Westview Press, 1985.

Rentz, G. "al-Kawasim." In *The Encyclopaedia of Islam.* Vol. 6. Leiden: E. J. Brill, 1978, pp. 777–78.

Ricks, Thomas M. "Slaves and Slave Traders in the Persian Gulf, 18th and 19th Centuries: An Assessment." In *Slavery & Abolition,* vol. 9, no. 3, December 1988, pp. 60–70.

"al-Rifaʿi." In H. A. R. Gibb and J. H. Kramers, eds. *Shorter Encyclopaedia of Islam*. Leiden: E. J. Brill, 1961, pp. 475–76.

Risso, Patricia. *Oman and Muscat: An Early Modern History*. London: Croom Helm, 1986.

———. *Merchants and Faith: Muslim Commerce and Culture in the Indian Ocean*. Boulder: Westview Press, 1995.

Roberts, Gaylard. "Mr. Roberts' Letter Giving an Account of His Journey Over the Desert of Arabia on His Way to England." In Douglas Carruthers, ed. *The Desert Route to India, Being the Journals of Four Travellers by the Great Desert Caravan Route Between Aleppo and Basra, 1745–1751*. London, 1929, pp. 44–47.

Roux, Georges. *Ancient Iraq*. London: Penguin Books, 1992.

al-Saʿidi, Ḥumud. *Dirasat ʿan ʿAsha'ir al-ʿIraq al-Khazaʿil*. Najaf: Maṭbaʿat al-Adab, 1974.

Salibi, Kamal S. "Middle Eastern Parallels: Syria-Iraq-Arabia in Ottoman Times." In *Middle East Studies*, vol. 15, no. 1, January 1979, pp. 70–81.

Sarkis, Yaʿqub. *Mabaḥith ʿIraqiyyah*. Vol. III. Baghdad, 1981.

Sassoon, David. "The History of the Jews in Basra." In *The Jewish Quarterly Review*, vol. 17, 1926–27, pp. 407–69.

———. *A History of the Jews of Baghdad*. Letchworth, 1949.

Sbahi, Aziz. *'Uṣul al-Ṣabi'ah (al-Manda'iyyin) wa Muʿtaqadatihim al-Diniyyah*. Damascus: Dar al-Mada, 1996.

Seyf, Ahmad. "Despotism and the Disintegration of the Iranian Economy, 1500–1800." In Elie Kedourie and Sylvia Haim, eds. *Essays on the Economic History of the Middle East*. London: Frank Cass, 1988, pp. 1–19.

Shaw, Stanford. *History of the Ottoman Empire and Modern Turkey*, vol. I: *Empire of the Gazis: The Rise and Decline of the Ottoman Empire, 1280–1808*. Cambridge: Cambridge University Press, 1976.

Sheriff, Abdul. *Slaves, Spices and Ivory in Zanzibar: Integration of an African Commercial Empire into the World Economy, 1770–1873*. Athens: Ohio University Press, 1987.

Sluglett, Peter. "al-Muntafik." In *The Encyclopaedia of Islam*. Vol. 7. Leiden: E. J. Brill, 1993, pp. 582–81.

Steensgaard, Niels. *The Asian Trade Revolution of the Seventeenth Century*. Chicago: University of Chicago Press, 1974.

———. *Carracks, Caravans and Companies: The Structural Crisis in European Asian Trade in the Early Seventeenth Century*. Denmark: Andelsbogtrykkereit i Odense, 1973.

———. "The Indian Ocean Network and the Emerging World Economy, c.1500–1750." In Chandra Satish, ed. *The Indian Ocean: Explorations in History, Commerce and Politics*. New Delhi: Sage Publications, 1987, pp. 125–50.

Stripling, George W. *The Ottoman Turks and the Arabs, 1511–1574*. Urbana: University of Illinois Press, 1942.

Subramanian, Lakshmi. "Capital and Crowd in a Declining Asian Port City: The Anglo-Bania Order and the Surat Riots of 1795." In *Modern Asian Studies*, vol. 19, no. 2, 1985, pp. 205–37.

———. "The Eighteenth-Century Social Order in Surat: A Reply and an Excursus on the Riots of 1788 and 1795." In *Modern Asian Studies*, vol. 25, no. 2, 1991, pp. 321–65.

Sullivan, Richard D. *Near Eastern Royalty and Rome, 100–30 B.C.* Toronto: University of Toronto Press, 1990.

al-Suwaydi, ᶜAbdul-Raḥman bin ᶜAbdullah. *Tarikh Ḥawadith Baghdad wa al-Baṣrah min 1186 ila 1192 A.H./1772–1778 A.D.* Baghdad: Ministry of Arts and Education, 1978.

———. *Tarikh Baghdad,'aw Ḥadiqat al-Zawra' fi Sirat al-Wizara'*. Baghdad: al-Zaᶜim Press, 1962.

Tabakoglu, Ahmet. "The Economic Importance of the Gulf in the Ottoman Era." In *Studies on Turkish-Arab Relations*, vol. 3, 1988, pp. 159–63.

al-Tamimi, ᶜAbdul-Malik. *Tarikh al-ᶜIlaqat al-Tijariyyah Bayn al-Hind wa Manṭaqat al-Khalij al-ᶜArabi fi al-ᶜAṣr al-Ḥadith*. Baghdad: College of Arts Publication, monograph no. 48, 1986–87.

Toledano, Ehud. *The Ottoman Slave Trade and Its Suppression: 1840–1890*. Princeton: Princeton University Press, 1982.

Torri, Michelguglielmo. "Trapped Inside the Colonial Order: The Hindu Bankers of Surat and Their Business World During the Second Half of the Eighteenth Century." In *Modern Asian Studies*, vol. 25, no. 2, 1991, pp. 367–401.

Tracy, James, ed. *The Rise of Merchant Empires: Long-Distance Trade in the Early Modern World, 1350–1750*. Cambridge: Cambridge University Press, 1990.

———, ed. *The Political Economy of Merchant Empires*. Cambridge: Cambridge University Press, 1991.

Tuson, Penelope. *The Records of the British Residency and Agencies in the Persian Gulf*. London: India Office Records, 1979.

Vida, G., and P. Sluglett. "al-Muntafiq." In *The Encyclopaedia of Islam*. Vol. 7. Leiden: E. J. Brill, 1993, p. 582.

Wallerstein, Immanuel. *The Modern World-System: Capitalist Agriculture and the Origins of the European World-Economy in the Sixteenth Century*. New York: Academic Press, 1974.

———. *The Capitalist World-System: Essays by Immanuel Wallerstein*. Cambridge: Cambridge University Press, 1980.

———. "The Incorporation of the Indian Subcontinent into the Capitalist World-Economy." In Satish Chandra, ed. *The Indian Ocean: Explorations in History, Commerce and Politics*. New Delhi: Sage Publishers, 1987, pp. 224–53.

———, Hale Decdeli, and Rasat Kasaba. "The Incorporation of the Ottoman Empire into the World-Economy." In Huri Islamoglu-Inan, ed. *The Ottoman Empire and the World Economy*. Cambridge: Cambridge University Press, 1988, pp. 88–97.

al-Wardi, ᶜAli. *Lamaḥat Ijtimaᶜiyyah min Tarikh al-ᶜIraq al-Ḥadith*. Vol. I. Baghdad: al-'Irshad Publishers, 1969.

Wink, Andrea. "Review Article: World Trade, Merchant Empires, and the Economy of the Indian Ocean." In *International History Review*, vol. 15, no. 1, February 1993, pp. 106–15.

Wolf, Eric. *Europe and the People Without History*. Berkeley: University of California Press, 1982.

Wright, Sir Denis. "Samuel Manesty and His Unauthorised Embassy to the Court of Fath ᶜAli Shah." In *Iran*, vol. 24, 1986, pp. 153–60.

Yapp, M. E. *The Making of the Modern Near East, 1792–1923*. London: Longman, 1987.

Yılmaz, Serap. "Osmanlı İmparatorlugu'nun Doğu İle Ekonomik İliskileri: XVIII. Yuzyilin İkinci Yarisinda Osmanlı-Hint Ticareti Ile Ilgili Bir Araştirma Fransiz Arşivlerinden." In *Belleten*, vol. 56, April 1992, pp. 33–68.

Young, Gavin. *Iraq: Land of Two Rivers*. London: Collins, 1980.

Yule, Henry, and A. C. Burnell. *Hobson-Jobson: A Glossary of Colloquial Anglo-Indian Words and Phrases, and of Kindered Terms, Etymological, Historical, Geographical and Discursive*. New York: Humanities Press, 1968.

Zahlan, Rosemarie Said. *The Creation of Qatar*. London: Croom Helm, 1979.

Zaki, Ahmad Kamal. *al-Ḥayat al-Adabiyyah fi al-Baṣrah, ila Nihayat al-Qirn al-Thani al-Hijri*. Damascus: al-Fikr Press, 1961.

al-Zulfa, Mohammed. "Omani-Ottoman Relations During the Reign of Imam Ahmad b. Saᶜid, 1741–83, in the Light of a Recently Discovered Exchange of Letters Between the Imam and the Ottoman Sultan." In *Arabian Studies*, vol. 8, 1990, pp. 93–103.

INDEX

SUNY Series in the Social and Economic History of the Middle East

Donald Quataert, editor

Ali Abdullatif Ahmida, *The Making of Modern Libya: State Formation, Colonization, and Resistance, 1830–1932.*

Rifa'at 'Ali Abou-El-Haj, *Formation of the Modern State: The Ottoman Empire, Sixteenth to Eighteenth Centuries.*

Palmira Brummett, *Ottoman Seapower and Levantine Diplomacy in the Age of Discovery.*

Palmira Brummett, *Image and Imperialism in the Ottoman Revolutionary Press, 1908–1911.*

Ayşe Burğa, *State and Business in Modern Turkey: A Comparative Study.*

Guilian Denoeux, *Urban Unrest in the Middle East: A Comparative Study of Informal Networks in Egypt, Iran and Lebanon.*

Hala Fattah, *The Politics of Regional Trade in Iraq, Arabia, and the Gulf, 1745–1900.*

Samira Haj, *The Making of Iraq, 1900–1963: Capital, Power, and Ideology.*

Caglar Keyder and Faruk Tabak, eds., *Landholding and Commercial Agriculture in the Middle East.*

Issa Khalaf, *Politics in Palestine: Arab Factionalism and Social Disintegration, 1939–1948.*

M. Fuad Köprülü, *The Origins of the Ottoman Empire*, translated and edited by Gary Leiser.

Zachary Lockman, ed., *Workers and Working Classes in the Middle East: Struggles, Histories, Historiographies.*

Donald Quataert, ed., *Manufacturing in the Ottoman Empire and Turkey, 1500–1950.*

Donald Quataert, ed., *Consumption Studies and the History of the Ottoman Empire, 1550–1922, An Introduction.*

Sarah Shields, *Mosul Before Iraq: Like Bees Making Five-Sided Cells.*